Public Planning in the Netherlands

Public Planning in the Netherlands

Perspectives and Change since the Second World War

Dr. Ashok K. Dutt
Professor of Geography and Urban Studies
The University of Akron, Akron, Ohio, U. S. A.
and
Dr. Frank J. Costa
Professor of Urban Studies and Geography
Director of the Center for Urban Studies
The University of Akron, Akron, Ohio, U. S. A.

OXFORD UNIVERSITY PRESS
1985

Oxford University Press, Walton Street, Oxford OX2 6DP

London New York Toronto
Delhi Bombay Calcutta Madras Karachi
Kuala Lumpur Singapore Hong Kong Tokyo
Nairobi Dar es Salaam Cape Town
Melbourne Auckland

and associated companies in
Beirut Berlin Ibadan Mexico City Nicosia

Oxford is a trade mark of Oxford University Press

Published in the United States
by Oxford University Press, New York

British Library Cataloguing in Publication Data

Public planning in the Netherlands: perspectives
and change since the Second World War.
1. Netherlands—Social policy
I. Dutt, Ashok K.   II. Costa, Frank J.
361.6'1'09492   HV308
ISBN 0–19–823248–9

Printed in Great Britain by
St Edmundsbury Press, Bury St Edmunds, Suffolk

Preface

In this book are pooled the planning experience and theoretical knowledge of a select group of scholars from the Netherlands, the United Kingdom, Australia, and the United States. It is the first book in English devoted to a comprehensive view of Dutch planning and this fills a significant gap in our knowledge. The editors have selected an interdisciplinary group of contributors representative of both practitioners and theoreticians. Though the contributors come from such diverse areas as architecture, geography, planning, law, sociology, economics, and the civil service, Jan Tinbergen, the Nobel laureate, rightly points out that the volume has a bias towards physical and social planning. The editors intend such a bias to provide a major focus, or binding thread, for the volume.

The idea of putting together such a book stemmed from the annual summer planning seminars, sponsored by the University of Akron, which were held in the Netherlands and Belgium and directed by Ashok Dutt since 1976. Almost all the Dutch contributors to this volume have given lectures to the seminar groups. Moreover, nearly all contributors have visited the University of Akron over the past six years. As a result of these meetings and interchanges, the book has taken shape.

The editors are thankful to Professor Tinbergen for going through the manuscript and making many suggestions for improvement. Andreas Faludi, Marc de Smidt, Coenraad van der Wal, and Jan kits Niewenkamp are owed particular thanks for suggestions concerning several parts of this manuscript. Dr. Th. Quené, Chairman of the Netherlands Scientific Council for Government Policy, provided valuable assistance in the preparation of the introductory chapter. M. Margaret Geib, Cartographer of the Department of Geography of the University of Akron, must be given special acknowledgement for her work in designing and preparing the maps and figures.

The Institute of Geography of Utrecht University has kindly permitted us to reproduce materials originally published in its *IDG Bulletin*. These are Figures 13-2 and 13-3. Figures 1-2, 1-3, 1-4, and 2-1 are reprinted from *A Compact Geography of The Netherlands*, Ministry of Foreign Affairs, the Hague, 1979.

Special thanks are given to Judith Sherman, Rebecca Campbell, and Hilda Kendron for their continual assistance in typing and retyping the manuscript in the various stages of its development. Teri Jares-Blount and Deborah Phillips are thanked for organizing the manuscript and for final preparation. We also want to acknowledge the important editorial assistance given to us by David Liversedge, Ramesh Vakamudi, and Ranjan Chakravarty. Dr. Allen G. Noble, Head of the Department of Geography, the University of Akron, is particularly thanked for his constant encouragement and help in the preparation of this book.

Akron, Ohio
April 15, 1984

Ashok K. Dutt
Frank J. Costa

Contents

1
Introduction

Ashok K. Dutt and Frank J. Costa

The Netherlands is decidedly the most planned country among the European nations. Only a few democracies of the world can match the planning apparatus of the Dutch government. Such a state of affairs is a product of circumstances created by harsh environmental constraints, a challenging history, conflicting socio-cultural forces, hard economic necessities, and the size of the country.

Planning can be defined as group cooperation toward the realization of common goals. The content of planning varies from one part of the world to another. Often the explanations for these variations may lie in divergent planning ideologies. More frequently they are the result of differing levels of economic development. Primitive societies have little need for planning because for them change is something to be avoided. Developing societies, on the other hand, frequently experience a 'revolution or rising expectations' and within such an environment change cannot come fast enough. At the same time, developed societies often also experience social and political movements which seek to *minimize* the onrush of change or, at the very least, to subordinate economic and technological change to the natural constraints imposed by the environment.

Within a specific nation, the content of planning policy changes as the nation evolves (Fig. 1–1). In the earliest stages of this process, cultural values remain strong; but as development forces begin to emerge, economic or profit-making values begin to surface and grow. Eventually public interest values, from which planning is derived, grow in strength as a response to both the needs and excesses of economic activity. Public interest values emerge in the developing or urbanizing phase of the evolution of a society, but more frequently they become dominant in the developed phase. Concern with the environment and with the elimination of pollution fosters strong political movements that alter the content of planning goals and activities.

Thus in underdeveloped societies, planners seek to prepare for development by planning for urban growth and for the economic infrastructure of roads, ports, canals, etc. While in developing societies, planners are more concerned with balanced growth, growth of primary and secondary production sectors, rural-to-urban migration policies, and housing. Continuing forward in the development cycle, planners in developed nations stress their concern with the quality of life and environmental protection.

The Netherlands, in its long history, has gone through all three phases of this development continuum. The Dutch began the long process of growth without any 'master plan'. Land reclamation and the protection of reclaimed or drained land as well

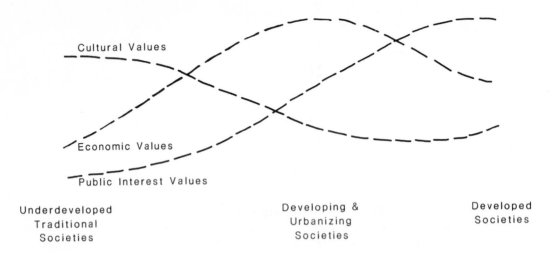

Fig. 1-1   Evolution of Human Values and Development

as the construction of canals for transport were the activities that occupied the Dutch people for centuries. Also created during this time was the unplanned but necessary network of cities—especially in Holland—which became the mercantile and manufacturing centers for the developing society.

The creation of the Dutch nation-state in the turbulent sixteenth century during the war with Spain and the unfolding of the Protestant Reformation, was another milestone along the path to a developed society. The mercantile and colonial expansion of the seventeenth and eighteenth centuries was followed by the creation of an industrial society at the end of the nineteenth century.

Over the course of the past century the Netherlands has evolved from an agricultural and mercantile society with a nascent industrial economy and a few important cities into a technologically advanced industrial economy in a highly developed and highly urbanized society. Dutch planning policy has also changed and evolved to accommodate societal changes.

BRIEF HISTORICAL SURVEY

The Netherlands presents a picture of tranquillity and order to its visitors, but much of its recent history has been anything but orderly and tranquil. In the early years of the nineteenth century, old religious quarrels between Calvinists and Catholics were still strong. In 1815, as a result of the Congress of Vienna, the Northern Netherlands (now the Netherlands) and Southern Netherlands (now Belgium) were united. This larger new state was expected to form part of an encircling bulwark around the borders of France to deter any new French aggression.

The unification process was plagued with problems from the start. Southern

Catholics objected to a constitutionally established Reformed Church. The northerners were also accused of providing for unequal representation in the Dutch Parliament where the Catholic majority had an equal voice with the Calvinist minority. Language rights of the French-speaking upper class in Flanders was another issue. Cultural differences and economic rivalries also fueled the movement for separation. Ultimately, the union was dissolved when the southerners, or Belgians, rebelled with the assistance of the French and established their own Catholic state. (The Dutch, in their time of difficulty, received no help from their British allies who were beginning to fear the mercantile competition from the unified Netherlands.)

The loss of Belgium and the growing industrialization of Europe caused important social and political changes in the Netherlands. A new constitution was adopted in 1848 which provided for complete freedom of religion. Old animosities still remained strong, however, when anti-Catholic riots greeted the reestablishment of the Roman Catholic hierarchy in 1853.

Over the course of the remainder of the nineteenth century, the Dutch came to grips with their religious problems in two ways. These were (1) the growth of a secularist community and (2) the 'pillarization' movement. The 'pillarization' movement is the denominational equivalent of the Swiss cantonal system. To minimize religious conflict, Dutch society was divided along religious lines. The Catholics had their own schools, social service agencies, communications media, etc. The same held true for the Protestants. Alongside these denominational pillars rose a secularist one which attempted to provide similar services for the religiously non-affiliated segment of the population. Thus, Dutch society was divided along religious and cultural lines.

Gradually, however, a national consensus on social welfare issues and urban development began to emerge. Governmental intervention was required to deal with issues of overcrowding and substandard housing in rapidly growing Dutch cities. The denominational 'pillars' had neither the means nor the inclination to engage these issues. A landmark piece of legislation was the Housing Act of 1901 which established standards for housing the Dutch people and initiated direct public involvement in the housing market through the public housing program. The direct relief provided to the poor by the state was another means by which central authority began to chip away at the 'pillars'.

In the course of the twentieth century, especially after World War II, a gradual shift away from the 'pillarized' society took place. Increasing public sector involvement in social welfare and the growth of a social work profession helped to hasten the process of 'hollowing out of the pillars'. After World War II, public direction of the social, economic, and physical reconstruction of the Netherlands resulted in the founding of the Dutch welfare state. Centralized direction and control of planning and housing created the edifice of planning institutions which are described in this book.

THE DUTCH POLITICAL SYSTEM

The Netherlands is a constitutional monarchy with a parliamentary government. The Parliament is bicameral with an upper house of 75 members and a lower house of 150 members. Election to the upper house is indirect, its members are selected by the Provincial parliaments. Each member serves for six years. Every three years elections are held when 37 or 38 members of the upper house retire. Election to the lower house is by popular ballot for which there is universal suffrage. Proportional representation of political parties is provided through the electoral laws of the Netherlands. This feature has frequently been cited as a reason for parliamentary instability and for the difficulty in forming governments in the Netherlands during the post-World War II years.

Governments are formed through parliamentary negotiation among the parties and must maintain the confidence of the lower house if they are to survive. Governments consist of a prime minister and a cabinet responsible for the various ministries of the government. The ministries are: (a) Foreign Affairs, (b) Defense, (c) Finance, (d) Economic Affairs, (e) Housing, Physical Planning and Environmental Planning, (f) Cultural Affairs, Recreation and Social Work, (g) Education, (h) Health, (i) Agricultural, Fisheries and Natural Conservation, (j) Traffic, Transport and Waterways, and (k) Home Affairs.

The Netherlands as of 1984 is divided into eleven provinces. There may be, however, thirteen provinces in the near future if Rotterdam and the Hook of Holland area is split off from South Holland and formed into a new province and the IJsselmeer polders are raised to the status of a province. The general administration of each province is carried out by a provincial council or parliament whose members are elected by popular ballot and proportional representation. A provincial executive and cabinet are selected from among the elected members of the provincial council and these must retain the confidence of the council to continue to function. The powers of provincial councils are delegated, though the central government controls financial allocations for the provinces.

Local administration is carried out by municipalities of which there are nearly 700. Legislative powers are vested in an elected municipal council while executive powers reside in a burgomaster who is appointed by the central government. Usually the burgomaster is a member of the most important political party in the municipality. As with the provinces, municipalities have powers of their own, but they rely on the national government for their funds. The provincial and national levels provide direction in some areas of planning and municipal development.

The Netherlands have a unitary and not a federal system. Although three levels of government are recognized, the powers of the lower two levels are granted by the upper level. Sovereignty resides in the central government alone.

GOVERNMENTAL FRAMEWORK FOR PLANNING

Planning in the Netherlands takes into account the economic, social, and physical or spatial elements of the society. The Dutch government has defined planning as public activity which guides the physical development of the country through a thorough understanding and review of the evolving economic, social, and cultural facets of Dutch society.

Though there are planning wings attached to several ministerial departments, which are responsible for organizing departmental projects for the future, four organizations, the Rijksplanologische Dienst (RPD), the Centraal Plan Bureau (CPB), the Sociaal–Cultureel Plan Bureau (SCP), and the Wetenschappelijke Raad voor het Regering sbeleid (WRR), are most important for national planning. The RPD or the National Physical Planning Agency is a part of the Ministry of Housing, Physical Planning and the Environment. It was the first established national planning

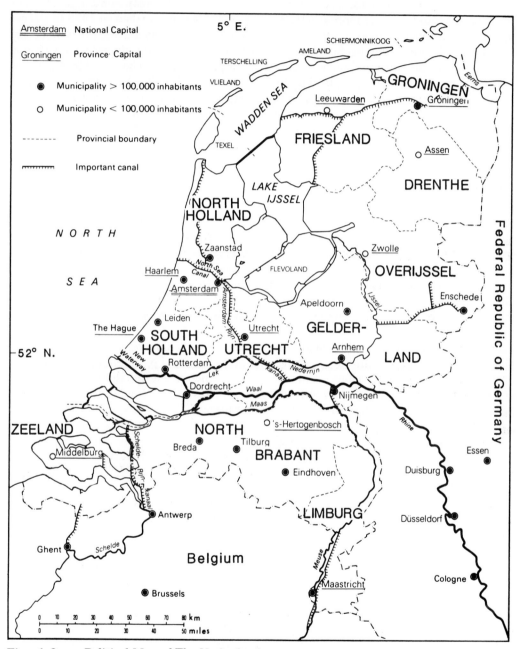

Fig. 1-2   Political Map of The Netherlands

organization in the country, dating from 1941. This agency provides guidance for the country's physical planning. The CPB, established in 1947 under the aegis of Jan Tinbergen, forecasts and analyzes the country's economic development. The CPB is a part of the Ministry of Economic Affairs. The SCP was established in 1973 to gather and analyze information, and select policy objectives for the social and cultural sector of national planning. The agency forecasts changes in the social life of the nation and evaluates proposed national policies and their implications for the social and cultural development of the Netherlands. The SCP operates within the Ministry of Welfare, Health and Culture. The WRR, or The Scientific Council for Government Policy, was set up in 1972. It reports directly to the Prime Minister and is assigned responsibilities for supplying scientific information and studies so that priorities may be established in framing general governmental policies.

PHYSICAL PLANNING

The Physical Planning Act of 1962 sets forth the legislative framework for physical planning at all levels of government. This act defines the role, scope, and responsibilities of each physical planning institution at the three levels of government—the national, the provincial, and the municipal. At the national level, primary responsibility for physical national planning is vested in the Ministry of Housing, Physical Planning and Environment. The national government determines national policy, which is then transmitted to the provincial and municipal levels of government in a variety of ways.

The Minister of Housing, Physical Planning and Environment Planning issues planning directives that are binding on provincial and municipal planning bodies. Involvement with the spatial distribution of activities and peoples is the dominant objective of national planning initiatives. Planned developments in a particular area are examined to determine their impact upon surrounding areas. There is not a binding national plan, rather national guidelines are set for the regional and municipal levels to follow in the formulation of municipal and regional plans.

Structural schemes for roads, electrical supplies, industrial water usage, etc. are made by the relevant ministries of the national government. The Minister of Housing, Physical Planning and Environmental Planning reviews the structural schemes in order to determine their overall spatial requirements and their likely effects on the provinces and the municipalities from the standpoint of overall national development objectives.

At the provincial level, the physical planning function is coordinative and regulatory. Provincial planners oversee the preparation and implementation of municipal plans and try to integrate these into an overall regional planning framework.

At the provincial level there are two general administrative bodies, the Provincial Council and the Provincial Executive. The Provincial Council is the legislative body and has elected members. The Provincial Executive is responsible for the daily administration of the Province. Regional plans and regulations and the approval of municipal plans are the function of the Provincial Executive. Each province is divided into one or more subregions for which physical plans integrating various municipal plans are prepared.

Recommendations to the provincial authorities from the national government are reviewed and modified and then applied through the process of regional planning and the approval of municipal plans. (Figure 1–4 depicts the process of increasing specificity in physical planning from the generalized regional level to the site-specific municipal level.) In this way the province acts as an intermediate review arm of the national government.

The Netherlands is composed of five major divisions containing eleven provinces. Within these provinces are many municipalities. Under this arrangement the provincial level can and does promote the activities of local administration. The provincial level can award subsidies to local private companies to develop utilities and supplies, besides taking the initiative in the preparation of municipal plans.

Responsibility for assuring that development proceeds in accordance with regional and national directives is the principal regulatory function of the local level of government. The municipal council of a city creates local physical planning by adopting first, a structure plan which is a nonbinding master plan, and secondly, a mandatory development plan which specifies the intended development of all undeveloped portions of the municipality and of areas intended for redevelopment. The master plan establishes general policies and a timetable for implementation. Its nonbinding character gives it a flexibility which can accommodate new policy as well as revisions to the development time-schedule. The binding development plan covers both land and water areas within a municipality and specifies future land uses, future road locations, and sites for planned public facilities. The development plan consists of a zoning map specifying locations for future lands and provisions for the internal uses of land and building. As a binding document it can be amended only through municipal legislative and provincial review processes.

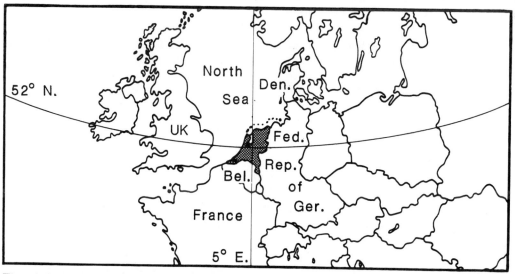

Fig. 1–3   The Netherlands in Europe

ECONOMIC AND SOCIAL PLANNING

The research for economic planning is carried out by the Central Planning Bureau (CPB). This bureau is responsible for economic forecasting, trend analysis, and cost-benefit analysis of special projects of the Netherlands. Preparation of an annual advisory national economic plan is the principal function of the bureau. Trend analysis of data with the objective of predicting future production, import–export price levels, and national income is an integral part of the work of this agency. From these data, the Central Planning Bureau prepares short- and long-term forcasts for the economy. These forecasts are made in the areas of wages and prices, short-term economic growth, and internal change within the Netherlands. Forecasts of output in various industrial sectors, energy and food supplies forecasts, and finally public costs forecasts for the services of the welfare state, for example education, national health, etc., are also made. The nature of the activities of the Social and Cultural Planning Bureau has already been explained.

PLANNING COORDINATION

Three facets of planning, physical, economic, and socio-cultural, must be considered when planning for the different sectors, such as transportation, recreation, housing, etc. In 1968 a national commission, known as the De Wolff Committee, prepared a long-range planning document. One of its recommendations was the establishment of an integrated national policy for the long-term development of the Netherlands. Consequently the Scientific Council for Government Policy (WRR) was set up in 1972 to provide an umbrella for physical, economic and socio-cultural planning. But by 1976, when the Dutch Parliament enacted a law formalizing the Council, the high expectations of the WRR had failed to materialize. Section 2 of the Act of Parliament of August 5 1976 states that the Council shall:

(a) Provide government policy-makers with information on developments which may affect society in the long term and draw timely attention to anomalies and 'bottlenecks' to be anticipated; define the major policy problems and indicate policy alternatives;

(b) provide a scientific structure for decision-making which the Government could use when establishing priorities and to ensure that a consistent policy is pursued;

(c) make recommendations concerning the elimination of structural inadequacies, the furtherance of specific studies and the improvement of communication and coordination concerning long-range planning in both the public and private sectors.

Although the coordinative function is mentioned, the WRR is not given any specific powers to coordinate. Thus since 1972, it has done little more that prepare research documents on multidisciplinary matters. Nonetheless, several of the reports issued by WRR have had an important impact on Dutch planning thought and on Dutch planning policy.[1]

Coordination of the planning facets remains unresolved, while the RPD, the CPB, and the SCP continue to plan at a national level in their own respective domains.

DUTCH SOCIETY TODAY

The Netherlands today is a highly developed nation which continues to provide an excellent standard of living for its citizens. However, several significant changes, in this generally happy and prosperous nation should be noted because they may be harbingers of a future different from that envisioned by most people only a decade ago. These changes concern population, the economy, and the Dutch social condition.

In recent years, the rapid population growth of the early decades of this century has declined to the point where current birth rates do not promise any substantial future growth. The impact of a stable and ageing population on long-held planning goals and on the provision of social services is only now being realized. The strong national desire to reclaim land from the sea is fading. The capability of an ever smaller number of working-age people to provide the finance necessary to maintain the elaborate social services network of the Netherlands is being called into question for the first time.

The Netherlands of the 1980s is still one of the wealthiest countries of the world, but its economic concerns are mounting. By 1983 the unemployment rate had reached 16 percent.[2] Not since the early post-war years have so many of the Dutch people been out of work.

The Netherlands may be entering a new economic era for which its people and institutions are unprepared. The optimism of life in a continually growing economy is being replaced by a concern for an economically and socially uncertain future. The welfare state legislation of the post-war years promoted equality and contributed to the leveling of differences within society. But it was carried out in the high growth period of the 1950s and 1960s when markets for industrial goods were expanding and competitors were few. Today the Netherlands is experiencing severe unemployment brought on in part by high labor costs and the non-competitiveness of its goods on world markets. This, coupled with the cost of maintaining the structure of the welfare state on declining revenues, has produced a severe shock to the Dutch economy and society. Some commentators foresee a decline in living standards as the only way to revise the economic tailspin.

ABOUT THE BOOK

These concerns find frequent expression in several chapters of this book. There is a crisis in both the theory and the practice of planning in the Netherlands. The old system so confidently built up in the 1950s and 1960s is no longer adequate. It required increasing resources from public coffers to keep it functioning. These are no longer forthcoming. The current economic crisis with its prospect of long-term economic stagnation during the decade of the 1980s is having a dramatic effect on the optimism of planners and their faith in planning institutions. These crises seem to be fueling an incipient shift away from centralized planning with a comprehensive scope to decentralized and incremental or piecemeal approaches in planning.

In chapter two Peter Hall calls attention to the spatial changes that geographically reflect the massive social changes of the post-war years, in his description of evolving urbanization patterns in the Netherlands. It has been the task of the Dutch planning

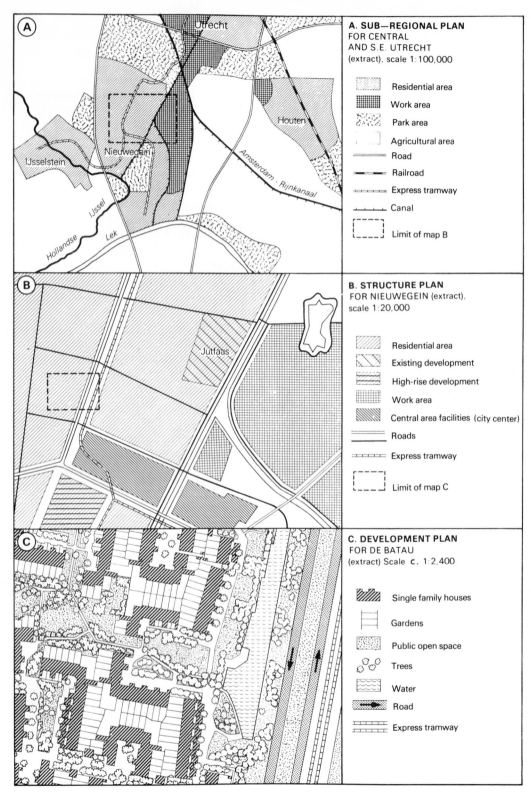

A. SUB—REGIONAL PLAN
FOR CENTRAL
AND S.E. UTRECHT
(extract), scale 1:100,000

- Residential area
- Work area
- Park area
- Agricultural area
- Road
- Railroad
- Express tramway
- Canal
- Limit of map B

B. STRUCTURE PLAN
FOR NIEUWEGEIN (extract),
scale 1:20,000

- Residential area
- Existing development
- High-rise development
- Work area
- Central area facilities (city center)
- Roads
- Express tramway
- Limit of map C

C. DEVELOPMENT PLAN
FOR DE BATAU
(extract) Scale c. 1:2,400

- Single family houses
- Gardens
- Public open space
- Trees
- Water
- Road
- Express tramway

Fig. 1-4   Example of (A) Part of a Regional Plan, (B) Municipal Structural Plan
and (C) Detailed Development Plan of a Section of Municipality

apparatus to deal with these massive shifts in the urbanization pattern. In undertaking this task, the Dutch have created a universally admired system of comprehensive and functionally integrated planning.

The evolution of the Dutch planning system is described by Hamnett in chapter three and Faludi and de Ruijter in chapter four. Faludi and de Ruijter describe the varied sources of the Dutch planning tradition. These disparate views on the development of Dutch society were, to a great extent, submerged during the extended period of post-war economic growth. In recent years, however, they have come to the forefront and now constitute a fragmented foundation underlying the apparently smooth surface of uniformity regarding the disposition of planning issues. Hamnett, in chapter three, carries this theme of a fragmented ideological base even further in his discussion of the political roots of Dutch planning. Ideological conflicts go deep into the Dutch past and have, in part, divergent religious orientations as their cause.

Chapter five, by Morris, is devoted to urban design. Although not specifically concerned with the post-war era, Morris describes the creation of several splendid townscapes. The recognition of the aesthetic quality of these old town centers was a contributing cause to the shift from decentralized development and urban renewal in the 1950s and 1960s to contained development and urban rehabilitation in the 1970s and 1980s.

The primary facets of Dutch planning are described in the chapters on physical planning, economic planning, and socio-cultural planning. Kits Nieuwenkamp, in chapter six, provides an extended perspective on physical planning and contrasts the earlier more optimistic era of consensus as to goals and availability of resources with the current period of confusion and austerity. He sees the current period as one of coming to terms with a new and unfamiliar environment of economic stagnation and reduced funding for the programs of the welfare state.

Timmermans and Becker, in chapter seven, provide an extended discussion of ideological and religious conflict in the provision of social services. The Dutch, in order to minimize the conflict, created the system of 'pillars' in which religious denominations provide, with state aid, a full range of social and cultural services for their members. This denominational 'cantonal' system has been gradually dissolving under the pressures of social change and secularization which became so pronounced in the Netherlands of the 1960s and 1970s.

This same contrast between post-war affluence and growth and current stagnation recurs in the essays by Timmermans and Becker on social planning and van Delft and Kwaak on economic planning. Van Delft and Kwaak, in chapter eight, distinguish several distinct periods of economic planning including the immediate post-war period of reconstruction in which the national government played a dominant central role. This was followed by the era of economic expansion which lasted nearly a quarter of a century, during which the private sector became the locomotive of the national economy. Dutch economic planning during this period was concerned primarily with stimulating and guiding private investment to overcome regional disparities. In recent years, however, economic planning has had to come to grips with a new reality of economic stagnation and unemployment. In this most recent period, Dutch economic planning is struggling in much the same way as Dutch physical planning in order to respond adequately and effectively to new economic realities.

A series of chapters in this book is devoted to special planning issues. Marc de Smidt, in chapter nine, examines the relatively new planning tool of the Integrated

Structural Plan (ISP) which attempts to bring together in a specific spatial context the physical planning, economic planning, and social planning efforts of the various responsible ministries. He examines the use of the ISP approach in the region of North Netherlands. Ambitious planning goals, in this case, do not translate into impressive results. De Smidt finds that the mechanisms of intersectoral planning still need some adjustment.

In chapter ten Hetzel gives an extended discussion of Dutch housing policy in which he calls attention to the early commitment on the part of the Dutch government to improve housing conditions for the poor and the workers. This commitment dates back to the passage of the pathbreaking Housing Act of 1901. Hetzel devotes the bulk of his chapter to housing policies since World War II. Once again, the familiar theme of a current crisis in the availability of resources for public planning activity, in this case housing construction, is sounded.

Van der Sluys and van Evert give us a municipal perspective on Dutch planning in chapter eleven. They look at the Hague and its planning. An extremely interesting case study of neighborhood renewal in the old painters' quarter of the Hague is included. Van der Sluys and van Evert foresee more local initiatives in Dutch urban planning which will shift the entire planning system away from a highly centralized mode to a less rigid decentralized mode for planning.

Another series of chapters in this volume deals in great detail with important project plans including the creation of new land from the IJsselmeer and the construction of the new sea defenses in the Rhine Delta. Dutt and Heal, in chapter twelve, trace the historical steps and the human catastrophes which caused the Dutch to undertake one of the world's most impressive civil engineering works—the Delta Project. The chapter provides an extended discussion of planning for the project. Dutt and Heal discuss how an initial consensus on planning goals eventually eroded into conflict with environmentalists ranged against the Dutch planning establishment, and who ultimately, forced a compromise.

Dutt, Costa, van der Wal and Lutz give an account of the reclamation planning and settlement policies for the IJsselmeer polders in chapter thirteen. The evolution of these policies is explained as a product of changing land use needs for the nation and the loss of consensus on overall goals for the reclamation of new lands from the sea. And then, van der Wal offers an analysis of changes in the objectives of town planning and urban design as reflected in the development of several new towns in the IJsselmeer polders in chapter fourteen.

The many perspectives on planning and planned change offered in this book are evidence of a healthy democratic process of debate and compromise in the Netherlands. Many points of view are the hallmark of a pluralistic society. The working out of accommodations among divergent points of view is the test of the democratic process. In this regard the Dutch have achieved a high level of democratic dialogue and consensus about national goals. There appears to be a testing of this consensus at the present time under the pressure of economic and social change. In many respects the current period is like the religiously divisive period of the mid to late nineteenth century. Today the conflict centers on the degree to which individual interests should be subordinated to the collective interest. This is a testing time for the Dutch but the successful outcome of past events and periods of natural catastrophe and ideological stress must make the informed observer optimistic about the future of the Netherlands.

NOTES

1. See especially, *Place and Future of Industry in the Netherlands*, The Hague, 1980.
2. *The Economist*, London, vol. 287, no. 7284, p. 63.

2
Dutch Urban Planning within the Perspective of European Development

Peter Hall

The evolution of the Dutch urban system since World War II in many ways anticipates that of the rest of Europe. Like Great Britain, the Netherlands has one of the most highly evolved and mature systems of cities in the whole European continent. It is small wonder then that certain tendencies were evident earlier in these two systems than in other European countries. The Netherlands and Britain, in fact, have led the flight from the cities into the suburbs. And in this pattern, the other European nations follow at varying distances behind.

These conclusions follow from a comparative study of urban evolution in Europe between 1950 and 1975, made cooperatively by the International Institute for Applied Systems Analysis (IIASA) and the University of Reading.[1] That study sought to analyze urban trends within a common framework of functional urban regions (or daily urban systems), similar but not identical to the Standard Metropolitan Statistical Areas long used for such analyses in the United States. Before discussing the results, however, it will be usefull to develop a theoretical pattern of urban evolution.

THEORY: SIX STAGES OF URBAN LIFE

The theory tries to relate urban change to the general economic and social evolution of a European (indeed, any) country in the period since the Industrial Revolution. In the initial stage—corresponding to the Agrarian and Industrial Revolutions—improvements in agricultural productivity, coupled with population increase, lead to a surplus farm population which pours off the land to look for work in the cities. In most rural areas, the local cities lack the industrial structure to absorb the bulk of this excess population, because at this stage there is a highly concentrated distribution of economic activity, with most industrial workers in one or two leading cities. The migration streams therefore pass on into these cities, enhancing their supremacy and fostering their rapid growth. At this stage, then, *the leading city grows rapidly, often faster than smaller cities.* However *smaller cities grow, while the population of their surrounding rural areas contracts.* There is thus a condition over much of the country of *centralization during the loss (LC):* using a metropolitan area framework,[2] the city increases modestly (or may in some cases contract), the rural ring around it loses massively, and the overall effect is one of contraction.

In the second stage, industrialization spreads down the urban hierarchy to second- and third-order cities, which now begin to absorb more of the surplus population of their surrounding rings. *The lower-order cities therefore show a faster growth rate* comparable to that of the leading city or cities. And their gain acts as a counterweight to the loss from their rings: centralization during the loss is replaced by a condition of absolute centralization *(AC)*, in which *the city grows faster than the ring loses, with growth overall.*

In the third stage, the economy progressively matures. Second- and third-order cities now show rapid growth, perhaps even exceeding that of first-order cities. And this growth begins to wash outside their boundaries, leading to suburbanization of the rural rings. Now, therefore, *both city and ring are growing, but the city growth is faster than that of the ring:* this is a condition of relative centralization *(RC)*.

With the fourth stage, this process naturally goes further. The growth of every city—whether first-, second-, or third-order—is now passing increasingly into the suburban ring. A reversal now takes place: *suburban growth is faster than that of the city itself*, so that a condition of relative decentralization *(RD)* prevails.

With the fifth stage, a significant change occurs. Urban redevelopment (for commerce at the center, for slum clearance and redevelopment in the inner city) joins with the search for better living standards to displace the urban population. For the first time, *the city population begins to fall*; there is a condition of absolute decentralization *(AD)*.

In this process, the largest metropolitan areas invariably lead the way: they tend to be the most congested, the ones with the most serious slum problems, and the ones in which commercial expansion at the center displaces the most people. Some second-and third-order centers, in older industrial regions with poor living conditions, may however join them in the vanguard of decentralization. It is no wonder therefore, that the sixth and final stage of the cycle should peculiarly—and perhaps exclusively—affect them. In this stage, *the decline of the city is so rapid that—whether or not the ring continues to grow—the entire metropolitan area begins to contract.* This stage, a perfect mirror image of the first, is appropriately termed decentralization during loss *(LD)*.

If the theory has any merit, most countries should pass more or less systematically through the six stages depending on the point at which they first experienced industrialization. Evidence from the United States, in the early 1970s, suggests that substantial numbers of older and larger metropolitan areas had in fact reached the final stage, while most other metropolitan areas were experiencing either relative or absolute decentralization.[3] These size and age effects were further reinforced by a regional effect, whereby metropolitan area contraction was most notable in the older industrialized and older urbanized areas of the North-East and East-North-Central (Mid-West) regions. Some observers also identified a new effect, whereby metropolitan area populations in the aggregate grew less rapidly than nonmetropolitan ones.[4] Census data for 1980 suggest that this is true in terms of a fixed set of metropolitan areas, but not if account is taken of the creation of totally new metropolitan areas in the 1970-1980 Census decade.[5].

All this can be explained by the fact that, in terms of the model, the United States is now a mature industrial–urban nation. But the evidence from the IIASA/Reading survey suggests that in comparison, Europe as a whole—perhaps surprisingly—is not. Different parts of it, in the 1950-75 period, were behaving in very different ways; in other words, they appeared to be at very different stages in the unfolding of the theoretical model. Great Britain stood at one end; Southern and Eastern Europe, and (perhaps surprisingly) France at the other. But, on this spectrum, it was perhaps significant that the Netherlands was closer to Great Britain than perhaps any other mainland European nation.

The evidence for this is presented in Table 2–1 which shows, for a sample of European countries and for various decades, the numbers of metropolitan areas falling into each of the six categories above.

The table shows clearly that Great Britain advanced earliest and most comprehensively along the road of decentralization. Already by the 1950s, 67 out of 138 metropolitan areas, or almost one-half, were exhibiting decentralization, and 14 were actually in the sixth stage of decentralization during loss. By the 1970s the corresponding figures were 102, or close on three-quarters, and 23. At the other end of the spectrum comes Spain, which in the 1950s showed only 4 areas out of 41 in the decentralizing category, and which exhibited little change even by the 1970s, with only about 9 out of 41: still less than one-quarter. In comparison with these two extremes, the Netherlands is clearly closer to the British end. Already in the 1950s, 12 out of 19 areas, or nearly two-thirds, were showing decentralization; by the 1970s all areas were in this category, and 12 of them were showing absolute decentralization with losses of central city populations. Sweden, the final example, is shown as an instance of a country that in the 1950s mainly exhibited centralization (21 out of 22), but that had switched very strongly by the 1970s to a decentralizing trend (20 out of 22).

Table 2–1   Selected European countries: population shifts (1950–75)

Nation	Decade	Type of Shift					
		LC	AC	RC	RD	AD	LD
Netherlands	1950–60	0	0	7	12	0	0
	1960–70	0	0	2	14	3	0
	1970–75	0	0	0	7	12	0
Great Britain	1950–60	8	8	55	39	14	14
	1960–70	4	1	30	57	34	12
	1970–75	3	1	32	54	25	23
Sweden	1950–60	3	11	7	1	0	0
	1960–70	3	3	13	3	0	0
	1970–75	2	0	0	2	14	4
Spain	1950–60	7	10	20	4	0	0
	1960–70	7	11	17	5	1	0
	1970–75	13	5	14	8	1	0

LC–Centralization during loss
AC–Absolute centralization
RC–Relative centralization
RD–Relative decentralization
AD–Absolute decentralization
LD–Decentralization during loss

Source: Hall and Hay (1980).

We can conclude from this that the Netherlands embarked almost as early on the path of decentralization as did Britain; but there was one important difference. Unlike Britain, the Netherlands has never had any metropolitan areas in the sixth, or LD, category. The urban areas of the Netherlands have neither of the characteristics that theoretically contribute to entry into this stage: large size, or a declining industrial base. The largest metropolitan areas had populations of less than 2 million, and none of them depended on a limited or precarious economic base. What was occurring in the Netherlands by the 1970s, therefore, was a simple process of core-to-ring decentralization, spearheaded by the larger cities (Amsterdam, the Hague, Rotterdam, Utrecht) which by this time were all losing population.

This indicates that the earlier stages of urban evolution were by then over. There is some evidence that in a few areas of the Netherlands in the 1950s they were still taking place. A number of metropolitan areas, almost all of them in smaller and in more rural eastern and northeastern parts of the country, were still exhibiting centralization, albeit only in a relative sense. These, almost certainly, were areas where the cities were still benefitting from migration off the land during a period of agrarian rationalization. But the evidence is fairly clear that by the 1960s that phase was over, for the number of such centralizing areas shrank to two. At this time, the great majority of metropolitan areas were in the intermediate stage of relative decentralization; it was only after 1970 that the absolute decline of central city populations began. This conclusion is independently confirmed by Dutch studies.[6]

THE RESPONSE OF THE DUTCH PLANNING SYSTEM

The evolution of Dutch planning policy since World War II neatly illustrates the reaction of the official planning machine to these changing circumstances. In the 1950s and early 1960s, a major policy aim was to encourage development in the areas of rural outflow in the south, east, and north-east, such as Breda, Nijmegen, Arnhem, and Groningen. Another was to attempt to contain the threat of intrusion on to valuable agricultural land caused by the suburban outgrowth of the biggest cities in the so-called Randstad (Rim City) Holland. This was to be achieved by both a stong policy of agricultural conservation in the 'Green Heart' of the Randstad, and the establishment of buffer zones between each pair of cities in the Rim City itself. To compensate for these policies, and to provide for the expected growth, planned urbanization was to take place in such areas as the drained IJsselmeer polders and in the Delta area south of Rotterdam–Dordrecht. These remained the basic principles of policy from the *First Report on Physical Planning in the Netherlands* of 1960 to the *Second Report* of 1966—though in the latter they were supplemented and amplified by an outline of a new settlement structure for the entire country, based on a principle of 'concentrated deconcentration'. What is really significant, however, is the radical change in approach between 1966 and 1974-6, when the *Third Report* appeared.

By that time, the Randstad was clearly no longer showing rapid growth; indeed there was large-scale migration from it, especially to the south and east of the country, though many people continued to commute back into the Randstad cities for work. Large-scale planned decentralization from the Randstad, then, disappeared as a policy objective. Instead, the main emphasis was on protecting the major Randstad cities from decay: their centers were to be built up, and new residential areas provided close by, so as to minimize both the time burden and the energy costs of commuting. The

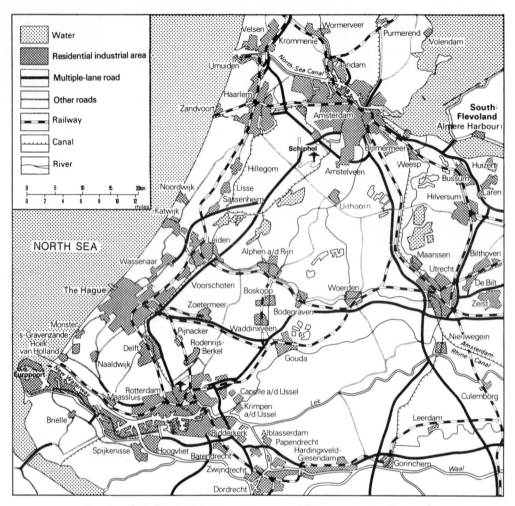

Fig. 2-1   Randstad Holland with Place Names and Transportation Network

great majority of new housing is now therefore to be provided in growth centers close to the major cities.

It is instructive to compare this shift of policy with what was occurring in Great Britain at the time.[7] In both countries, there was a sudden realization that the fall in rate of population growth (occasioned by drastic and unforeseen reduction in the birth rate), coupled with an equally unexpected out-migration from the larger cities, would require a major revision of national planning policy objectives. There was a new emphasis on the economic and physical revitalization of the major cities. There is of course no guarantee that government action can be successful in this aim—and the urban history of the United States, during the 1960s and 1970s, offers some cautionary lessons in this regard. Nevertheless, it is broadly true that in beginning to grapple with these problems, the Netherlands and Great Britain are some way in advance of most of their European neighbors.

NOTES

1. P. Hall and D. Hay, *Growth Centres in the European Urban System*, London, Heinemann Education, 1980.
2. The system utilized in the IIASA/Reading study assumes a fixed definition of Metropolitan Areas over the twenty-five-year study period, to ensure consistency.
3. B. J. L. Berry, 'The Counter-Urbanization Process: Urban America since 1970', in B. J. L. Berry (ed.), *Urbanization and Counter-urbanization* (Sage Urban Affairs Annual Review, 11) Beverly Hills and London, Sage, 1976; W. Alonso, 'The Current Halt in the Metropolitan Phenomenon', in C. L. Leven (ed.) *The Mature Metropolis*, Lexington, D.C. Heath, 1978; K. F. McCarthy and P. A. Morrison, 'The changing Demographic and Economic Structure of Non-metropolitan Areas in the United States', *International Regional Science Review*, 2, 1977, pp. 123-42; K. F. McCarthy and P. A. Morrison, *The Changing Demographic and Economic Structure of Non-metropolitan Areas in the United States*, R-2399-EDA, Santa Monica, Rand Corporation (Mimeo), 1979; G. Sternlieb and J. Hughes, *Post-Industrial America: Metropolitan Decline and Inter-Regional Job Shifts*, Brunswick, NJ, Rutgers University, 1975; G. Sternlieb and J. Hughes, "New Regional and Metropolitan Realities of America", *Journal of American Institute of Planners*, 43, 1977, pp. 227-40.
4. D. R. Vining and A. Strauss, 'A Demonstration that the Current Deconcentration of Population in the United States is a Clean Break with the Past', *Environment and Planning*, A, 9, 1977, pp. 751-8; D. R. Vining and T. Kontuly, 'Increasing Returns to City Size in the Face of an Impending Decline in the Size of Large Cities: Which is the Bogus Fact?', *Environment and Planning*, A, 9, 1977, pp. 59-62.
5. P. M. Hauser, 'The Census of 1980', *Scientific American*, 245/3, 1981, pp. 53-61.
6. O. Ayodeji and F. Vonk, *Metropolitan Employment Developments: An Inquiry into some Aspects of Economic Change in the Larger City-Regions of the Netherlands*, Delft, Planologisch Studiecentrum T.N.O., 1980.
7. P. Hall, *The World Cities*, New York, McGraw-Hill, 1979, p. 116.

3
Political Framework and Developmental Objectives of Post-War Dutch Planning

Steve Hamnett

This chapter traces the development of spatial planning policies in the Netherlands since the last war against a changing political and economic backcloth. Its central concern is to examine the way in which political and institutional factors have promoted or inhibited the adoption and implementation of national spatial planning policies, the reform of land use planning legislation, and the integration of spatial planning with other sectors of governmental policy.

Problems of pursuing long-term planning goals are related to the greater short-term political priority of housing and unemployment issues at times of recession. Problems of implementing national policies, and of integrating national spatial planning policies with policies in other sectors and at other levels of government, are discussed in terms of departmentalism and the difficulty of coordinating the activities of provincial and municipal authorities under a constitution which guarantees local autonomy. The paradox which the foreign student of post-war Dutch planning encounters initially is that planning is well developed in many fields, despite a system of government by shifting and grand coalitions of several political parties which tend to have a bias against strongly interventionist programs. A deeper exploration of Dutch political culture is required to attempt to resolve this paradox and the chapter begins with such an exploration. Subsequent sections follow the development of national spatial planning policies over time and attempt to distinguish a number of separate stages in the evolution of policies, characterized by different political and planning priorities.

POLITICS AND GOVERNMENTAL PLANNING

The pluralism of the Netherlands is the factor which shapes the political context of planning. Dutch society has been divided for much of the century into four main *zuilen* or social groups—Catholic, Protestant, Socialist, and Liberal. Membership in one of these groups could mean spending most of one's life with little contact with members of others. Schools, hospitals, trade unions, and other social organizations still reflect this *verzuiling* or fragmentation and the resulting social cleavages have been of considerable, if declining, importance in the structure of political parties.

Prior to the last war, government in the Netherlands was dominated by conservative coalitions of religious parties, joined on occasion by the Liberals. Not until 1939 was the first Labor minister included in a cabinet. The Catholic party (KVP) has been a constant element in post-war cabinets, sharing power with different combinations of the other major parties. The Labor party (PvdA) was included in most of the cabinets of the fifties, but its exclusion in 1959 marked the beginning of a period of right-of-center government which lasted throughout the sixties, apart from one brief period in 1965–6.

The balance between the main political parties in Parliament used to lead to 'centrist and depoliticized policy-making processes'.[1] In Arend Lijphart's phrase, the Netherlands exhibited the 'politics of accommodation'.[2] This accommodation began to break down, however, in the late 1960s, as challenges to the status quo came first from the Poujadist 'Boerenpartij' and then, more dramatically, from the 'Provo' movement which attracted international attention. In the late sixties, also, the Labor party lost interest in seeking compromise with the Catholics and the Liberal VVD and began to forge a new left-wing coalition with a number of smaller parties. This 'new left' has attempted to fight elections since 1967 on the basis of a program agreed in advance with potential coalition partners, instead of being arrived at in the traditional way through compromise in the period between the holding of elections and the formation of a cabinet. Political polarization has also been a consequence of efforts, recently successful, to form a single Christian-Democratic Alliance from the various religious parties—a task made urgent by signs of the gradual breakdown of traditional loyalties and evidence that an increasing number of Catholics and Protestants are voting for the secular parties.[3]

Labor made gains in the 1972 elections at the expense of the Catholics and took the initiative in forming a cabinet based on a radical program. The cabinet eventually came to include both the Catholics and one of the major Protestant parties, however, and like most post-war cabinets in the Netherlands, it failed to survive for its full four-year term, falling in 1977 on the principal issues of land policy and abortion. The 1977 election saw further gains for Labor, but a coalition program could not be agreed with the obvious partners at that time, the Christian Democrats, and a Liberal–Christian-Democrat cabinet was eventually formed instead. In 1981 a new interim cabinet was formed, made up of Christian Democrats, Socialists, and Democrats '66' with the Christian Democrat Van Agt as prime minister. In the 1982 elections, the Social Democrats became the leading party with 30.37 percent of the vote as opposed to the Christian Democrats with 29.36 percent.

Disagreement between coalition partners is common, even after a cabinet has been formed. Where consensus on a particular issue seems unattainable, moreover, there is a tendency to avoid the threat of veto by a cabinet member by postponing decisions.[4] Recourse to the electorate is unlikely to offer a solution because, under the Dutch system of proportional representation, the relative strength of different parties in Parliament is unlikely to be altered significantly after an election. Delay and the avoidance of decisions are, of course, common criticisms of coalition systems. Lijphart, however, argues that in the long run 'consociational democracies' of the Dutch type may be more effective in their decision-making than adversarial democracies of the Anglo-American type:

> In the short-run an adversarial system may be a great deal more decisive and effective ... Conversely, consociational democracy may appear slow and ponderous in the short-run but has a greater chance to produce effective decisions over time, particularly if the leaders learn to apply the mutual veto with moderation.[5]

The argument is that, in the absence of strong single-party cabinets, there have arisen important extra-parliamentary advisory and coordinating bodies in most fields of economic and social policy in the Netherlands. Compromises are sought between the major parties on the basis of expert advice from a number of semi-independent committees and organizations. Before the last war there existed in the Netherlands strong anti-liberal and anti-parliamentary movements and support for forms of corporatism came from both the religious parties and the emergent Labor party. After the liberation there was a reaction against the centralized institutions which had been established during the German occupation, but it still proved possible to set up a number of important semi-public organizations alongside the restored institutions of pre-war government. In the field of economic policy, in particular, a Socio-Economic Council and a Central Planning Bureau (CPB) were established to advise government on the preparation of indicative economic plans.[6] The development of central advisory bodies in the field of spatial planning did not occur until the early 1960s, for reasons explained later in this chapter.

Recent additions to the machinery of central government planning followed the publication of the report of the 'Commission for Research on Future Societal Structure' (the De Wolff Committee) in 1970. This called for greater rationality in governmental decision-making through the conscious adoption of planning; policy analysis within and between departments; the establishment of a social planning agency; and the integration of the policies pursued by sectoral planning agencies in the economic, spatial, and social fields. Largely as a result of this report, a social planning agency was set up and a commission was established to promote and carry out policy evaluation within central government (COBA). In 1972 the government also took steps to promote long-term societal planning by setting up the 'Scientific Council on Government Policy' (WRR), a sort of 'think tank' with the task:

> To advise the government on the likely long-term development of Dutch society ... to identify problems for policy-makers in good time and to propose alternative policies to deal with those problems; to develop an integrated long-term framework within which government priorities can be determined and which will enable government to pursue a coordinated and responsible course of action.

The relationship between planning and politics in the Netherlands can be summarized as follows. Incrementalism has been the traditional political style of the country because of societal pluralism and the resulting form of coalition government, but the need to find compromises between coalition members has created a demand for extra-parliamentary planning and advisory bodies in a number of fields. Planning and inter-departmental coordination are encouraged, moreover, by the predictability of Dutch politics—civil servants can undertake long-term planning without fearing a major change of political direction every four or five years. Planning in all fields has remained no more than indicative, however, because of the constant presence of the conservative religious parties in post-war governments.

A further factor which has discouraged *dirigiste* planning has been the apparent reluctance of central government in the Netherlands to force local authorities to comply with its policies. Local autonomy is of great formal importance in the Netherlands. The constitution of 1848 established that the country was to be a 'decentralized unitary state'.[7] The 11 provinces and the 700 or so municipalities guard their autonomy jealously and resist fiercely any attempt to reduce it. Much-needed local government reform has been delayed, largely because of opposition from municipal and provincial organizations, and attempts to create a better system of local functional units have now been abandoned in favor of a continuation of piecemeal reform of municipal and provincial boundaries. New provinces are being created at present in the eastern area of Twente and in the Rotterdam harbor area, administered since 1964 by the multipurpose 'Rijnmond' authority, but no major changes are likely in the rest of the country in the foreseeable future, despite the small size of many municipalities and the outdatedness of provincial boundaries.

In other ways, however, the Netherlands is a highly centralized country and real local autonomy seems to have been seriously eroded during the present century. In particular, municipalities have very few independent sources of finance and are heavily reliant on central government grants and loans. The overall pattern of central–local relations, therefore, is one which aspires to partnership between the three tiers of government, where municipalities and provinces are legally autonomous, but where local dependence on central finance is higher than in any other West European country. Central government's reluctance to use its financial powers coercively testifies to the residual importance of constitutionally guaranteed local autonomy.

SPATIAL PLANNING IN THE NETHERLANDS FROM 1945 TO 1960

The inter-war years saw a progressive increase in the planning powers of local authorities in the Netherlands to control urban expansion into rural areas, encouraged by agricultural interests which commanded strong support from the religious parties. Interest in regional planning also developed during the thirties under the influence of British, American, and German ideas, and advocates of national land use planning were gaining support as the war drew near. The process of adopting strong central powers for land use planning was speeded up immeasurably by the German occupation, however. On 15 May 1941, an agency was set up to produce a national land use plan—the *Rijksdienst voor het Nationale Plan*—and shortly afterwards the Germans created the power to produce binding provincial and municipal plans and to enable the central authority to prevent undesired developments at the municipal level.

National planning powers and much of the organization established in 1941 were retained intact after the war. The Rijksdienst voor het Nationale Plan found itself in a weak position, however, partly because of its origins but also because of the greater priority of reconstruction work.[8] There was a delay in reforming the wartime legislation and it became necessary to pass an interim act in 1950 which retained the hierarchical system of national, provincial, and local plans set up by the Germans. Demand for reform continued to grow during the fifties, but a response was slow in coming because of conflict between the need perceived by propagandists of planning for a modified but still hierarchical system, with a strong central planning authority, and the post-war support for the restoration of the decentralized pre-war system which allowed the municipalities more autonomy.

There was no general consensus on a coherent set of land use planning principles at the end of the war and national spatial planning did not have the same political importance as economic growth, housing, and the provision of aid to depressed industrial and rural areas with high unemployment—in the latter case through an active industrialization policy operated by the Ministry of Economic Affairs. Not until the 1950s was a link gradually established between industrial development policies and land use planning as the problems of congestion in the towns of the Western Netherlands—the Randstad—came to be appreciated. Influential reports were published in 1956 and 1958 by joint teams of the Rijksdienst voor het Nationale Plan and the Central Plan Bureau which made clear the relationship between the growth of the West and high unemployment and out-migration from other parts of the country—in particular the northern provinces. As a consequence the aims of regional economic aid policies were changed in 1959 to embrace not only unemployment relief in the depressed areas but also the dispersal of industry from the West. The Sixth Industrial Report marked a further change from the provision of indiscriminate assistance throughout the peripheral areas to a system of aid based on primary and secondary growth poles. Grants to encourage migration from the high unemployment areas to the West were also supplemented by grants to individuals who wished to move within the assisted areas to one of the growth poles. There was no support at this time for the idea of linking inducements to firms to locate outside the West to restrictions on location within the West, however, because of the primacy of the economic growth goal and continued political reluctance to interfere with the freedom of choice of industrialists.

By the end of the fifties, then, the Netherlands possessed an agency charged with preparing a national plan, but no agreed national planning policy; a regional policy which was based only on incentives to industrialists and workers to move to designated areas and which, as the responsibility of the Ministry of Economic Affairs, gave low priority to spatial planning considerations; a housing policy geared primarily to increasing production by whatever means possible; and a physical planning system which dated in most of its elements from 1941. The 1960s were to see some important changes in several of these fields, although the tide was to continue to run against central direction of physical planning and towards the restoration of provincial and municipal autonomy for some time to come.

1960–1970: CONSENSUS, OPTIMISM, AND GROWTH

Land, Planning, and Housing

Further attempts were made after 1950 to abolish the wartime legislation, but these were frustrated by cabinet changes or overtaken by new ideas on the appropriate form of plans at national and local level. Most of the features of the hierarchical wartime planning system were replaced, however, by the Physical Planning Act, 1962 (*Wet op de ruimtelijke ordening*) which came into effect on 1 August 1965. Prior to 1965, plans at national, provincial, and municipal levels were required to be detailed and binding—although little progress had been made towards producing such a plan at the national level. Under the new act, however, only the municipal *bestemmingsplan* was to be legally binding on the actions of individual citizens. Central government and the provinces were to be concerned henceforth with 'policy', to be set out in indicative *streekplannen* at provincial level and in whatever form the government thought appropriate at central level.

The new act, which gave the municipalities responsibility for the major statutory planning instrument, represented the culmination of the post-war pressure to restore municipal planning powers.[9] Somewhat paradoxically, however, the act also required government to take on a more active role in framing national planning policy at the same time as it relinquished its tight control over the actions of the provinces and municipalities. Physical planning at the national level was to be more than the prevention of undesirable development. The act made it clear that the minister responsible was to pursue 'a coherent and consistent national planning policy which would provide clear guidance for the activities of provinces and municipalities'.[10]

Central government policy was to be based on the research and advice of its technical agency, renamed 'Rijksplanologische Dienst' (RPD) in 1964. Important attempts to provide better coordination of spatial and other forms of planning were included in the act and there were also measures which sought to improve the level of popular discussion of planning issues. Coordination of the activities of different ministries in pursuit of planning ends was to be the task of the 'Rijksplanologische Commissie' (RPC), a committee of senior civil servants. Since 1958 there has been a cabinet committee for spatial planning, the 'Raad voor de Ruimtelijke Ordening'. A third body created at this time was the 'Raad van advies voor de ruimtelijke ordening' (RARO), an advisory body in which are represented academics, business interests, trade unions, nature protection groups, the armed forces, and experts and observers from a wide range of other government and private bodies. RARO has the twin tasks of advising the government on its planning policy and of disseminating this policy to a wide popular audience. Since 1965 RARO has published reports on over thirty topics, including local government reform, major planning policy, and ways of involving the public in the planning process. It has grown in stature over this period and now plays a major role in the evaluation of planning proposals.

Coordination between central, provincial, and municipal authorities was a key theme of the new planning system. It was to be promoted, in part, by five new government inspectors of planning, each of whom was to be responsible for a different part of the country. These inspectors were to be ex-officio members of advisory commissions, similar in composition to RARO, in each of the provinces, and one of their tasks was to ensure that *streekplannen* conformed to national policy guidelines. The *streekplannen* themselves were given a key role in relating national policies to municipal plans, although critics at the time and since have complained that the provinces were denied adequate resources to pursue positive policies themselves.

At the local level *bestemmingsplannen* were required to be prepared for all the unbuilt areas of a municipality. Once such a plan had been adopted, it was to provide the basis for the granting or refusal of permission to develop land. *Bestemmingsplannen* were also to provide the basis for municipal land acquisition by compulsory purchase. The 1962 act sought to speed up the process of compulsory purchase but it remains slow, in accord with the bias in Dutch law towards legal certainty and the safeguarding of the rights of individual property owners.

An attempt was made during the short life of the Labor-led Cals cabinet (1965–6) to alter the basis of compulsory purchase from market value to existing-use value, but without success. This was an isolated incident of cross-party disagreement on land planning policy in a decade which was otherwise characterized by general support for policies aimed at maintaining the high rate of increase in GNP and standards of living which had been recorded since the late fifties. Consensus extended also to housing policy. The characteristics of early post-war policy were maintained until 1963—*ad hoc* building wherever municipalities could assemble land at the right time to take advantage of fluctuating levels of financial aid from government. In 1963, however, new figures appeared which indicated that there was still a housing shortage, qualitative and quantitative, of between 280,000 and 350,000 dwellings.[11] The seriousness of this shortage led to urgent attempts to increase housing production. Additional labor was to be found by granting exemption from military service to building workers; more and larger contracts were to be given to firms able to use industrial building techniques on a large scale; and, progressively, controls on private sector development were relaxed, so that the share of public sector housing in total housing production diminished in the latter part of the decade. These measures had some effect. The number of dwellings completed in 1964 was 100,000, in 1966 the figure was 120,000. At the same time the share of industrial building systems in the market increased—as housing production increased from 80,000 in 1963 to 125,000 in 1969, the share of systems builders rose from 8 percent to 23 percent. Much of this increase occurred in public sector projects in the Randstad, leading to complaints about the poor quality of the housing environments being created. Rent control was relaxed in 1965, providing a further inducement to private investors and developers to become involved in the private and privately subsidized housing sectors.

Finally, as the end of the decade approached, both the right-wing de Jong cabinet and the Labor party turned their attention towards urban renewal. Financial contributions towards the reconstruction of town centers and the acquisition of slum areas for demolition had been available from central government since the early sixties. The cabinet statement on 'Toekomst van het Oude Woningbestand' (1968) and the Labor party paper on 'Nieuw Wonen in Oude Wijken' (1969) were both concerned with the replacement and renovation of older housing areas, a concern which was to attain greater political urgency in the seventies.

National Spatial Planning Policy in the 1960s

The studies of the relationship between the West and the assisted areas of the late fifties led to pressure in Parliament for a statement of national spatial planning policy. This came in 1960 when the de Quay cabinet published the *Nota inzake de ruimtelijke ordening* (usually referred to in English as the 'First Report on Physical Planning in the Netherlands'). Its main principle was the endorsement of the dispersal policy which had been adopted in the regional policy statements the previous year, in pursuit of a 'more harmonious balance' of population across the country. Proposals for the protection of the agricultural 'Green Heart' of the Randstad and for the future development of Randstad towns were also adapted from the earlier studies. The '*Nota*' is important as the first attempt to frame a comprehensive statement of national land use and regional planning policy at national level, but its practical effects were limited, since it consisted of little more than a collection of generally accepted aims, unsupported by carefully thought-out means for their achievement. The importance of coordination with the plans of provinces and municipalities, and also between land use planning and other sectors of government policy, was given much emphasis in the report, but coordination of an unspecified nature was unlikely, alone, to bring about the harmonious balance sought.

There were some encouraging signs in migration trends at this time, even so. The Sixth Industrialization Report, also published in 1960, contained figures which indicated a slowing down of the rate of migration to the West. This trend was confirmed in the Eighth Industrialization Report in 1963 which also showed that the provinces of Brabant and Gelderland were attracting increasing numbers of migrants. Out-migration from the North was still steady, however.

More influential than the First Report on Physical Planning was its successor, the Second Report of 1966 (*Tweede Nota over de ruimtelijke ordening in Nederland*), produced because of dissatisfaction with the lack of specificity of the First Report and also in order to take account of the provisions of the new Physical Planning Act which had come into effect in the meantime. The Second Report was shaped by current high population forecasts. It anticipated that population would increase from about 12.5 million in 1966 to 20 million by the year 2000. It assumed that the changes in the pattern of internal migration noted in 1963 would persist, but projections of population by region led to the conclusion that an active dispersal policy would need to be continued. The purpose of dispersal policy was now explicitly the pursuit of equality between the different parts of the country. It was no longer primarily intended to relieve pressure on the West but sought, rather, to allow peripheral areas to realize their full potential. For the North this meant a greatly increased population target of 3 million by the year 2000. Dispersal was to be promoted through regional incentives and through the provision of new sites outside the West for harbor-based industries. The Green Heart of the Randstad was again a major concern of the report, but this time seen as part of a continuous, central open-space which included most of the areas of high environmental quality in the west and south of the country, all of which were to be protected.

The suburbanization of the Green Heart was to be prevented by a policy of encouraging urban growth to occur radially outward from the Randstad, northward toward Alkmaar and the southern IJsselmeer polders and southward toward the islands of Zuid-Holland and West Brabant. This concept of 'concentrated deconcentration' was the major new policy in the *Tweede Nota* and it has been a central element of spatial planning policy ever since. Its purpose was to provide a variety of living environments in city-region zones, capable of satisfying the needs of an increasingly mobile and affluent population and thereby discouraging them from seeking homes in the accessible but sensitive Green Heart.

The Second Report was a more specific policy document than its predecessor, but it was still largely a statement of intent, unsupported by real powers of implementation. The indicative 'structure sketch' which accompanied the report was for the guidance of provinces and municipalities who, it was hoped, would be persuaded by the good sense of the report and would comply with its proposals. The 1962 Act had provided powers for central government to issue directives to provinces on the content of their *streekplannen*, but there was no suggestion in the report that these powers would be widely used if it were found that provincial and municipal plans were not consistent with national policy. Central government remained committed during this period to minimal intervention in the affairs of lower-level authorities.

The Second Report included a statement of the government's commitment to the principle of integration of physical and economic planning. It became clear soon afterwards, however, that such integration had not yet been achieved in practice, as the Ministry of Economic Affairs continued to pursue policies which were primarily responsive to changes in the national economy and only thereafter, if at all, to spatial planning objectives. Thus, the *Nota inzake de sociaal-economische aspecten van het in de jaren 1969–72 te voeren regionale beleid*, responding to a brief downturn in the economy, noted that 'the fight against structural unemployment in peripheral areas remains the most fundamental aim of policy'.[12]

The areas to which regional policy aid was to be provided were restricted somewhat in the late sixties. No longer was the problem a matter of 'the West and the Rest'. Areas adjacent to the western provinces which had benefitted from a measure of spontaneous decentralization were now excluded from regional policy benefits. Incentives were now available only in the northern provinces of Friesland, Groningen and Drenthe, part of Overijssel, and also in Zuid-Limburg, an old coal-mining area in the South which had been severely affected by pit closures. The old textile area around Tilburg was included in 1968. Attempts were made also to reduce the number of growth poles, which had originally been too large because of municipal pressure for designation. This could not be achieved fully until 1972, however, because it was the secondary poles which were to be scrapped which suffered the most from the increase in unemployment in the second half of the sixties.[13] Other changes made in 1968 included a new subsidy system which favored capital-intensive industries and a reintroduction of migration grants, this time to encourage workers from the West to move to the assisted areas.

By the end of the sixties dispersal was clearly occurring. The flow of migrants to the western provinces from other parts of the country had been reversed and there was a net flow out of the West, partly concealed by the influx of migrants from overseas. Amsterdam, Rotterdam, and the Hague stopped growing in the early sixties and the Randstad towns as a whole showed a net population decline after 1968.[14] The influence of policy on this reversal is difficult to assess, but evidence seems to indicate a natural movement to the assisted areas in years when the labor market was tight in the West, encouraged by the availability of incentives. The movement was overshadowed, however, by the expansion of industry and urban development in areas adjacent to the West throughout the period, made possible because of an absence of strict controls on such expansion, related in turn to successive governments' industrialization and economic growth priorities.[15]

THE NETHERLANDS SINCE 1970: NEW GOALS AND NEW PROBLEMS

The beginning of the new decade saw a move toward tougher controls on the location of industry in the Randstad. Migration from the North had been halted, but incentives alone were not generating a significant flow of population in the North, despite the aims of the Second Report. Protestant politicians are especially concerned with policies for the North, despite the absence of a local constituency system, just as Catholic politicians take a particular interest in the affairs of the predominantly Catholic southern provinces, and it was partly as a result of pressure from the Protestant parties that a pledge was made to impose restraints on industrial location in the West in the course of the negotiations that led to the formation of the five-party, right-of-center Biesheuvel cabinet in 1971. The following year the cabinet honored this pledge by proposing a selective investment tax on the construction of industrial buildings in most parts of the three western provinces. The rate was set initially at 40 percent. The intention, as in 1966, was to encourage mobile firms to establish themselves in the problem areas and thereby to avoid further damage to the residential environment in the West. An additional argument introduced in support of the tax was that the serious labor shortage which had arisen in the West in the early seventies was producing inflationary wage settlements which were then generalized across the country.

At the same time the cabinet took a tougher line on the decentralization of government jobs. Sixteen thousand were to be relocated from the Hague within twelve years, mainly to the North, but with a significant number going to Zuid-Limburg. Both proposals were greeted favorably by Parliament and when the Biesheuvel cabinet fell in November 1972, the new Labor-led cabinet under Joop den Uyl endorsed them. Ironically, it was the Labor party which was subsequently obliged to reduce the proposed rate of tax from 40 percent to 25 percent in the face of opposition from the business community which argued that the higher rate would drive firms not to Groningen but out of the country. A further criticism was that the tax was not selective enough, since it would penalize those firms which had no choice but to locate in the West. There was also opposition from the Hague and the province of Zuid-Holland which were worried about the position of the Hague as a center of international cultural and commercial organizations. Both were also critical of the decentralization of government jobs and the effects that these would have on the population and unemployment structure of the city. The cabinet stood firm on the issue of government jobs but deferred the introduction of the tax until, in 1973, the economy slackened and the restraint measures lost some of their logic. In 1974 the government announced that the tax would be applied only in the Rijnmond area. Elsewhere direct licensing controls would be applied to firms.

At the same time that tougher measures were being contemplated to increase the flow of jobs into the North, new attitudes to the future of the northern provinces were gaining support (see *Nota Noorden des Lands*, 1972). It was argued that the target population of three million for the North by the year 2000, set in 1966, was unrealistically high and that its pursuit could be harmful to an area which was becoming increasingly valued for its attractive environment and ecological importance. Unemployment rates were low throughout the country in the early seventies and it was easier under such circumstances for widespread support to grow nationally for environmental and ecological goals, in reaction to the dominance of the economic growth in the sixties. These new priorities were acknowledged in the Third Report on Physical Planning, part one of which was published in 1973. This first part—the *Orienteringsnota*—was an attempt to draw up a set of national goals and policy choices and to expose these to public debate. In September of the previous year the government had obtained the approval of Parliament for a process of public participation in 'fundamental planning decisions', based on widespread publicity and a network of local discussion groups. These *planologische kernbeslissingen* were to represent a step towards more open and accountable central government decision-making. The *Orienteringsnota* was the first policy document to go through this process.

A review of spatial planning policy was required in the early seventies for a number of reasons. Since the Second Report had been published there had been a decrease in the natural growth rate of population, at an accelerated rate after 1970. Total annual population growth was also decreasing, despite increased immigration from the Dutch territories of Surinam and the Netherlands Antilles. The changed pattern of internal migration was a further factor. In addition to these general demographic trends, a number of significant developments were discernible in housing and density standards. The average occupancy rate of dwellings fell from 4 to 3.46 between 1960 and 1970; there was an increase in the average size of new dwellings and a related fall in the density of new development. The *Orienteringsnota* concluded that:

> These data point to a trend in dwelling habits towards greater individual privacy and account for the rise in popularity of the single-family dwelling and the small communi-

ty. These trends and the shortage of housing in the major cities have led to increased suburbanization and a failure to achieve the goal of concentrated deconcentration. The effects on the old urban areas have also been adverse—the residential function has deteriorated with depopulation and the loss of young people, and the symptoms of ghetto formation require urgent action.[16]

The report also noted that the number of passenger cars had increased from half a million in 1960 to two and a half million in 1970, while the small motorcycle or *brom-fiets* had doubled its numbers to two million. Public transportation usage had shown a corresponding decline. All these housing and mobility figures indicated that the urban area was growing at a much faster rate than the population. The response was to recommend a set of policies based on reducing mobility by creating better links between home and work, increased housing densities in and around urban areas, and a switch back towards public transport. The Labor-led cabinet of den Uyl, in drawing up the *Orienteringsnota*, explicitly embraced a 'limit to growth' philosophy. The introduction to the report contrasted the optimism of 1966 with the realization in 1973 that raw materials were finite, the physical environment was of restricted capacity, governmental finance was limited, and that generally:

> Human society is part of the totality of animate and inanimate nature and is thus also dependent on the proper functioning of other parts of this totality, the ecosystem.[17]

Concentrated deconcentration remained a central policy in the *Orienteringsnota*, but with more emphasis on concentration. It was clear from the evidence of the years since 1966, however, that this policy had not been successful. The pace of suburbanization had been unchecked and the Green Heart had been further eroded as many of the small municipalities which were to have been restricted to a maximum annual growth of one percent had in fact grown by much more. In other words, coordination with the provinces and municipalities had not succeeded in implementing national policy. Municipalities had sought growth, under pressure of the threat of amalgamation if they remained too small, and had found that growth was possible in many cases under the terms of expansion plans produced before 1966. The provinces had not succeeded in preventing this growth. Zuid-Holland had never fully endorsed the targets of the Second Report in any case, but even in Noord-Holland and Utrecht it had been found that the instruments available to the provinces were not adequate for the task of controlling municipal growth—at least in the years immediately after 1966.[18] Many *streekplannen* predated the Second Report and allowed for more growth that the 1966 policy permitted. The financial statement required as part of a *bestemmingsplan* was also used by some municipalities to support the argument that they could not build enough public sector housing for their own population without allowing for an equal or larger number of private or partly subsidized dwellings from which the costs of the public housing could be cross-subsidized.

A crucial reason for the unplanned growth of many small municipalities was also to be found in central government housing policy. It was noted earlier that the late sixties saw a drive to increase total housing production by relaxing controls on the private sector. Public housing was still subjected to a system of annual quotas—finance for housing was allocated to provinces and municipalities each year to enable a specified number of dwellings to be begun. When it became clear that several designated growth centers just outside the Randstad were failing to meet their growth targets, provinces were encouraged to allow development in small municipalities where capacity existed, in order to maintain total housing production.[19]

The towns designated for 'concentrated deconcentration' were failing to meet their target populations in the late sixties and early seventies for a number of reasons, including high land costs, a shortage of administrative staff, difficulty in arranging boundary extensions, problems in attracting private developers, and, in particular, a lack of extra financial support from central government to meet the high initial investment costs associated with accelerated growth.[20] The problem of the poor preformance of the growth centers was partly responsible for a number of steps in the seventies toward better coordination of housing and planning policies at national and provincial level. Provincial housing advisory commissions were set up in 1970 to coordinate the allocation of housing finance to municipalities[21] and these commissions have taken more account of planning policies in arriving at their allocations than was previously the case. Provincial planners have also gained experience with the new *streekplannen* provisions of 1965 and the western provinces are gradually being covered by a set of plans which are less land use based and blueprint-like than their predecessors. A housing policy statement in 1972, the *Nota Volkshuisvesting*, announced special coordinating measures to improve the performance of the growth centers themselves. An interministerial working group was set up with responsibility for speeding up development in thirteen designated growth towns around the Randstad. This group—the 'Interdepartmentale Werkgroep Knelpunten Woningbouw'— also included provincial representatives. Lastly, the *Orienteringsnota* contained details of new proposals for integrating policies at central government level, using terminology derived from the De Wolff Committee report. Indicative spatial 'structure sketches' were to be produced and were to be complemented by 'structure schemes' for policy sectors such as civil aviation, housing, and transport. All were to be subject to the *kernbeslissingen* procedure and the 'schemes' were required to conform to the national spatial 'sketch'.[22]

The first 'structure sketch', or indicative spatial policy statement, to follow the adoption of the *Orienteringsnota* in 1975 was the Urbanization Report or *Verstedelijkingsnota* which formed the second part of the Third Report on Physical Planning. Published in 1976, this report had the purpose of translating the policies of the *Orienteringsnota* into specific targets for different parts of the country. Its targets were based on the forecast of a population of a little over fifteen a half million by the year 2000, compared to the estimate of twenty million in 1966. Its main proposals were, firstly, to reduce the target population for the North, although the town of Groningen was to serve as a growth center and Eemsmond was to provide an alternative location for port-based industries unable to find space in the Randstad. The decentralization of government departments to Limburg and the North was now to be phased over sixteen years instead of ten. A distinction was also made between growth centers around the Randstad and 'growth towns' further afield. The latter included Zwolle, Breda, and, eventually, Amersfoort, which are in the intermediate area between the Randstad and the peripheral areas, thus in part acknowledging that there was more likelihood of diverting significant amounts of growth to this sort of area than to the peripheral areas themselves.

The growth of migration to the eastern areas of Brabant and Gelderland caused the authors of the Urbanization Report some problems. The consequence of allowing this migration to continue unchecked would be increased commuting back to the Randstad along already strained road and rail links. The alternative, however, was to provide more building land in the West. This alternative was chosen to some extent in the designation of additional growth centers in the southern Randstad along the railway line from the Hague to Rotterdam via Pijnacker and Nootdorp. The protection of the Green Heart now, as previously, depends on the successful development of these and other growth centers in line with their targets.

Critics of the report have argued that there is still inadequate attention paid to the local interests and political pressures which led to the failure of the Second Report to restrict the growth of small municipalities. Not only new instruments but a willingness to use them were required. Powers given to central government to issue directives to provinces on the content of their *streekplannen* had been little used since 1965. The government now sought additional powers to make similar directives on the content of municipal plans, without the intermediacy of the provinces. This proposal indicated a shift back from the position of municipal autonomy in planning which had been established in 1962. It has not been implemented, however, because the den Uyl government fell in 1977 and its legislative program was abandoned, including this and other proposed changes to the Physical Planning Act.

The polarization of Dutch politics which occurred in the late 1960s and early 1970s had its effect on party attitudes towards planning policy. The Labor party, in particular, committed itself to a radical reform of land policy and the den Uyl cabinet put forward proposals for changing the basis of municipal land acquisition from market value to existing-use value. The proposals were not far-reaching enough for the left of the party—there were too many exemption clauses and there were no related proposals to give municipalities the financial resources necessary to pursue an active and positive land policy. More significantly, however, the Catholic party in the coalition sought to amend the proposals in favor of the rights of landowners, and farmers in particular. The draft legislation was delayed on a number of occasions and, like the proposed changes to the Physical Planning Act, was finally frustrated by the fall of the cabinet.

Since the publication of the Urbanization Report, the Netherlands has experienced the general economic *malaise* which has affected most West European economies in the second half of the seventies. This has had its effects, inevitably, on regional economic policies. The *Nota regionaal sociaal-economisch beleid*, published in 1976, stressed in its introduction the importance of a continued commitment to the integration of economic, physical, and social planning, but its policy proposals were largely concerned with the provision of additional short-term assistance to the traditionally depressed areas. Many subsidiaries of national and multinational firms which had located in the North in the sixties have closed down and unemployment has risen again, this time without the prospect of industrialization to bring relief. The gap between the West and the old problem areas has opened again. Unemployment in the West is still below the national average, although this conceals the high unemployment in the old inner part of the major Randstad cities.

The annual report of the 'Rijksplanologische Dienst' for 1980 noted that migration from Noord and Zuid-Holland has not been as great as the Urbanization Report had expected over the period 1975–80, nor had the rate of migration to Brabant and Gelderland been as high as anticipated. This suggests that more people are satisfying their housing needs in the Randstad or in the growth towns. There is evidence to suggest that, as previously, a certain amount of development is still occurring on the inner edge of the Randstad. There is also evidence, however, that the growth towns are performing better than previously in attaining their housing targets, thanks to the new coordination arrangements and working groups.

CONCLUDING COMMENTS

The preceding description of the development of Dutch national spatial planning policy has been selective and provides only a superficial sketch which other chapters in this book fill in. A longer account might have devoted more attention to the specific problems of housing, transport, the rural areas, and old inner towns, as well as to a range of other policy issues. Such an account would reveal that these problems are common to most urban societies in Western Europe, in character if not in degree. What is significant about the Dutch experience, however, is its national spatial planning policy which attempts to provide a coordinated response to these problems—to relate in one policy statement, for example, measures for the stimulation of population growth in the North, motorway construction in the East, and housing density increases in the Randstad. More ambitious still is the attempt to integrate this spatial planning policy with national economic and social policies and with the concerns of ministries and departments responsible for the sectoral planning of airports, pipelines, waterways, and a range of other functions.

That this coordination is difficult to achieve in a liberal democratic state should not be surprising. The preceding description of post-war planning policies has revealed conflict on occasion between the priorities of housing and spatial planning policies, and between the long-term aims of urbanization strategy and the short-term aims of unemployment relief measures. Priorities are determined politically and the weakening of political consensus since the mid-sixties has not made coordination easier. The openness of decision-making in the Netherlands and the attempts since 1972 to expose planning issues at national level to full public discussion creates the further possibility of delay in a policy-making process in which delay is already endemic because of the nature of Dutch coalition politics. Nor is it the case, as planners might on occasion hope, that a better-informed public is more likely to accept whatever rationally derived proposals are placed before it.

It was argued earlier that coordination and planning as principles are readily accepted in a 'consociational democracy', but Dutch attempts to implement planning policies in the sixties were thwarted in part because of the greater strength in practice of the ideal of local autonomy compared to the ideal of coordination. There are signs, however, that progress has been made recently towards greater coordination between activities of different tiers of government. This does not mean that the Urbanization Report is likely to attain all its goals. It does provide grounds for hoping that some of its goals will be attained, however—or at least for hoping that failure will not be the consequence of compartmentalized decision-making at different levels and in different departments, as occurred after 1966. And it is worth emphasizing again that the Dutch have a strong capacity for learning from their past failures because of their explicit goal formulation and the openness of their decision-making. Few of their neighbors have as great a capacity.

NOTES

1. H. Daalder, 'The Netherlands', in S. Henig (ed.), *Political Parties in the European Community*, London, George Allen and Unwin, 1979.
2. Arend Lijphart, *The Politics of Accommodation*, 2nd edn., Berkeley, University of California Press, 1975.
3. J. Th. van den Berg and H. A. A. Mollemans, *Crisis in de Nederlandse politiek*, Alphen aan den Rijn, Samsom, 1975.
4. Arend Lijphart, *Democracy in Plural Societies*, New Haven, Yale University Press, 1977.
5. Lijphart, 1977, *op. cit.*, p. 52.
6. J. G. Abert, *Economic Policy and Planning in The Netherlands*, New Haven, Yale University Press, 1969.
7. A. F. Leemans, 'The Dutch decentralisation system in transformation', *Planning and Development in The Netherlands*, vol. 6, no. 2, 1972, pp. 93–107.
8. Peter de Ruyter, 'De Rijksplanologische Dienst: instelling en ontwikkeling', *Verkenningen in planning theorie en onderwijs, No. 5*, Afdeling der Bouwkunde, Technische Hogeschool Delft, 1975.
9. J. A. C. de Jonge, 'Naar de eigen taak van het Rijk', in H. van der Weyde (ed.), *Ruimtelijke Ordening in Nederland*, Alphen aan den Rijn, Samsom, 1976; and P. Glasbergen and J. B. D. Simonis, *Ruimtelijk Beleid in de Verzorgingsstaat*, Amsterdam, Kobra, 1979.
10. *Wet op de ruimtelijke ordening*, The Hague, Staatsuitgeverij, 1962, Article 2.
11. P. Friese, *Socialistische woonbeleid*, Deventer, Kluwer, 1976, p. 24.
12. Ministerie van Economische Zaken, *Nota inzake de sociaal-economische aspecten van het in de jaren 1969-72 te voeren regionale beleid*, The Hague, Staatsuitgeverij, 1967, p. 17.
13. A. Hendriks, 'Regional Policy Planning in The Netherlands', in N. M. Hansen (ed.), *Public Policy and Regional Economic Development*, Cambridge, Mass., Ballinger, 1974.
14. H. F. L. Ottens, *Het Groene Hart binnen de Randstad*, Assen, van Gorcum, 1976; J. L. Sundquist, *Dispersing Population: What America can Learn from Europe*, Washington, Brookings Institute, 1975; and H. van Engeldorp Gastelaars and C. Cortie, 'Migration from Amsterdam', *Tijdschrift voor Economische en Sociale Geografie*, vol. 64, no. 4, 1973, pp. 206–17.
15. A. Hendriks, *op. cit.*; J. J. van Duin, 'De doelmatigheid van het regionale beleid in Nederland in de jaren zestig', *Tijdschrift voor Economische en Sociale Geografie*, vol. 66, no. 5, 1975, pp. 258–71; and N. Abcouwer, M. de Smidt, and F. Vonk, 'Bezinning op het Regionaal Beleid', *Stedebouw en Volkshuisvesting*, Sept. 1977, pp. 413–24.
16. *Derde Nota over de ruimtelelijke ordening*, Deel 1 (*Orienteringsnota'*), The Hague, Staatsuitgeverij, 1974, p. 4.
17. *Ibid.*, p. 10.
18. Glasbergen and Simonis, 1979, *op. cit.*
19. *Ibid.*
20. RARO, *Advies over woonplaatskeuze en woonmilieu*, The Hague, 1972.
21. Friese, 1976, *op. cit.*
22. P. G. Meijer, 'Structure schemes for infrastructure', *Planning and Development in The Netherlands*, 1977, no. 2, pp. 149–68.

4
No Match for the Present Crisis?
The Theoretical and Institutional Framework
for Dutch Planning*

Andreas Faludi and Peter de Ruijter

> If there is such a thing as intellectual autonomy then it must be seen against the
> background of the conditioning control of organized intellectual life by a variety of
> groups in society. For knowledge to grow (change, move, etc.) we must be able to under-
> stand and separate the intellectual and institutional conditions of organized knowledge
> in the past.[1]

Dutch planning as a distinctive trend has not developed coherently and cumulatively
in a proper progression over the years. The Netherlands is too small and too open to
foreign influences for this to occur. Besides, the institutionalization and professionalization of urban and regional planning have not yet fully taken place. This is as
much true for the practice as it is for the theory of planning. The absence of a coherent
body of planning thought, while in no way having caused the present crisis in Dutch
planning, may be partially responsible for the lack of adequate responses.

In the introductory section to this chapter, the planner's paradise which the
Netherlands once was will be shown to exist no more. Then follows a description of the
disparate traditions of Dutch planning, which do still exist, adding to the fragmentation of its institutional framework. Because of this fragmentation, Dutch planning
cannot cope well with the phenomenon of 'negotiative planning', which is next described. We conclude by reiterating the point that the perspectives for Dutch planning are
very much in the balance. A fundamental rethinking of its rationale and approaches
seems certainly in order, but one must not be too optimistic as to the adequacy of the
response.

PLANNER'S PARADISE LOST

Dutch planning casts a favorable image abroad. The preconditions for public planning
seem to exist. The Dutch are disciplined and used to control, in particular over land
and development. The government machine is manned by generally competent public
servants. There is a long tradition of central planning. The achievements in terms of
physical development seem particularly unassailable.

*The authors owe their thanks to S. L. Hamnett and J. L. M. kits Nieuwenkamp, and
G. Verduijn for their helpful comments on earlier drafts of this paper. The historical
part of it is based on work by P. de Ruijter which is still in progress. The text describes
the situation in 1982.

There is, however, a great deal of crisis talk. A survey carried out in 1982 among professional and managerial personnel showed widespread pessimism about the future, much more so than in comparable polls taken in the United States. And for many years the feeling of crisis was foreshadowed by the mood in circles more immediately concerned with urban and regional planning.

Dutch planning may generally be seen in terms of a response to perpetual crisis. A country whose most developed parts are below sea level needs to be defended day in and day out. If that country—being one of the most densely populated in the world—also experiences a shortage of land (opinion differs as to whether this is real or imagined), then government intervention and control become uncontroversial. Dutch planners tend, indeed, to be envied by their foreign colleagues for their apparent status as well as for their achievements. Next to the British new towns, it is the Dutch sea defenses, land reclamation schemes, and housing developments which draw the greatest international acclaim. Far from suffering from a crisis, Dutch planning seems to be thriving.

In actuality, Dutch planning faces more intricate challenges today than it has in earlier times and is at the same time suffering from a crisis of confidence. The challenges result from a breakdown of consensus as to the need for further large-scale measures of the kind which have kept the Netherlands—literally speaking—afloat and flourishing in the past.

The Delta Plan enacted by law in 1958 as a response to the catastrophic spring tide of 1953 is now not going to be completed as originally conceived due to massive protest against the closure of the Eastern Schelde estuary. The next phase of the reclamation of the former Zuiderzee (now IJsselmeer), the Markerwaard, is attracting much criticism because of, amongst other reasons, its effects on the ecology of the area. To the embattled authority responsible for these works it must seem ironic that this ecology is man-made, as is the largest bird sanctuary in Northwest Europe, which formed spontaneously in the polders of Southeast Flevoland. The latter is now being guarded jealously by naturalists against further reclamation. The second national airport scheme has been halted by similar hostility to large-scale development, as have many road construction proposals. Finally, articulate proponents of a philosophy of no-growth supported by popular mistrust of technology are now giving attention to atomic power stations. In the second half of 1981, these were beleaguered by thousands of demonstrators asking for their closure.

Apprehension about technology is fueled by the realization that poisonous waste has been dumped all over the country for many years. A number of such discoveries have hit the headlines, sometimes requiring the evacuation of entire neighborhoods, the renewal of the topsoil, and medical checks on numerous affected people. In one instance, the authorities admitted that simply nothing could be done about the particular dump in question. This has all come to light within a short space of time and in a small country. The feeling, therefore, of sitting on an ecological powder keg is widespread.

The massive and orderly expansion schemes that have seemingly catered so admirably for the needs of the most rapidly expanding population of any of the Western industrial nations after World War II have also come under fire. The satellite town of Amsterdam, Bijlmer, is a symbol of this type of development and has become the target of scathing comments. Nor have the incremental additions to smaller towns and cities found much approval. Cumulatively, they eroded the open countryside, in particular the 'Green Heart'—the area of open land surrounded by the 'Rim City', the towns and cities of the Randstad Holland (see Fig. 4-1).[2] With the increasing use of the private car, this area had become accessible to middle-class people working in the cities who wished to take advantage of better housing and environmental conditions. Smaller municipalities and developers were only too willing to cater to them, skillfully evading restrictive government policies on the way. It is only now when the pressure for development has eased due to the present economic slump that controls appear to be more effective.

The big cities—Amsterdam, Rotterdam, the Hague, and Utrecht—are facing the consequences. For years there have been repeated pleas for urgent attention to their problems. (Their position with respect to the rest of the country is well recognized, as

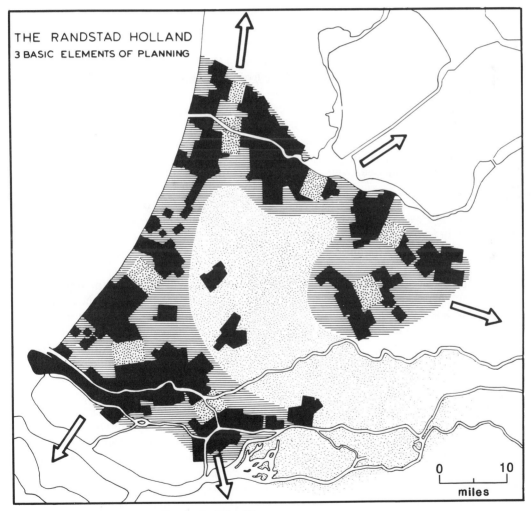

THE RANDSTAD HOLLAND
3 BASIC ELEMENTS OF PLANNING

Fig. 4-1   Randstad Holland: the Rim-City
(Source: Rijksplanologische Dienst, The Hague)

is the fact that they suffer from the added problem of a growing population of immigrants and 'guest workers', largely from Mediterranean countries.) Nevertheless,
governmental response has so far been slow and half-hearted.

The crisis seems to be worsened by the fact that housing need is all but decreasing.
Nobody expects the population to reach the twenty million mark by the year 2000
anymore. But even with this figure having been lowered to fifteen million, at present
there are fourteen million inhabitants, there is talk about a housing crisis, albeit one of
a different kind.

This new crisis reflects rapid social change during the past fifteen years. In the
1950s and early 1960s, the Netherlands could be portrayed as industrious, quiet,
somewhat boring, family centered, and *petit bourgeois*.[3] Since then, religion and the
family have disappeared from the center of the social stage. The sexual revolution has
been a sweeping success, mores have changed, marriages are breaking up at a rapid
rate, and young people are leaving home early. The demand for small housing units
has increased. Not only are they expensive on a per capita basis, but also the people
concerned are on the whole the financially weaker. Until a very short time ago,
building costs were increasing more rapidly than most other indices. (Since 1981 they
have been leveling off due to the economic slump.) Besides, the land being brought into
development programs (marshes, etc.) is not of genuinely habitable quality, the costs
of redevelopment are high, and increasing labor costs weigh heavily. The reaction of
the young, in particular, among the affected groups has drawn considerable attention.
They squat in empty offices, disused warehouses, and even luxury apartments
awaiting sale. The spirited defense of these *krakers* against being evicted by the
police—sometimes directing masses of supporters by their own illegal radio stations—arouses sympathy as well as anger at the apparent prevalence of lawlessness in
society.

Not only has Dutch planning so far been unable to meet this present crisis, but there
is also severe unease about its procedures. Planners in this environment have seen
themselves in a regulatory role, adjudicating between various claims on land.[4] As will
be shown, this self-image has been particularly prevalent since the beginning of the
1970s.

The adjudication of claims on land, often made by, or voiced through, departments
of government, does seem necessary, especially where that land is thought to be
scarce. Citizens rightly demand that the government know its mind and act accordingly. The general public does not wish to know about breakdowns in communication or
conflicts between departments or levels of government. They may also expect plans to
be adhered to, once they have been adopted. After all, legal philosophy in the
Netherlands, as in other countries on the continent of Europe, leaves little scope for
flexibility and governmental discretion. Plans, therefore, have a tendency to create
rights and obligations. When the plans are proven to be ineffective at actually guiding
developments, and when they are departed from (often circumventing legal requirements), Dutch planners tend to invoke a conspiracy theory. Politicians are not
sticking to their guns, powerful interests are presumed to act behind the scenes, or the
old enemies of physical planners, the spending departments in fields such as housing
or transport, are said to have gained the upper hand. These allegations are obviously
not entirely without foundation. At the same time they distract planners from the
soul-searching so necessary to the development of the planning profession. Thus there
is little general appreciation of, or sympathy for, the limitations of planning that are

revealed when it is faced with cumulative uncertainty arising in situations where many factors are involved. There is also little sympathy for selective consultation and coordination.

A recent commission investigating central government organization reporting in 1982, found no less than sixty-nine coordinative tasks being fulfilled by ministers, while an earlier report identified several hundred advisory bodies. Also, a survey at the end of 1982 showed central government to have 538 powers of control over provinces and municipalities as laid down in sixty-eight Acts of Parliament. In addition, 505 regulations for some form of participation are to be found in forty Acts. Finally, there are 51 regulations concerning the making of various plans.

These figures do *not* include the activities of central government itself. Here too, powers of control, regulations, and plans are plentiful. The proliferation of policy documents is particularly noticeable in the field of physical planning, in which they are used as a means of coordinating spending departments. Each becomes the object of a participation exercise. By 1981, four had been formally adopted after parliamentary debates involving hundreds of questions and motions. A further six awaited debate, while eight were in various phases of preparation. (One, on energy, was withdrawn pending the outcome of broader discussions on the use of nuclear power.) One of the earlier schemes was up for review in 1982. The whole exercise of piloting these reports through a complex procedure is rapidly becoming a chore for government officials and the spokesmen of relevant interest groups alike.

Time should be at a premium when planning in a turbulent environment. One therefore can only be amazed at the time some decisions take. For instance, the present Physical Planning Act was finally adopted in 1962 after having been under preparation in various forms for eighteen years! Amendments, which were proposed in 1977, have not yet been adopted. A similar fate overcame the Urban Renewal Bill which in 1982 was still under discussion. Its preparation reaches back well into the 1960s.

The reorganization of the provinces is another long-standing reform issue. Proposals to create forty, twenty-four, or twenty-six provinces were dropped in favor of the suggestion that two out of the eleven existing ones should be divided into two each. But, in late 1981, a new Minister reopened the debate about the advantages of creating more provinces after all.

However, it is not only legislation that takes time. The planning process is also a long, drawn-out procedure. Provincial structure plans take about five years, which is speedy compared to some local plans. The latter can be appealed against to the Crown. Ten years for such an appeal is perhaps exceptional, but is not unheard of. In the meantime, policy-makers circumvent and/or break laws to allow development to continue,[5] leaving planners, such as there are (we shall deal with the question of who the planners are later), bewildered, questioning the usefulness of planning altogether.

Similar feelings are prevalent among the public at large as well. A general appeals procedure against decisions of all governmental bodies, introduced in the mid-1970s, is being used increasingly to challenge government action in the field of housing and planning. What seemed an excellent idea to improve legal certainty is rapidly becoming a cause of further delay and legal wrangling, and of new uncertainties and frustration—not in the least for the public at large.

It would be wrong, of course, to make it seem as if these crisis symptoms were limited to urban and regional planning. As emphasized earlier, they are reflections of a

real or imagined crisis which has befallen Dutch society in general. It has been described as a crisis of the concept of the welfare state. Demands are said to be increasing, as
witnessed by a growing number of interest groups, without there being an adequate
political response. Indeed, the support necessary for the political system to be able to
respond seems to be lacking. Symptoms of this *malaise* are widespread tax evasion,
moonlighting, the rise of an informal economy, and sit-in demonstrations sometimes
ending in clashes with the police (as during the coronation of Queen Beatrix on 30
April 1980).

Though the crisis in Dutch urban and regional planning is, in essence, part of a more
general crisis, its challenges and responses are worth studying. Since the late sixties it
has become a testing ground for political theories as well as the object of professional
concern. The crisis provides a lesson in the hopes and failures of a significant period,
apparently drawing to a close at the beginning of the 1980s.

DUTCH PLANNING: DISPARATE TRADITIONS

This section describes the development of Dutch urban and regional planning in terms
of its various traditions. As mentioned earlier, the gulf between them has been, and
still is, such as to prevent the proper institutionalization of planning. It is even difficult to answer the simple question as to who the planners are.

The planning function, especially at local and provincial level, tends to be spread
over a number of departments of government, each emphasizing a particular aspect of
planning (on the central level, similar but less clear-cut divisions exist). Typically,
planning is the domain of architects or engineer/planners; research, that of social scientists; and the packaging of plans into neat legal language, that of people with the relevant legal and administrative training. The first two types of people tend to be found,
respectively, in municipal works departments and in provincial planning agencies.
They pass their work on to legal departments supporting their corresponding executive bodies. The differences of style dividing the first two groups are enforced by
the traditional gulf between on the one hand, architects and engineers, educated as
they are at technological universities, and on the other, social scientists, coming from
universities without engineering facilities. Indeed, the development of Dutch planning
may be characterized as a struggle between these two groups for predominance, with
the legal specialists keeping discretely in the background; though with urban and
regional planning becoming such a prominent part of public policy during the last
decade, the situation is changing rapidly. The application of legal and administrative
theory to solving planning's intricate problems is becoming a recognized field of
specialization, and perhaps the only source of original planning thought in the
Netherlands.

None of this was evident in earlier days. As in other places, planning in the
Netherlands has developed from reformist arguments, in particular about housing provision. Late in the nineteenth century people from various backgrounds were happily
united in pleading for more government intervention in the field of housing. In so doing, they defined the area of concern of urban and regional planning. Little attention
was paid by this band of activists to planning as such. A modicum of concern as to
how to go about policy-making (once the desired powers were conferred upon
municipalities) was to be found in the arguments for creating the necessary factual
base for intervention in the form of housing statistics.

The methodology of planning became an issue only after the efforts of the reformists had come to fruition. The milestones in this respect were the Housing Act and the Public Health Act, both enacted in 1901, which provided for housing subsidies and controls. The Housing Act also introduced the expansion plan (*uitbreidingsplan*). This provided a base for deciding on the land for new housing schemes and for directing their development. From such innocent beginnings, the present welfare state developed, with its dozens of controls and projects. A 1982 count showed that there were then 537 forms of subsidies!

With these two acts, the question of what municipalities should do with their new powers gained importance, as well as that regarding what methods they should adopt in deciding the planning issues involved. The former question is different from that which occupied the reformers, i.e. what the powers of government should be. It could be broken down further into questions as to what should be the type and location of housing and its concomitant facilities. A constructive design task emerged which was taken up by municipal engineers and by architects in private practice working under commission, who had already been involved in the more incidental schemes and projects of the late nineteenth century.

With the entry of engineers and architects into planning, the first conflict arose around the proper perspective on planning. Engineers were aiming for a kind of systematic approach while architects argued for the primacy of the creative approach. In so doing, the former took a leaf from the book of the German engineer/planner Baumeister,[6] whereas the latter referred extensively to the Austrian Sitte,[7] who emphasized visual appearance. The debate had much in common with contemporary arguments in Germany.[8]

At first municipal engineers seemed to be in the more advantageous position. As officials they were accustomed to having to justify their proposals. They were also pragmatic and, at the same time, were inclined to look for research results. Their traditional reliance on technical standards fitted in well with the reformers' concern for better sanitary conditions. Some of the early plans (for example for a northern expansion of Amsterdam and a general expansion of Tilburg, a medium size textile town in the South of the Netherlands) bear their mark. (Both plans, dating from 1903 and 1916 respectively, are based upon analyses of available information, including uncertainties prevailing in the environment. Both take account of various alternatives. Thus from a methodological point of view each has a modern ring.)

Architectural designers had little taste for the pedestrian and bureaucratic side of planning. In their writings they argued for recognition both of the central role of creativity and the individual architect as the master designer. Berlage, famous the world over for many of his projects, clearly took this stance.[9] Like Sitte before him, he recognized the need for some kind of research to provide a basis for design, but he took pains to separate this task from design, assigning it to the engineering department! Research can follow bureaucratic procedures, but a plan cannot be made in such a way, so the argument went.

If planning has anything to do with rational argument concerning policies, then the architectural tradition does not qualify as a *planning* school of thought. It rejects the suggestion that design might issue from argument, sometimes even militantly so. Granpré Molière,[10] in this respect Berlage's equal, would disagree that the urban designer needed such worldly things as information. Rather, he had direct access to truth: 'For his work he has all necessary knowledge; his technique is flawless, his patience endless, and his spontaneity never lets him down'.[11] But whether we think it right or not, a large part of planning work, in particular on the local level, has been and continues to be done by architect planners.

Given the choice between these two traditions, the present authors are openly partial to the engineering tradition. With its emphasis on systematic methods of work, it resembles current notions of planning. Above all it has provided the impetus for expanding planning, in terms of both scale and depth. The expansion in the scale of planning to include the citywide, the regional, and finally the national level of planning, has already been described in Chapter 3.

To the engineer/planner, research and design—or analysis and synthesis—are two sides of the same coin. When the expansion plans were being proposed in 1898, Tellegen, later to become burgomaster of Amsterdam, stated this doctrine.[12] Plans had to take into account 'all needs of the municipality in the widest sense'. He also referred to norms to which the plans must conform, analogous to technical standards used to determine the choice of materials and dimensions in engineering design. Today we know them as planning standards. Finally, he mentioned ideas concerning the proper relationship between the elements of a design (for example of main and secondary roads). They clearly prefigured our present planning concepts.

What were absent, however, were any clear notions as to the overall organization of planning work or the logic of its presentation—what we would now call the planning process. Instead, plans were defended or criticized for the way in which they conformed to recognized standards and/or established concepts, with research, inter alia, contributing towards the acceptance of both standards and concepts.

As the scope of planning grew, problems concerning the logic and organization of planning work also increased. A structure plan for an entire town or city is obviously more involved than that for a simple housing scheme on its outskirts. In the absence of clear ideas as to how plans on this scale should be approached, architects with their reliance on creativity got the upper hand.

Engineers slowly retreated from the planning process, particularly at the local scale. But they did so only to regroup around a new notion. Research needed to be conducted not so much into concrete situations in the present, but into the broader questions concerning the relationship between variables on a citywide level both now and in the future. Van Lohuizen[13] and Angenot[14] in particular engaged in this kind of work which came to be described as a 'survey'. The 1935 General Expansion Plan for Amsterdam (Fig. 4-2),[15] the product of successful teamwork between Van Lohuizen and the architect Van Eesteren, known for his affiliation with the 'Congrès Internationaux d'Architecture Moderne' (CIAM) (and therefore a 'rational' designer), formed the high point of this development.

The intention was laudable, but nevertheless the work showed methodological shortcomings. Who was to decide on which surveys to conduct? Are 'the facts' objective? How do they give rise to the proposals in the plan? None of these questions were posed explicitly. Perhaps this was partly due to the happy cooperation between researcher and designer. The affinity of the engineer/researcher with design problems must have contributed in no small measure to the avoidance of these issues. The engineer/researcher simply knew intuitively which empirical material was relevant and which was not.

There was little discrepancy at the outset between survey research and planning. This situation changed when social science researchers entered the scene. Initially they were expected to fit in, much as engineer/researchers had done. But how could

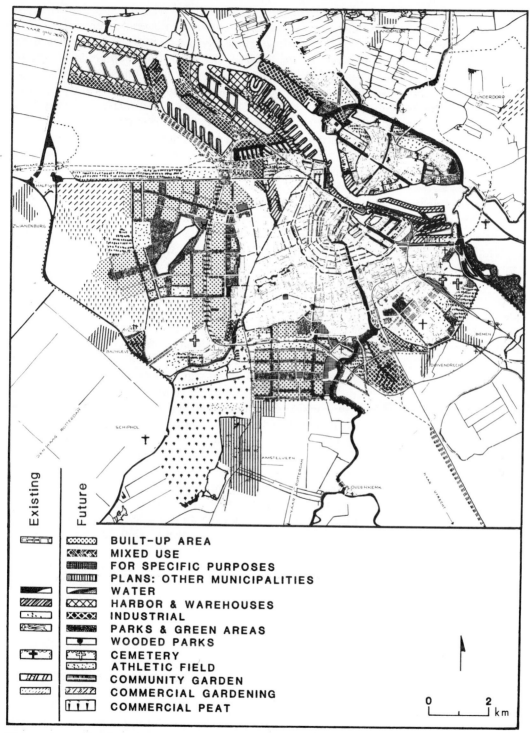

Existing / **Future**

	BUILT-UP AREA
	MIXED USE
	FOR SPECIFIC PURPOSES
	PLANS: OTHER MUNICIPALITIES
	WATER
	HARBOR & WAREHOUSES
	INDUSTRIAL
	PARKS & GREEN AREAS
	WOODED PARKS
	CEMETERY
	ATHLETIC FIELD
	COMMUNITY GARDEN
	COMMERCIAL GARDENING
	COMMERCIAL PEAT

0   2 km

Fig. 4–2   The General Expansion Plan of the City of Amsterdam (1935)
(Source: Dienst Ruimtelijke Ordening, Amsterdam)

they? They had neither the ability to design, nor an affinity with design; their concern was primarily the quality and breadth of their empirical research. What designers should, or indeed could, *do* with the results of their labors was of secondary concern. In the positivistic tradition of their grand master, the social geographer (*socio-graaf*) *Steinmetz,*[16] they tended to assume that policy would flow from knowledge naturally. Thus, in not attending to this step, they were no better than architectural designers.

So the engineers abdicated their research role to social scientists as they had previously lost their design role to the architects. They remained on the scene, however, to design (and later plan) infrastructural works, not the least important task in the Netherlands! Meanwhile, social researchers and architectural designers entered into a new struggle for leadership. At the outset this seemed an unequal contest. Conceptually as well as hierarchically, research was a handmaiden to design. Also, planning was a statutory task, grinding on irrespective of whether research had taken place. This put designers into a more favorable position.

Fortunately for the researchers, the situation was not static. Particularly on a regional and national scale, planning in the design tradition was perceived as too cumbersome and too concerned with blueprints and land use. Since World War II, planning has been seen more and more as public policy-making. With changing styles of policy-making, it is now more a matter of systematic argument than of intuitive design. Both tendencies find their expression in the Physical Planning Act of 1962.

Social researchers actively contributed towards changing the balance of power between themselves and the architectural designers. Steigenga, in particular, formulated a theoretical, social-science-based paradigm for planning: 'From Social Analysis to Social–Physical Construction' was the title of his inaugural lecture at the University of Amsterdam in 1962.[17] In doing so, he allowed himself to be influenced by American planning thought. The onetime visiting professor at the University of Minnesota seemed impressed by the so-called systems approach represented by Stuart Chapin.[18] Later he would also follow closely debates in Germany concerning the role and responsibilities of social scientists. A geographer himself, his interest reached far beyond that of survey research. He clearly shared the concern which planning theorists were beginning to show for the organization and procedures of planning.

With his view that planning, both urban and regional, is a task fit for social scientists with the proper sort of education (Steigenga set up the first social-science-based planning course in the Netherlands), it was to be expected that he would run up against opposition from architectural designers. From their stronghold at Delft University of Technology, the latter defend their primacy in urban design up to the present day, carefully avoiding specification of the borderlines of planning. Thus maintaining the distinction between design and research, between creative work and verbal analysis, becomes a matter of ideology.

Unfortunately, Steigenga never succeeded in rallying social scientists within planning to an all-out attack on their restrictive role as survey researchers. The reasons for this are complex. Distancing oneself from design and policy-making—while at the same time complaining that survey reports are not being acted upon—is perhaps not too uncomfortable a position; one avoids taking responsibility for policies which might come under attack. Above all, the existence of separate research departments on various levels of government militates against fusing the intelligence function with the making of plans and policies.

The 1970s were a turbulent decade, and a new role for the social scientist came to the fore: that of critic. Planning under present-day conditions of capitalism was doomed to fail, or so it was argued. Attention shifted away from the theme of how to plan and on to the preconditions of planning—or the lack thereof. The discussion was in terms of societal control. This change applied to academic staff and students in particular. For a time the differences between technological and university schools of planning seemed to disappear. Design without attention to its social context became unpopular, among architectural planners as well. Everybody seemed equally concerned with the broader issues. Nobody wanted to be labeled a technocrat. German and French neo-Marxist thought, in particular Althusser's structuralism applied to urban sociology by Castells,[19] was particularly influential.

Again, attention to procedural and organizational matters became more a domain of practicing planners, with the National Physical Planning Agency taking a clear lead. The British systems school, as represented by McLoughlin[20] and Chadwick,[21] gained particular acclaim. Its achievements in the field of methods received attention in the agency's trend-setting annual reports and other publications. These developments were followed by only a handful of planning academics.

It was on the same level of central government planning that the latest newcomer among the competing schools of planning thought entered the scene: coordinative or negotiative planning. In 1970 a government commission concerned with the organization and procedures of policy-making and planning spelled out an appealing theory of planning. There are various sectors of government concern, such as housing, education, and transport, each representing a concrete area. They regularly touch upon the same facets: finance and the use of land being the most obvious ones. Because of this, the need for coordination arises. Consequently, a distinction should be drawn between sector planning, concerned with concrete action, and facet planning, the assumption being that the latter would coordinate the former regarding its own area of concern. Together they would form a kind of matrix organization. At the apex of this system, according to this view, a bureau for integrated planning should be established. A more modest version of the latter was introduced in due course under the guise of a Scientific Council for Government Policy, and the new Social and Cultural Planning Bureau also owes its existence to the commission's report. Perhaps the greatest beneficiary was the National Physical Planning Agency. Facet planning seemed to be a ticket upon which one could tackle stubborn spending departments jealously guarding their autonomy against interference from urban and regional planners. One should bear in mind that the Dutch constitution subscribes to the principle of individual ministerial responsibility. Not even the prime minister, let alone another minister endowed with some coordinating role, can force a plan or policy on his colleagues. In this situation any suggestion of a hierarchical relationship such as the one provided by the pair of concepts, sector planning and facet planning, is welcome.

This particular suggestion was meat for the legal and administrative theorists in planning mentioned earlier. Not only was coordination between departments of government in need of attention, there was also the question of vertical coordination. The demise of long-standing efforts to devise a national plan had shown that physical planning had to rely to a great extent on the provinces and the municipalities for the amplification and implementation of policies. The Physical Planning Act of 1962 acknowledged this by eschewing any suggestion of central guidance other than through research, negotiation, guidelines, and, (very rarely used) reserve powers for giving directives. This conformed better to the other principle underlying Dutch constitutional thinking, i.e. that the Netherlands is a 'decentralized unitary state'. Implementation of this principle and of the provisions of the 1962 act required a great deal of coordination between different levels of government.

Both horizontal coordination (between departments of government on the same level) and vertical coordination receive a great deal of attention from Dutch planners. Fitting them into the system of sector and facet plans, and squaring coordination generally with the jealously guarded division of responsibilities, poses challenging problems. On the one hand, the extensive negotiations conducted largely by public administration officials fits in well with the traditional Dutch pattern whereby many issues are removed from the political agenda. After all, the political system is very fragmented, and party politics is weakly developed, as explained in Chapter 3. Unfortunately, the perfectionism which was said earlier to form a feature of Dutch administration, has had its effect here, too. We suggested in the previous section that the feeling of crisis in Dutch planning partly stems from the stifling effect of overambitious efforts at coordination.

There is also a mismatch between so much coordination, on one hand, and the idea that all these efforts will finally culminate in a clear cut plan, on the other. This emphasis on the plan, reflecting as it does the quest for legal certainty, is counterproductive. Not all coordination can go via a formal plan. Moreover, when politicians and interest groups get involved in discussions concerning the plan, they rapidly find that it reflects the results of prior and behind-the-scenes negotiations among officials, so that their say is limited. Consequently, interest in urban and regional planning may decline, particularly on the left of the political spectrum where dissatisfaction with the traditional Dutch ways of policy-making by officials is greatest. This, then, is what the crisis in Dutch planning is actually comprised of. It may be said to be a crisis which would have erupted, even without the current economic *malaise*.

NEGOTIATIVE PLANNING

For a while it appeared that the Netherlands would embrace a form of planning where solutions to problems instead of being imposed by the use of statutory powers, are the result of negotiations between the many parties concerned. This was not only applicable at the central government level, but at the local and provincial level as well, where fewer constitutional issues arise. The question was one of political theory, i.e. whether representative government should not make way for participatory democracy. Community groups, neighborhood councils, and other experiments abounded, sometimes with considerable support from central-government-financed welfare workers. Some even now see decentralization of powers and responsibilities as the best way of solving the present crisis. In any case, the Dutch are motivated by the best of democratic intentions, which form a solid base for this method of planning, sometimes labeled 'communicative planning' in the vein of Habermas's critical theory.[22] 'Negotiative planning' is another term of great currency in the Netherlands, having fewer overtones and encompassing the many dealings between various departments of government, rather than focusing solely on the relations between government and citizens.

Negotiative planning seems realistic in a complex, pluralist society. Any combination of the quest for coordination with the insights of procedural planning theory, in particular regarding the limitations of and the political factors involved in planning, would lead on to the conclusion that negotiations are the bread and butter of effective planning. Literature from abroad confirms this. But there are factors militating against it. Negotiative planning is a messy affair. Dutch planners seem to be perfectly willing to compromise in practice, but to accept untidiness in principle runs against their grain. Thus negotiative planning knows many practitioners but few theoreticians. Rather it tends to be attacked for letting the real issues disappear behind a cloud of words, for preventing things from getting done, and for removing planning issues from the political arena to the negotiating table (as if politics were something other than negotiating solutions, or negotiations were somehow *not* political).

Rather than rallying representatives of the various traditions in Dutch planning, the crisis described in the first section seems to divide them yet again. Urban designers see it as a chance to enhance their professional status, sensing that an emphasis on 'getting things done' rather than talking might improve their standing and thus allow them to act out their visions. Already, designers in private practice are being asked to design entire plans by municipalities as competent in planning as Amsterdam: 'No questions asked—just give us the scheme!'

Other groups join in eagerly, emphasizing the need for more research to provide a basis for better plans, more political muscle for planning, more courage for responsible politicians. What remains doubtful is what negotiative planning should be replaced with. Indeed, what is not clear is what the causes of the current crisis are, nor is there any structured debate about the crisis taking place. The disparity of traditions and the incompleteness of the institutionalization of planning militate against it. Thus the title of this paper: Dutch planning thought may indeed be no match for the present crisis.

The authors cannot but think of planning as involving negotiations and, of course, politics. If for no other reason, this is because one cannot assume that problems and solutions can somehow or other be defined in an objective way. Planning problems can only be defined from subjective points of view, reflecting the perspectives of those involved. Where cooperation is needed, some adjustment of perspectives is necessary, and such adjustment requires negotiation.

Equally inescapable are the limitations under which planning functions. Though necessary, negotiations wither away important resources, particularly time. The conventional answer is selectivity in negotiation. Recognizing this and standing by the decision not to attend to certain issues and not to negotiate with every conceivable interest are difficult indeed.

Theorists can do little other than point out these facts of life. Marginal improvements are possible in the field of planning approaches and methods, where systematic selection of issues for further consideration should be the watchword. Thus, the professional element in planning needs strengthening, but the most urgently needed contribution remains at the philosophical level. Planners must be reconciled to the fact that they have limited capacities for knowing what they think they ought to be doing: finding hard-and-fast solutions to what are essentially messy problems.

Perhaps, though, the future may hold in store a rather different development for Dutch planning. A hard-nosed realism, devoid of theory, might lie ahead. This might be greatly supported by the urgent need to build more housing quickly and cheaply.

The cosiness and attention to detail which characterize recent housing schemes, attempting to give a sense of the amenity of old Dutch towns, are on the way out. Participation and responsiveness to consumer demand, which have done much to bring this 'soft' style about, are being questioned, especially by architectural planners. So are coordination and planning generally.

Unfortunately, Dutch planners are poor defenders of their trade. Not only do housing interests take over, but environmental concerns are being articulated by agencies other than physical planning. Energy falls within the area of responsibility of yet another ministry, while the links with economic planning are traditionally weak. On all these fronts the need to get things done may prevail over rational and, at the same time, humane planning.

If policy in the Netherlands turns this way, and obviously the new realism is not limited to urban and regional planning, then something valuable would be lost. The Netherlands is a highly civilized society, articulate and concerned at the same time. The welfare state has institutionalized much of this. Beyond basic needs, the quality of life in a more general sense is being taken seriously. Care for this quality in all its various aspects has been one of the parents of negotiative planning (the other being pluralism). It would be a great pity if negotiative planning turns out to have been merely a bubble which burst in the current economically depressed world.

CONCLUSIONS

The tone of this chapter has not been overtly optimistic. Perhaps the pessimism which has been shown to prevail amongst the Dutch professional and managerial classes has also afflicted the present authors. Be this as it may, the case of Dutch planning is puzzling and disturbing at the same time. How could things go wrong, when conditions were so favorable?

The disparate traditions of Dutch planning may partly account for this. The same traditions still prevent it from coming to terms with the challenges of the present. Instead of following the negotiative planning style fit for a pluralist society, even at a time of crisis, each of them seeks to gain advantages out of this crisis by emphasizing its own contribution. In a small country where it is difficult anyway to assemble the critical mass necessary for an attack on the theoretical problems posed by the current crisis, this may prove a lamentable mistake.

NOTES

1. J. Bailey, *Ideas and Intervention—Social Theory for Practice*, Routledge and Kegan Paul, London, 1980, p. 23.
2. For works in English on this characteristically Dutch phenomenon, see G. L. Burke, *Greenheart Metropolis—Planning the Western Netherlands*, Macmillan, London and St. Martin's Press, New York, 1966; and P. Hall, *The World Cities*, Weidenfeld and Nicolson (2nd edn.), London, 1972.
3. For a standard text in English, see J. Goudsblom, *Dutch Society*, Random House, New York, 1967.

4. See D. L. Foley, 'British Town Planning: One Ideology or Three?', *British Journal of Sociology*, vol. 11, 1960, pp. 211-31; and A. Faludi, *A Reader in Planning Theory*, Pergamon, Oxford, 1973, pp. 69-93.

5. The favorite means for allowing desired development to occur irrespective of plans is provided by an article in the Physical Planning Act giving the municipal executive the power to anticipate a future plan when issuing a building permit. Subject to the provincial executive's approval, this power has been used to issue a very substantial proportion of all building permits of the last decade.

6. His best known work is: R Baumeister, *Stadterweiterungen in technischer, baupolizeilicher un wirtschaftlicher Beziehung*, Berlin, 1876.

7. His main work is: C. Sitte, *Der Städte-bau nach seinen künstlerischen Grundsätzen*, Verlag von Carl Graeser & Co., Vienna, 1889. See also G. R. Collins and C. Craseman-Collins, *Camillo Sitte and the Birth of Modern City Planning*, London–New York, 1965.

8. G. Fehl, 'Stadtbaukunst contra Stadtplanung', *Stadtbauwelt*, no. 65, 1980, pp. 451-62.

9. Important publications of Berlage in this respect are: H. P. Berlage, *De kunst in Stedenbouw* (4 articles), *Bouwkundig Weekblad*, 1892, pp. 87-91, 101-2, 121-4, 126-7; and *Stedenbouw* (4 articles), *De Beweging*, 1914, pp. 1-17, 142-57, 226-47, 263-79.

10. A number of articles of Granpré-Molière in *Woorden en Werken van prof. ir. Granpré-Molière* (bijeengebracht door zijn vrienden en leerlingen/collected by friends and students), DeToorts, Heemstede, 1949.

11. Granpré-Molière, *Woorden en Werken*, p. 31. Nor did the urban designer/planner need any special form of education. As a leading professor of architecture at Delft University of Technology, Granpré-Molière successfully opposed moves in this direction in the inter-war period, saying that 'synthesis must be a power of the mind, and not an object of study'. It was well after World War II before students at Delft could specialize in urban design.

12. See his important paper for a conference held in 1908: J. W. C. Tellegen, 'Vereeniging voor de Staathuishoudkunde en de Statistiek', in *Pre-adviezen*, Mart. Nijhoff, 's-Gravenhage, 1908.

13. Van Lohuizen sets out his point of view in: Th. K. van Lohuisen, *Het wetenschappelijk onderzoek in den stedebouw*, Amsterdam, 1940, and even more explicitly in *De eenheid van het stedebouwkundig werk*, Van Waesberge, Rotterdam, 1948.

14. See L. H. L. Angenot, 'Het wezen van de moderne stedebouwkunde', *Forum*, vol. 4, 1959.

15. The General Expansion Plan for Amsterdam was published in 1934 and approved by the Amsterdam Council in 1935. It was preceded by a number of research documents and was followed by many others. A comprehensive study (and evaluation) is still missing. See for the plan: *Algemeen Uitbreidingsplan van Amsterdam* (2 vols.), Nota van Toelichting and Bijlagen, Amsterdam.

16. S. R. Steinmetz, *Inleiding tot de sociologie*, F. Bohn, Haarlem, 1931.

17. His main work is W. Steigenga, *Moderne planologie*, Het Spectrum, Utrecht–Antwerpen, 1964 (2nd edn., slightly revised, 1968).

18. F. Stuart Chapin, *Urban Land Use Planning*, University of Illinois Press, Urbana, 1965 (2nd edn.).

19. M. Castells, *The Urban Question: A Marxist Approach*, Cambridge, MIT Press, 1977.

20. J. B. McLoughlin, *Urban and Regional Planning—A Systems Approach*, Faber and Faber, London, 1969.

21. G. A. Chadwick, *A Systems View of Planning*, Pergamon, Oxford, 1970.

22. See also the work of the Dutch political theorist H. van Gunsteren, *The Quest for Control*, John Wiley, New York, 1976.

5

Historical Roots of Dutch City Planning and Urban Form

A. E. J. Morris

...some are born planners, some achieve planning, and some have planning thrust upon them...

This account of the historical roots of Dutch land use planning and urban form takes as its theme a quotation adapted from William Shakespeare; a presumptive liberty which is permissible in this context because to change from his original wording 'born great', to the wording 'born planners', is to do no more than to equate greatness with planning—an equivalence long accepted by the Dutch. Futhermore, the adaptation also serves to make clear at the outset of this chapter that the Dutch have always seen a need for planning, in contrast either to those other nations which have only tardily accepted it, of whom the British are a notable example, or to those which, having been able to resist it until yet more recent times, are now, inevitably, having more and more planning thrust upon them, of whom the USA is an outstanding example.

The prepartion of this chapter has necessarily involved reference to only English language material. References generally are in notes to the text.[1] Two works that combine text and numerous illustrations are *The Making of Dutch Towns*, by Gerald Burke, and *The Netherlands*, as part of Volume VI in the International History of City Development, by E.A. Gutkind, to both of which readers are referred for plans and photographs additional to those few key illustrations included here. Of Dutch histories consulted, I have found *The Dutch Nation*, by G.J. Renier, to be most helpful for my purpose, in particular as a study in national consciousness, analyzing 'what the Dutch felt and thought about themselves at the time of the Republic'—the essential period of this chapter. I knew Gustav Renier while at University College London, where he was one of my wife's history professors, and it was at his urging that the first of many visits to the Netherlands was made. It is from these informative and always enjoyable firsthand experiences that I have gained my extremely high regard for the Dutch, in history and today, as land use planners, and the creators—both deliberately and instinctively—of a uniquely national urbanism.

In showing how it was that the Dutch took so naturally to land use and city planning, the historical emphasis in this chapter centers on the sixteenth and seventeenth centuries, the period when the Dutch Republic was formed; though it is useful to look first at the origins of settlement in what became the Spanish Netherlands (or 'Low Countries'). It was the division of the Spanish Netherlands that produced, as separate countries, the Netherlands, Belgium, and Luxemburg (with a remaining southern portion going to France). 'Holland' proper, as two parts, North and South, comprises two of the provinces of the Netherlands. In this context, reference is made to Dutch history, planning, cities, etc., and to either *the Netherlands* or the *Dutch*. The main principles of Dutch land use and city planning are next established, and characteristics of the urban form are described, with emphasis accorded the 'Old' and 'New Netherlands' systems of fortification. Amsterdam is introduced at some length, together with shorter mentions of other important urban centers. I then conclude with a brief summary of the eighteenth and nineteenth centuries, the immediate background to 'modern' twentieth-century planning.

Land-use planning is a generally unambiguous term, deriving in the main part from the national preoccupation with 'land-making' and subsequent land retention. Urban form on the other hand, needs some explaining. It embodies the end-product results of both 'city planning', the organization of two dimensions of urban land use (which is another familiar term) and 'urban design' concerned with the third dimension of buildings and related landscape elements. The term 'urban design' is unsatisfactory for general *historical* purposes, since it implies that the buildings comprising the main part of urban third dimensions were necessarily designed in pursuance of a collectively (or 'politically') agreed aesthetic objective, when, even in the Netherlands, that was not necessarily the case. The word *urbanism* (from the French) is greatly to be preferred, embracing both the *planned* (deliberate) and *unplanned* (organic growth) building activity of a particular historic period. From which it follows that 'urban form' is the result of that activity at any moment in history.

In this connection, 'vernacular building' is another useful term, as applied to the readily identifiable characteristic regional ways of building during a given period of the past. (Dialect in speech is a closely comparable analogy.) Ordinarily such building did not aspire to formal architectural values: it was the natural local way of building, using locally available materials to meet local requirements. It can be argued that the most beautiful instances of vernacular building in Europe in the sixteenth to eighteenth centuries are Dutch, with Amsterdam as an outstanding example.

THE LOW COUNTRIES: A GENERAL BACKGROUND

Few readers will have come to this subject without some knowledge of the importance of water in Dutch history, whether that water be the North Sea or the major European rivers, or connected with the exceptionally high water tables. The compelling imagery created by the rather improbable story of a boy holding his finger in a vulnerable dam must have remained with many from school-days past. However, as Renier cautions: 'One can exaggerate the influence of geography upon the history of the Dutch, and far too much is said about climate by those who study comparative national character.' Nevertheless, he adds, 'the fact that the Dutch fought the sea and fought their rivers, and are fighting them still, did put its mark upon their character...ever since the Romans taught them to construct dikes, the people of the Low Countries have built defenses against the sea and the rivers and have continued to wrest portions of territory from the waters. Every man had to be a soldier in this war, every soldier was permanently on sentry duty.'[2]

North of the main Rhine waterways, the Lek and the Waal, the Low Countries had nothing to interest the Romans. Indeed, from the observations of Pliny the Elder, who went there in AD 47, it is difficult to see that there was much of interest to anybody, other than sparse communities of early settlers, occupying a region where 'twice in each period of a day and a night the ocean with its vast tide sweeps in a flood over a measureless expanse, covering up Nature's age-long controversy, and the region disputed as belonging whether to the land or to the sea. There a miserable race occupy elevated patches of ground or platforms built up by hand above the level of the highest tide experienced.'[3] South of the river barriers the Romans were more active, with Nijmegen *(Noviomagus)* of major importance since it controlled a strategic crossing of the Waal.

The 'elevated patches of ground' are know as *terpen*, of which more than one thousand had been constructed by the first century AD. The North Sea coast at the time was formed by a continuous bank of dunes, approximating to the modern coastline, which more or less permanently protected the low-lying *geestgrond*. There was a drained lagoon—the *Flevo lacus*—which was to form the nucleus of the larger Zuiderzee. From the fourth century AD the level of the land gradually sank while that of the sea was rising. These changes, combined with exceptionally severe storms, created breaches in the line of the dunes, opening up the Zuiderzee behind the Wadden Sea and the chain of newly formed islands in the North West, and creating the Schelde estuary and the archipelago of Zeeland in the South. Hence to a considerable extent the continuing program of Dutch land formation is one of reclamation back from the sea. Before the reclosing of the Zuiderzee, more than one-third of the Netherlands lay less than three feet above the average high-water level at Amsterdam. In the western region, behind the dunes, a quarter of the land is still below Amsterdam Zero, some areas as much as twenty feet below.

Land formation north of the Rhine was being undertaken by Frisian tribes from the eighth century; at first it would seem through expansion of *terpen*, followed by early experiments with diking to protect farming land vulnerable to seasonal flooding. The damming and reclamation of tidal marshes was logically the next step. The Frisian laws recognized a need to enforce constant vigilance in the war against water, embodying the oath: 'With five weapons shall we keep our land; with sword and shield, with spade and fork and with the spear. Out with the ebb, up with the flood, to fight day and night against the North King (the sea) and against the wild Viking.'[4] An alternative version defends the land with the spade, the handbarrow, and the fork.

From collaborative effort required to make land for building, it was axiomatic to agree collectively on its best use, and from the twelfth and thirteenth centuries there was *natural* acceptance of the need for 'planning'. 'Rugged individualism', explains A.J. Barnouw, 'does not make for civil liberty'.[5]

Community action was also needed not only to organize the driving of countless timber piles to well below water level, in order to provide consolidated building foundations, but also to ensure subsequently the maintenance of agreed water levels in order to prevent the piles drying out and rotting. One of the most important public appointments was that to the water-level office; another was that of the local dike master who was responsible for the planning of new works and the safe condition of existing dikes. 'Diking produced its own code of law,' writes Masselman, 'when a break occurred, drums sounded for all men to pick up their spades and rush to the scene. At such times all feuding had to be suspended on pain of death. A man who rebelled was instantly killed or buried alive in the breach with a pole through his body. It was a matter of dike or die'.[6]

The concentration of the population on manmade land, over much of the area of the future Dutch territory, meant that 'by the end of the Middle Ages the majority of people were living in urban centres'. At the beginning of the sixteenth century, in Holland and Belgium, Barnouw continues, there 'numbered no fewer than 208 fortified towns and 150 large villages which, but for the lack of walls, might pass for towns'.[7] That at a period when the great majority of the Western European population was living in rudimentary rural villages, where they were to remain until the late eighteenth- and nineteenth-century industrial revolutions. The centuries during which Dutch towns received their municipal rights are given by C.H. Peters as follows: before the thirteenth century, twelve; during the thirteenth century, sixty-two; during the fourteenth century, sixty-seven; during the fifteenth century, forty-four; and two, the new towns of Willemstad and Klundert, were created in the sixteenth century.[8]

One extremely important result of the exceptionally early Dutch urbanization was that the feudal system was broken far earlier in the Netherlands than in Europe generally. The firmly established, self-governing communities of staunchly independent Dutch burghers were ready and able to capitalize on their geographical location as European trade expanded, and they were also able to weld themselves into an effective union in their successful war of independence against Spain. The 'democratic' political context was also to become a primary determinant of the uniquely Dutch urbanism of the sixteenth to seventeenth centuries, as described below.

From the thirteenth to the fifteenth century the area of new land added each century was of the order of about 40,000 hectares, and during the sixteenth century that increase was almost doubled. Each area protected by a system of dikes constituted a *polder* and was the responsibility of a polder-board of local landowners. The reclaimed land was often difficult to drain naturally, by opening sluices at low tide, for example, and the early hand- or animal-powered 'mills' for raising water were inefficient. However, during the early fifteenth century Dutch technical ingenuity developed the first of the countless windmills which have been, and indeed many still are, used to power increasingly efficient pumps.

Already by 1673 when Sir William Temple wrote 'Of their situation' in his book on the Dutch, he found that: 'The Soil of the whole Province of Holland is generally flat like the Sea in a calm, and looks as if after a long contention between Land and Water, which It should belong to, It had at length been divided between them: For to consider the great Rivers, and the strange number of Canals that are found in this Province, and do not only lead to every great Town, but almost to every Village, and every Farmhouse in the Countrey; And the infinity of Sails that are seen every where coursing up and down upon them; One would imagine the Water to have shared with the Land; and the People that live in Boats, to hold some proportion with those that live in Houses.'

Sir William observed this to have great trading advantages, because 'one Horse shall draw in a boat more than fifty can do by Cart, whereas Carriage makes a great part of the price in all heavy Commodities: And by this easie way of traveling, an industrious man loses no time from his business, for he writes, or eats, or sleeps while he goes; whereas the Time of labouring or industrious men, is the gratest Native Commodity of any Countrey.'[9]

During the peaceful period of the Burgundian Dominion, full economic advantage was taken of both a geographical location astride the main river routes to German and other markets, and the ease with which a canal system could be extended. This endured until 1477 when Charles the Bold was killed in defeat, after which the greater part of the Low Countries was carried as a dowry by his daughter Mary into the growing empire of the Spanish House of Hapsburg. As will be related next, it was the successful revolt of the northern provinces of the Spanish Netherlands that created the Dutch Republic.

URBAN ORIGINS AND GROWTH

When, at the end of the sixteenth century, the territory of the future Dutch Republic became a part of the Spanish Netherlands, its urban settlement pattern, in common with that of Western Europe generally, had for some time since been firmly established. But there are important differences between the ways in which Dutch towns achieved their jealously valued urban status and the general circumstances. In Western Europe four main types of town can be identified by origin: first, and in the great majority, those which originated from villages; second, towns which were the reestablishment of a Roman foundation; third, civil townships connected with a *burg* (military stronghold) or a monastery; and fourth, 'new town' foundations, settlements created with instant urban status.

In the Netherlands, compared to the rest of Western Europe, far fewer towns were of Roman or military or religious origins, for reasons already introduced. The small number of medieval 'new towns' perhaps accords with the European average, thus we can see that a significantly higher proportion of Dutch towns achieved urban status from village origins. (For the crucial distinction between 'urban' and 'rural' status, see Morris, *op. cit.*, and Gideon Sjoberg, *Cities*.[10] For the present purpose it will suffice that an 'urban settlement' has a trading (market) function, whereas a 'rural settlement' (village) does not.

Although important, the above difference from usual European circumstances is overshadowed by three other urban characteristics which are uniquely Dutch. The first and second concern the physical, two-dimensional nature of settlement origins and subsequent growth, and the third, described later, concerns the constituents of Dutch urbanism.

In general, the physical growth of a settlement can be either along *unplanned* lines, or it can follow the predetermined directions of *planned* intentions.[11] Until recent decades, in international urban history the former process has greatly dominated the latter, with important national exceptions, the most noteworthy of which concerns the achievements of Dutch city planning and urbanism (for which the extra-special national circumstances have been previously established).[12]

Where the physical characteristics of settlement in the Netherlands differ from those of western Europe generally (and indeed is still so with the creation of new land) is in the 'planning' not only of an unusually high proportion of the original villages, but also the subsequent extensions of many of those that grew into towns. The only truly 'unplanned' villages were those which were established on existing high ground, and the only organic growth consonant with Western European tradition was that which was possible before all the available land had been taken up. The historic nuclei of present-day Haarlem and Leiden are outstanding examples of unplanned urban development, as clearly revealed by old maps, and are still there to be visited.

Villages founded in connection with land reclamation works—or where the cause and effect were reversed—ordinarily involved the construction of one or more dikes for

land drainage and the creation of a safe land route, with adjoining building plots, raised above the high-water level. The simplest form was that of a canal lined by buildings
on one side only. Variants included land routes and buildings raised above both sides
of the canal; a cross form, where the dike intersects an existing land route, Burke cites
Sloten as a clear example;[13] and a combination of dikes and a dam, whereby the main
flow of a river is diverted along both sides of an enclosed 'harbor'. The latter required
the greatest resource investment and was accordingly employed very rarely, by far its
most important use was in the creation of Amsterdam.

The resultant village, or eventual urban form, was not necessarily 'planned' to the
extent, for example, of a thirteenth-century *bastide* in South-Western France, where
the market square and the layout of streets and building plots were variously predetermined. Nevertheless neither was the form the result of unplanned processes; rather it
was a uniquely Dutch modification of organic growth, controlled along lines determined by the all-important 'water factor.'

Of greater consequence than the shaping of urban nuclei—because of the comparatively extensive areas involved—was the need to control the reclamation and use
of new suburban land. This brought the 'water factor' into even greater prominence
during the urban expansion phases of the fourteenth to eighteenth centuries. Not only
were new canals required in order to drain land and provide excavated soil for land formation, but they were also necessary so as to provide water-transport access up to a
considerable proportion of the building which were to serve both as the residences and
the warehouses and workshops of burgher families. Moreover, the outermost canals
characteristically performed the additional function of a 'wet moat' within the defensive system of that time. The Dutch term for the 'water towns' is *grachtenstaden*,
from the *grachten*, or drainage canals, which were excavated either for the foundation
or extension of towns.

In numerous instances, the plan of a new urban district was determined by the
preexisting layout of ditches (*sloten*) for draining the adjoining agricultural land over
which the expansion was to take place. Typically, these had been dug as parallel
straight lines, a uniform distance apart, and when widened and deepened, a proportion
were upgraded as *grachten* serving the new district. The regular *sloten* are the uniquely Dutch counterpart of the haphazard English field hedgerow patterns. As is to be expected, these two fundamentally different types of 'pre-urban *cadastre*' (to use a term
coming into general use) resulted in the creation of fundamentally different urban
forms. The sketch-map of Delft, (Fig. 5-1), illustrates this Dutch pre-urban *cadastre*.

Amsterdam, the largest by far, and the most famous *grachtenstaden*, is described
below. Alkmaar (Figure 5-2) is an example of a nucleus on high ground to which an
enclosing ring of new districts was added. Delft is regarded by Burke as 'the classic example', with major extensions in 1350 and 1395. Leiden, (Fig. 5-3), with a population of
some ten thousand was the largest city in the Netherlands at the end of the fourteenth
century, by which period from *burcht* origins it had acquired several physical extensions, and there were also to be further major extenions in the seventeenth century.

The Eighty Years War

In 1506 the Burgundian Dominion passed to Spain through the marriage of Mary of
Burgundy into the house of Hapsburg. By mid-century her great grandson, Philip II
of Spain, ruled a vast empire which included the main portion of the Netherlands, in
addition to the newly discovered Americas. Renier believes that in the light of the

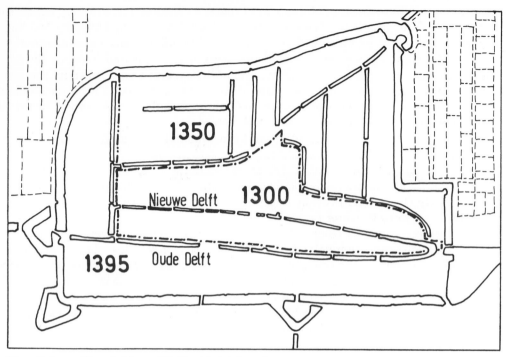

Fig. 5–1   Sketch Map of Delft, 1650 (after Johannes Blaeu)

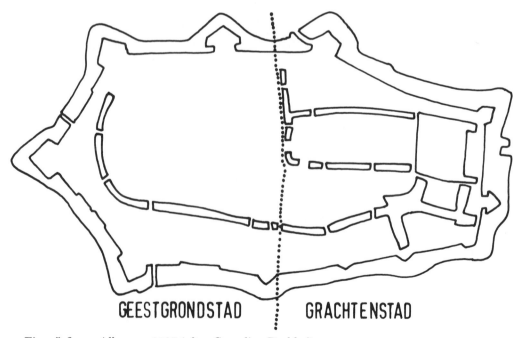

Fig. 5–2   Alkmaar, 1597 (after Cornelius Drebbel)

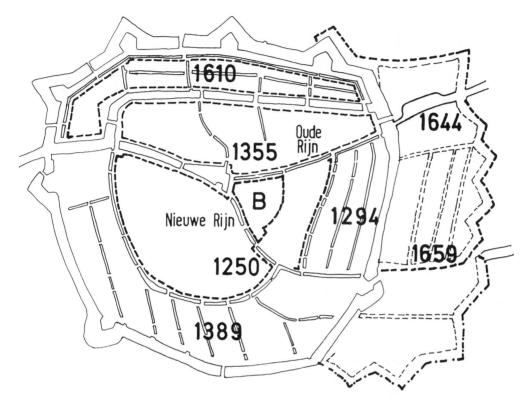

Fig. 5-3   Leiden, 1640 (after Johannes Blaeu)

time, 'Philip of Hapsburg was a progressive ruler (who) tried to unify his dominions and to rationalise their administration'.[14] But in seeking to impose on the Netherlands the same monarchist government that had been achieved in Spain, through the creation of a united Kingdom of the Netherlands with its capital at Brussels, he misjudged the independent spirit of the Netherlands, the whole of which rose against him in 1568. In the North, the revolt was successful, and out of the Eighty Years War (as the Dutch still call it) was created the Dutch nation. In the South the revolt failed and independence came much later.

Of the contributory reasons for the northern success, two of present relevance are: (1) the comparatively high proportions of urbanization in the key provinces of Holland (50 percent plus), Flanders (45 percent plus), and Brabant (35 percent plus), urbanization which had led to strong trading communities who had most to gain from independence; and (2) the fortunes of geography whereby water, on this occasion, could be used in the defenses against Spain. In the drier, less urbanized South, local resistance was powerless against Philip's highly trained, veteran professionals, whereas in the North, Dutch nationhood had secure roots in the natural redoubt formed by the seaward provinces of Holland and Zeeland. Christopher Duffy quotes Bentivoglio, who wrote in 1678: 'It is almost impossible to enter either of those provinces in force, because not only the chief places, but even the commonest towns are environed either by the sea, rivers or lakes, or by earth, than which there can be none more low, or more miry'.[15] (The role of fortification in Dutch city planning and its effects on urban form are described later in this chapter.)

The war against Spain lasted until 1648, concluding with the Peace of Münster when Spain gave *de jure* recognition to the Dutch Republic. Already since 1609 the Dutch had enjoyed *de facto* independence north of the frontier separating them from the reconquered southern provinces, a frontier which had been stabilized from the early 1590s.

DUTCH URBAN FORM OF THE SIXTEENTH TO EIGHTEENTH CENTURIES

The political context for Dutch urban form of this period (and also, incidentally, that in England) was markedly different from most other European countries. Combined, in the Netherlands, with uniquely national physical constraints on the use of urban land, it is hardly surprising that Dutch cities evolved along uniquely national lines. In contrast to circumstances in other Continental countries, where centralized, all-powerful monarchies could impose themselves on their capital cities and provincial centers through the self-aggrandizing construction of vast palaces, grand avenues, and impressive statued squares, in the republican Netherlands burgher communities were successful in creating impressively unified cities. Writing of Amsterdam, Steen Eiler Rasmussen, perhaps the most perceptively analytical of urban historians, observed that 'while it entirely lacked the one dominating body, every building in it was part of a harmonious whole, the entire city one great composition'.[16]

Democratic self-government and shortage of urban land were twin determinants of that character. The *grachtenstaden* could not afford to provide for space merely for monumental effect. Expensively acquired land had to be put to work in order to recoup investment and to produce revenue for further expansion. In other locations, where land was not at such a premium, civic spaces usually served the purpose of market squares, notable examples of which are at Delft, Amersfoort, and Gouda. Architectural dominance, where it occurred, was mainly in the form of town and market halls. The one exceptional urban palace, at Amsterdam, built originally as the State or Senate house between 1648–64, is characteristically modest for all its size, prompting Geoffrey Cotterell to observe that it 'looks down pretending to be a large post office; for how can a palace be a palace without a grand entrance—without at least a courtyard? Seven little doors are ridiculous!'[17]

The characteristic basic component of historic Dutch urban form is the individual burgher's house, and it was the organization of these houses as a 'harmonious whole' that prompted Rasmussen to write of Amsterdam as 'one great composition'. In this respect Amsterdam must be regarded as the outstanding Dutch city, if only because of the exceptional extent of its historic central districts. Leaving size aside, however, Amsterdam is but one of several claimants as the most beautiful Dutch city, and there are numerous more modest historic centers which have their own particular attractions as variations on the uniquely national theme. To experience Amsterdam alone is not enough: it must be seen in the context of other historic cities if its qualities are to be fully appreciated.

The traditional urban scene is a blend of buildings and public open spaces. The great majority of Dutch buildings originated as multipurpose combinations of residence and warehouse (and workshop, if the owner were involved in small-scale domestic industry); and the open space was the canals required to provide them with the vital waterway access. Fortunately, indeed in effect 'miraculously' as compared with the commercial and wartime devastation of urban history in other countries, the many changes of use from original purpose have been accommodated behind the historic facades with remarkably little effect on external appearances. Similarly, the canals have not been filled in, as must have been their fate in other countries. The greatest change that they have seen, intrusive as it is, has been the use of onetime quaysides as open-air car parks.

Each building fronting on to a canal had its right to that waterway and quayside. Minor building plots fronting cross-streets were on literal 'backwaters'; as shown in Fig. 5-4. A description of an average merchant's house in Amsterdam is provided by Cotterell: 'It would have a cellar, a ground floor where he and his family lived and slept, an upstairs apartment which was probably his workroom but possibly included a bedroom, and above that an attic beneath the gable which was his private warehouse-goods went up and down by pulley. The street, whether it faced a canal or another row of houses, was an extension of his house. In fact it was like a large room belonging to all the inhabitants: They sat out in it, worked in it, and played in it. The air, though this was unnoticed, was a trifle stuffy. Their beds were large, rather coffin-like affairs, attached to or recessed into the wall—a version of pull-out beds in one-room apartments. Some houses had privies. If not, the matter had to be attended to with commodes and chamber pots. Washing was no problem. Nobody washed. Or, at least very little'.[18]

The buildings were formed into continuous terraces, each plot having the narrow frontage and considerable depth as a result of the high medieval real-estate value plac-ed on frontage, whether it be to a canal or a street. Because of the narrow width, the side (or party) walls were the only load-bearing walls required, with the floor joists spanning across between them. Adjoining building owners usually shared the cost of the piled foundations needed for side walls. At the front and back of the building, elevational construction was kept as lightweight as possible, in order to avoid the need for expensive piling, and the resultant dominance of glazed-window openings com-pared with solid wall areas is characteristically Dutch in appearance. So also are the variations on the stepped-gable theme, as forming the ends of steeply pitched roofs.

Although as described here, the building plots of *grachtenstaden* were created as a result of carefully coordinated city planning processes, the elevations themselves were neither determined by municipal legislation, nor were they formally designed by ar-chitects as such. Other than a usual requirement to use specified fireproof materials, individual designs were the interpretation by the builder concerned of accepted local methods expressed in the 'local vernacular' of the period. Variety with order is one way of summarizing urban form of the period. Rasmussen's alternative is that 'tree-line canals and unified block fronts of solid, unpretentious houses reflected the diligence and energy of the Dutch community and the commercial genius of its people. The town was like a great and flourishing corporation in which each citizen owned shares'.[19]

Fig. 5-4   Sketch showing Relationships among Buildings, Streets and Canal

Urban Fortification

Just as when viewed from the air, or interpreted from large-scale maps, the Dutch
countryside is marked by self-evident lines of 'battlefields' from wars against the sea;
so the forms of the inner nuclei of most modern Dutch cities show signs of fortification
against military attack, there are still traces of walls, moats, and bastions. Fortification by a ruling élite against *internal* uprising, that required the construction of
castles and citadels (notably those for the Spanish Duke of Alva at Antwerp, Valen-
ciennes, Ypres, and other cities in the disputed Southern Netherlands), was never a
characteristic of Dutch defensive systems which were there to protect the entire urban
community against *external* attack. Duffy notes an exception at Groningen where in
1600 the States General went so far as to build a citadel of their own, as punishment
for the citizen's refusal to pay their contributions, prompting the French envoy to ex-
claim: 'Even the Spanish Archdukes would have been prevented from taking such
measures in the towns subject to them'.[20]

The construction of a new urban defensive perimeter requires organized community
action akin to that required for water control. Hence it is hardly surprising to find that
from the 1570s, when Spanish counter-revolutionary operations began in earnest,
hitherto unversed Dutch engineers rapidly became European leaders in the science of
urban fortification. In this work their old enemy, water, became an essential ally, providing at an economic level of investment the basis of first the 'Old' and then the 'New
Netherlandish' methods of fortification. Dutch military engineers became much
sought-after international consultants, advising Berlin, among other city clients, on
the design of its new system of 1653-8.

Until 1453, when at Constantinople the besieging Turkish army used artillery to break down the defensive walls, urban fortification was at the comparatively simple, inexpensive scale of the wall enclosed within a moat, arguably best filled with water. The wall raised the defenders above their attackers, giving them such advantages that successful sieges usually required the assistance of starvation, disease, dissension, or treachery of the besieged, until, that is, the revolutionary advent of artillery.[21] Vulnerable Dutch cities requiring fortification were secure within simple brick walls supplementing their natural water defenses, or easily excavated wet ditches. At that time, fortification of a community was ordinarily carried out by the community; another instance of the necessary acceptance of 'planning' by the Dutch. At Naarden, a small town famously refortified later, an ordinance of 3 May 1442 required that 'no one can be accepted as a citizen without making a donation of 20,000 bricks to the town to be paid within two years'.[22]

The acquisition of land by a community for the construction of its new defenses, or the extension of an existing system, involved its citizens in 'compulsory purchase' legislation; a process which is the legal prerequisite for modern urban and rural planning (in the Western world) and one with which the Dutch have been reconciled ever since the thirteenth and fourteenth centuries. In 1271 the town of Dordrecht was granted the right to acquire land for a new moat, regardless of existing uses, with 'right of free access to and use of land needed for this purpose'. A fair price was to be paid to the owners of the land, which, it is to be believed, 'did not considerably exceed its *agricultural* value' (author's italics).[23] There is a comparable record of 1386 from Leiden whereby the granting (by the feudal lord) of the right to acquire land compulsorily for extended fortifications instructed that 'compensation fixed by the Aldermen, should be paid'; at not much more than agricultural value, according to E.A. Gutkind.

In addition to the recognition of the need to pay fair compensation for private property acquired in the common interest, Dutch city councils also evolved a complementary system whereby 'betterment' payments should be made towards the cost of an urban improvement by those neighboring owners who would benefit from the increased value of their property. Alkmaar exemplified this process, when in 1558 the cost of compulsorily acquiring seven houses for the area of the new market square was apportioned between 119 landowners in the nearby streets who were deemed to gain from the development.

After Constantinople's fall in 1453, the additional dimension of *width* of a defensive system had to be added to that of *height*, in order not only to ensure a reasonably safe distance between the vulnerable, soft civilian urban interiors and the besieging batteries—a dimension that had to be continually increased from the seventeenth to nineteenth centuries—but also to provide for the geometric intricacies of enfilading defensive crossfire. Naarden refortified in the late seventeenth century as the mainstay of Amsterdam's outer defenses, shows how the area of land required for defense greatly exceeded the extent of the town. It also demonstrates the role of water in Netherlandish fortifications, of which Naarden is the best complete surviving example (although many other partially bastioned remains are to be found incorporated into open spaces).

The special need for the late sixteenth-century fortification of major Dutch cities was the threat of Spanish invasion to reconquer the seven northern provinces. Duffy notes four phases of increasing elaboration in the evolution of Netherlandish fortification, 'the salient characteristics of which were the employment of the earthen rampart and the wet ditch...features that met the most pressing demands of the theatre, which were for a kind of fortification that was suited to a flat terrain with a high water table, and for one which could be thrown up in a short time and at a low cost'.[24]

The first phase, from the outbreak of war in 1566, involved expedient strengthening of medieval *enceintes*, to be followed from the early 1570s by the early versions of what was to become known as the 'Old Netherlands' method. That second phase was also an expedient response to need and involved the construction of earthen ravelins and detached bastions of regular design, added in front of the medieval walls. Most of these early Netherlandish examples were in the disputed South Netherlands, notably at Ghent, Bruges, Dunkirk, and Oudenarde.

The third phase is that which in its fully developed forms of the end of the sixteenth century became famous throughout Europe as the 'New Netherlands' method. It represented Prince Maurice of Nassau's culminating achievement in fortification, for which he was fortunate to have been able to call on the services of several notable military engineers, including Simon Stevin of Bruges (his onetime tutor in mathematics and fortification) who was appointed Quartermaster General of the Dutch army. Together, in January 1600, they set up a chair of surveying and fortification at Leiden University. The new method was foreshadowed, writes Duffy, 'by the unrevetted fortifications which Count Henry of Nassau built at Breda in 1533',[25] and resulted in the complete earthen fortress so well suited to Dutch ingenuity and economic circumstances. Coevorden, as reconstructed for Maurice, was considered 'without peer in the Netherlands', when completed in 1605 (see Fig. 5-5).

The New Netherlands method was both quick and economic in its application. Duffy quotes the Huguenot captain La Noue's statement of 1587 that the earthen fortifications of Ghent constructed in the late 1570s required only two years and an investment of 300,000 florins, compared with the twenty years which would have been needed for masonry work, at a cost twenty times as great. In the short term, earthworks and wet ditches provided adequate and above all cheap defensive systems. But in the longer term, this method was vulnerable to a slow, imperceptible, but nonetheless inevitable erosion of the earthworks by rain and an accompanying silting-up of the ditches. Thus the final phase of Dutch fortification was the strengthening of earthworks and ditches with low masonry scarps in demi-revetment.

Amsterdam

Amsterdam is by far the most important city of those with origins as dike and dam settlements.[26] The river Amstel was dammed in 1240, creating the Damrack and the Rodin as outer and inner harbors respectively. The dikes to the east and west determined the lines of the two main streets of the original fishing village (see Fig. 5-6). Characteristically, they are today still much higher than adjoining streets. During the thirteenth century Amsterdam was only a small fishing village at a time when Leiden, Delft, and Haarlem were already important towns.

During the fourteenth and fifteenth centuries the growth of Amsterdam as a trading center required the extensions of 1367, 1380, and 1450, which in total added some 140 hectares to the existing area of about 40 hectares. This early expansion took a unique form, later also to be the basis of seventeenth-century development. New canals were excavated at a more or less constant distance out from the existing perimeter, eventually to be complete as a ring to the west and south. East of the original nucleus, the

Fig. 5-5   Late Sixteenth Century Coevorden: an Outstanding Example of a Star-
shaped Urban Fortification

pattern was modified by the construction of larger basins and docks. A first formal
defensive system was commenced in 1482 and contained the city until the seventeenth
century.

Extensive fires in 1451 and 1452 destroyed or damaged nearly all the city buildings.
In 1521 a law was introduced requiring brick and tile construction in place of timber
and thatch; an improvement that predates by a century and a half London's comparable reaction to its Great Fire of 1666. An ordinance of 1533 also sought to improve
public health in Amsterdam in response to the separate occupation of upper floors of
buildings. Through lack of sanitary facilities, families at the tops of houses were forced
to dispose of their slops by emptying buckets out of windows into the canal or street.

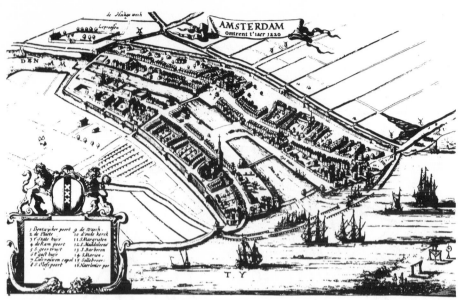

Fig. 5-6   A Thirteenth Century Sketch of the Oldest Core of Amsterdam on the
Estuary of Amstel (Source: *Amsterdam planning and development in a
nutshell*, Amsterdam, Public Works Department, p. 1)

The legislation obliged building owners to install sinks emptied by lead soil-pipes and
it also forbade the construction of covered drains or sewers unless they were fitted at
suitable intervals with removable inspection covers. Later, in 1565, but still centuries
in advance of most other countries, further legislation required that piled foundations
be approved by municipal inspectors; that one privy should be provided for each plot;
and that charges should be levied for the making of roads, pavements (sidewalks), and
canal embankments.

   This legislation was firmly enforced. In so doing, the city created the respect for collective decisions that was to be invaluable during implementation of the seventeenth-
century master plan.

   In 1576 the Spanish destroyed Antwerp, the leading port in the Netherlands. This
led to an immediate increase in the trade handled by Amsterdam, which by 1600 had
taken over the dominant role of Antwerp. Such rapid growth in trade and wealth during the last quarter of the sixteenth century could have resulted in urban expansion
pressures beyond the control of the city authorities: as occurred, for example, in
countless instances throughout Europe during the Industrial Revolution, when individual short-term commercial gain was considered before community interest.
Amsterdam, however, was able to control its future development. Three main factors
were responsible for this unique historical achievement—two of these derived from the
function of the city, its site, and the need for a defensive system; the third decisive factor was that Amsterdam was like a great flourishing corporation in which each citizen
owned shares. Inevitably, as will be noted later, there were those who saw possibilities
for personal gain, but there were few such people and the collective spirit prevailed.

Plan of the Three Canals

Amsterdam developed from its late sixteenth-century area of around 180 hectares to an early nineteenth-century total of nearly 725 hectares, in accordance with the 'Plan of the Three Canals'. Hendrik Jz Staets was responsible for this plan, adopted by the city council in 1607, but not without objections from certain speculators among the councillors who had bought up land in anticipation of development. The layout of the new parts of the city was determined by the the first two of the three factors referred to above. Amsterdam's trading function required direct water access to each merchant's house and warehouse. This was only possible through communal action in the construction of canals; linear expansion along existing waterfronts, for example, was precluded. Organized excavation of these canals required a plan, and the considerable investment needed for a defensive system imposed a limit on the extent of the planned expansion.

The three canals of the 1607 plan are the Herengracht, the Keizersgracht, and the Prinsengracht, named in sequence out from the center. The Herengracht, 24 meters wide (80 feet), had been excavated in 1585 and the Keizersgracht, 27 meters wide (88 feet), in 1593. Both therefore predate the plan itself and were located in the city according to the controlled organic growth pattern that produced a system of concentric canals. The third canal, the Prinsengracht, also 24 meters wide (80 feet), was excavated later, in 1622. The three main canals were linked by radial waterways and all had spacious quays and roadways on both sides. Outside the ring, to the west, there was the Jordan, an area zoned for industry. Around the entire area and encompassing the harbor district in the south-east was constructed an eight-kilometer-long (5 mile) defensive system with twenty-six bastions and seven gates.

It is easier to draw up a physical plan than to create the legislative framework to put it into practice. Amsterdam obtained for itself vital practical help through the introduction of compulsory land purchase powers in 1609. As Burke tells us, the city exercised these powers as it became necessary to do so for various parts of the scheme. Having acquired an area, the council prepared the land for building, divided it into plots of convenient size and shape, and then sold these on the open market subject to special conditions. Purchasers had to enter into covenants, which bound their successors in title also, to the effect that the land would not be put to any other use than that stipulated, that the plot coverage would be kept within prescribed limits, that the plot would not be subdivided by lanes or alleyways, that party-wall connections would be afforded to developers of adjacent plots, and that only certain types of brick would be used for external walls. The civic administrator most responsible for implementing the scheme was the surveyor general, Daniel Stalpaert (1615–76).

The planned growth of seventeenth-century Amsterdam is a clear example of the rule that societies get the kind of cities they deserve. It is proof, if any is still required, that theoretical planning expertise is of little significance in the absence of community resolution. Without political direction, expressed in suitable legislation, plans are just so much paper.

POSTSCRIPT: THE EIGHTEENTH AND NINETEENTH CENTURIES

When the Plan of the Three Canals was completed during the closing decades of the seventeenth century, the area within the fortification was almost 800 hectares, making Amsterdam the fourth largest city in Europe. That area was to more than suffice through into the nineteenth century, since the exceptional prosperity of the city's 'Golden Age' gave way to poverty. This was because first, a succession of debilitating local wars had their effect on commercial activity; and second—and more importantly—the gradual silting up of the Zuiderzee coincided with the increase in draught of oceangoing ships, thereby making access to the port of Amsterdam increasingly restricted.

Amsterdam, fortunately, was both too important and too big just to fade away completely—like Winchelsea, England's onetime leading south-coast port reduced to a small village; or Aigues Mortes in France, slumbering quietly for centuries until revived by tourism. There was ample residual commercial and political momentum to ensure revival when circumstances changed with the mid-nineteenth-century consolidation of European industrial revolutions.

In 1876 the North Sea Canal was opened, enabling the port once again to receive oceangoing ships; and in 1889 the new Central Railway Station was constructed on a series of man-made islands in the IJ, directly opposites the historic entrance to the Amstel, and the heart of the city. Earlier, between 1848 and 1858, the extensive Haarlemmermeer, between Amsterdam, Haarlem, and Leiden, had been drained, providing Amsterdam with a greatly enlarged agricultural hinterland and greatly improved main road access.

As a result, the city's population, which had only increased from 201,750 to 255,450 during the period 1810 to 1870, then doubled during the next thirty years to reach 510,000 in 1900. The built-up area more than doubled, from 800 to approximately 1,700 hectares. Amsterdam spilled over seventeenth-century moat with monotonous working-class housing districts, at the same time as the historic core became, in large part, grossly over-populated. Circumstances that were to be repeated, on a smaller scale, with the other major Dutch cities, and which are the ones which have faced twentieth-century Dutch city planning.

ORIGINAL FORMS OF FIVE DUTCH CITIES

The chapter concludes with summary descriptions of five major historic Dutch cities, with accompanying sketch-maps based on sixteenth and seventeenth-century town maps. These cities—Alkmaar, Delft, Haarlem, Leiden, and Nijmegen—have been chosen to illustrate main themes in Dutch urban history.

First, Alkmaar in 1597, from the map published by Cornelius Drebbel (Fig. 5-2). This smaller city, located some 30 km. north-west of Amsterdam, and 8 km. inland from the North Sea, beautifully exemplifies that characteristic process of historic Dutch urban development whereby a *planned grachtenstad* extension (in lighter line) was added to an essentially *unplanned geestgrondstad* nucleus.

The *geestgrondstad*, which had grown up on the eastern end of a sandspit, largely surrounded by marshland, is known to have had a market as early as 1134. A charter was granted by Count William II in 1254. *The geestgrondstad* has a more uniform street pattern than is usual with early medieval unplanned urban form, with the Langestraat, an impressive straight main street, linking the Grootekerk, and its monasteries, with the quay of the early town on the Mient, to the east. This regularity of layout is perhaps suggestive of a controlled origin?

By the early sixteenth century—the exact year is unknown—the related needs for more residential land and improved port facilities, had resulted in a city council decision to develop a main *grachtenstad* extension to the east of the Mient, with additional new area south of the Oude Gracht. A new moat and rampart defensive perimeter was completed, it is believed, by the 1560s. The new market square of 1558, mentioned before as an early example of Dutch increment-value tax ('betterment' in British planning practice) is also on the sketch-map. The surrounding marshland was drained in the last decades of the seventeenth century and Alkmaar became a prosperous market center, notable for its export trade in cheese.

Second, Delft in 1650, from the map published by Joannes Blaue (Fig. 5-1). The name derives from a shallow ditch (*delve*) that had been excavated, perhaps as early as the ninth century, to connect the rivers Schie and Vliet. The first settlement was on the eastern bank of the Schie. A moat and walls were recorded in 1071 and a charter was granted in 1246.

Delft is an excellent example of a *grachtenstad;* its form determined by three main waterways: the Oude Delft; the Nieuwe Delft, some sixty meters to the east; and a minor stream, parallel in part to the Oude and Nieuwe Delft; together with the regular east–west alignment of the surrounding polder ditches. (The role of minor drainage ditches as a characteristically Dutch urban-form determinant has been described above.) At the beginning of the fourteenth century the urban nucleus was approximately rectangular in outline, contained between the Oude Delft and the parallel stream, and divided lengthways by the Nieuwe Delft. Expansion at mid-century to the east and south-east, beyond the Verversdijk, was controlled on the 'planned' basis of deepening and widening the existing polder ditches into new commercial-frontage *grachten*. Similar extensions to the north and west which were carried out at the end of the century made Delft the third largest Dutch city at that time.

Third, Haarlem in 1647, from the map engraved by F. de Wit, published by Pieter Wils (Fig. 5-7). A bend in the river Spaarne enclosing marginally higher ground was chosed by the Counts of Holland as the site of their residence, the Bakenesse, which they occupied from the eleventh to thirteenth centuries. The town which established itself alongside the castle was defended by a ditch, the Bakenessegracht, cut across the river bend. A charter was granted by Count Willem II in 1245.

The first extension was to the west of the Bakenessegracht, centered on a new market square known as t'Sand, denoting its position on a dry ridge. A new wall and moat, the Oude Gracht, enclosed an area of about 90 hectares in 1250. In 1335 and 1360, two *geestgrond* districts were added across the Spaarne to the east, and then at the beginning of the fifteenth century there followed the extensive new area to the west and south of the Oude Gracht, (which became a commercial canal), enclosed within the wall and moat of the Raamsingel and Zijlsingel. The total area was then nearly 365 hectares. Haarlem's historic nucleus was completed during the last decades of the seventeenth century when, from 1671, a further 200 or so hectares were laid out according to a plan prepared by Salomon de Bray in 1644.

Fourth, Leiden in the mid-seventeenth century; abstracted from the map published by Joannes Blaeu, with the dotted outline of subsequent seventeenth-century extensions (Fig. 5-3). Blaeu's map shows a defensive perimeter approximating in outline to the ideal circular shape, enclosing an essentially 'formless' city, lacking any centrally unifying element, that had grown by the addition of a number of successive new districts. Summarized, this complex example of Dutch urban form was successively a *burcht*, a dike-town, and a *grachtenstad*.

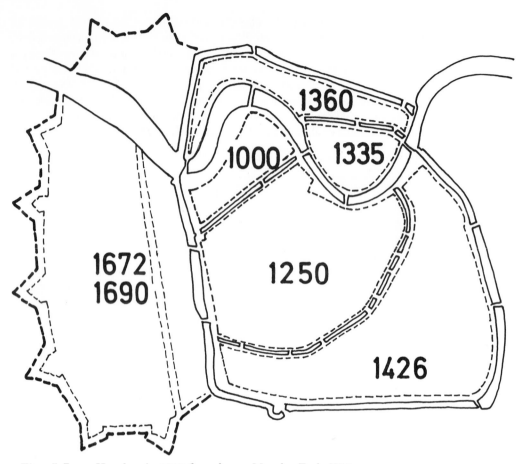

Fig. 5-7   Haarlem in 1647 (based on a Map by F. de Wit)

The location was at the confluence of three rivers: the Old Rhine, the New Rhine (the Vliet), and a minor stream, the Mare. Early village settlement is believed to have taken place on naturally higher ground between the Rhine branches, and there is an unsubstantiated possibility of an earlier Roman trading-post at that location. By the later twelfth century a *burcht* was well established on that higher ground, with a huddle of cottages comprising the trading village. Early in the thirteenth century a first extension was developed on the left bank of the New Rhine using the dike for the Breestraat, a curving street some 700 meters in length, and the lower, protected land for the Gravensteen—a residence of the Counts of Holland. A moat and wall were constructed from 1266 along the line of present-day Rapenburg.

From 1294, in response to rapidly increasing prosperity based on textile trade, a *grachtenstad* extension was planned to the south of the *burcht*, making use of the old *sloten* (drainage ditches) as the basis of four approximately parallel canals, the outer one of which, the Heeren Gracht, formed the moat of the Blaeu map. Two fourteenth-century extensions are shown which, with that of the early seventeenth century, comprised Blaeu's Leiden. With a population exceeding ten thousand, Leiden by 1500 had become the largest city in the Netherlands. Later still, between 1644 and 1659, three

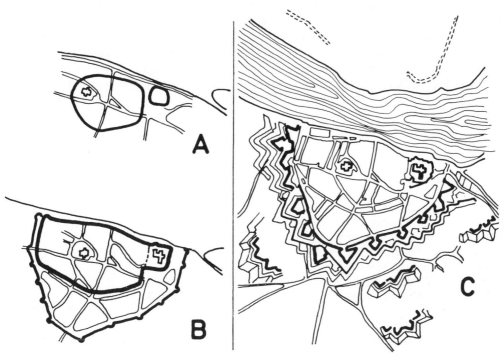

Fig. 5-8 Nijmegen: Three stages in its Evolution; (A) the Original Gallo-Roman Town, (B) the Medieval Town and (C) the Mid-fifteenth Century Town showing New Fortifications

further new districts were added across the southern side of the city. The total urban area was then approximately 170 hectares.

Fifth, Nijmegen (Fig. 5-8) is located some 90 km. south-east of Amsterdam on the southern bank of the river Waal (the Dutch name for the German Rhine). The city's historical development is a major European example both of multi-nuclear origins and also the effect of successive fortification systems as urban form determinants.

The name is of Gallo-Roman origin, derived from Noviomagus (or 'new market') and the first recorded settlement was established by the Romans at the point where a major military road crossed the Waal by ferry. The crossing retained a strategic importance and Charlemagne controlled it through an imposing castle (the *burcht* constructed on the heights above the ferry). Characteristically, beneath its walls a trading town (the *portus*) became established, unfortified at first until fortification was required by twelfth-and thirteenth-century commercial prosperity.

Expansion took place initially to the west, where an extensive new district was developed during the first part of the fourteenth century; and also up to the castle walls to the east. A new defensive perimeter was constructed between 1334 and 1356 unifying the *burcht* and the enlarged *portus*. By 1450, in response to the city's increased trading activity, a *Nieuwstad* had become established along the river bank, and the wall was extended. In turn, the enclosed area became congested and ribbons of suburban development grew up along the radial routes from the city gates. New land was incorporated, and the suburbs protected, within a new circumvallation completed in 1468, which ambitiously provided enough area to suffice through to the eighteenth century. A cleared, defensive fire zone (the *glacis*) was rigorously maintained around the ramparts, whose land was then available in the early eighteenth century for the final, complex artillery fortifications designed by Menno van Coehoorn and Anthoniszoon.

NOTES

1. For general reading concerning the European context, see H. A. L. Fisher *A History of Europe* (to 1713), London, Eyre and Spottiswoode, 1935; Lewis Mumford, *The City in History*, New York, Harcourt, Brace & World, 1961; S. E. Rasmussen, *Towns and Buildings* , Cambridge, Mass., MIT Press, 1969; and conscious as I am of this select company, my own *History of Urban Form*, London, George Godwin Limited, 1979.
2. G. J. Riener, *The Dutch Nation*, London, George Allen & Unwin (for the Dutch Government Information Bureau), 1944.
3. See Pliny, *Naturalis Historia*, tr. H. Rackman, Books XVI-XVII.
4. J. van Veen, *Dredge, Drain, Reclaim*, The Hague, Nijhoff, 1962.
5. A. J. Barnouw, 'The 17th Century: the Golden Age', in *The Netherlands*, ed. Bartholomew Landheer, Berkeley, California, University of California Press, 1943.
6. H. L. Masselman, *The Cradle of Colonialism*, New Haven, Yale University Press, 1963.
7. Barnouw, *op. cit.*
8. C. H. Peters, *De Nederlandsche Stedenbouw*, vol. ll, 1909 (quoted in Gerald L. Burke, *The Making of Dutch Towns*, London, Cleaver-Hume Press, 1956).
9. Sir William Temple, *Observations upon the Provinces of the United Netherlands*, 3rd edn., corrected and augmented, 1676, republished Cambridge University Press, 1932.
10. Gideon Sjoberg, 'The Origins and Evolution of Cities' in *Cities: Their Origin, Growth and Human Impact*, New York, Scientific American Books, 1967.
11. For further descriptions of these two types of urban form through to the nineteenth century, see A. E. J. Morris, *History of Urban Form*, vol. 1, London, George Godwin, l979, and New York City, Halstead Press, John Wiley and Sons, 1979.
12. For other special national circumstances where 'planned' towns were in the majority over 'unplanned' towns see: for the USA, J. W. Reps, *The Making of Urban America*, Princeton, N.J., Princeton University Press, 1965, and Morris, *op. cit.* (in the USA, 'planned-for' rather than 'planned' is a more useful term for the early urban settlements); for the thirteenth-century *bastide* new towns of Europe, see M. W. Beresford, *New Towns of the Middle Ages*, Lutterworth Press, 1967, and Morris, *op. cit.*
13. Burke, *op. cit.*
14. Reiner, *op. cit.*
15. Christopher Duffy, *Siege Warfare: the fortress in the early modern world*, London, Routledge & Kegan Paul, 1979.
16. S. E. Rasmussen, *Towns and Buildings*, Liverpool, University Press of Liverpool, 1951.
17. Geoffrey Cotterell, *Amsterdam: the life of a city*, Farnborough, England, C. C. Heath, l973.
18. *Ibid.*
19. Rasmussen, *op. cit.*
20. Duffy, *op. cit.*

21. For further development of this crucial topic, see Morris, *op. cit.*, and Ian Hogg, *The History of Fortification*, London, Orbis Publishing,1981.

22. E. A. Gutkind, *Urban Development in Western Europe: the Netherlands and Great Britain*, vol. Vl, International History of City Development, New York, The Free Press, London, Collier-Macmillan, 1971.

23. *Ibid.*

24. Duffy, *op. cit.*

25. *Ibid.*

26. For Amsterdam in history, see W. Dougill, 'Amsterdam: its town planning development', in *The Town Planning Review*, vol. XlV (June 1936); Cotterell, *op. cit.*; Rasmussen, *op. cit.*

6
NATIONAL PHYSICAL PLANNING: ORIGINS, EVOLUTION AND CURRENT OBJECTIVES

Jan kits Nieuwenkamp

RUMOR IN CASA

Following upon the physical expansion period of the 1960s and the ideological certainties of the 1970s, Dutch physical planners in the 1980s 'do not seem to know which cake they are baking anymore'.[1] Thus, the former physical-planning chief Theo Quené expressed his concern in 1978. Since then, many articles, not only in the professional literature but also in popular newspapers, have appeared that discuss the future perspectives of physical planning. These discussions begin with the planning framework so carefully shaped in the sixties and early seventies. A leading institution in that shaping, the Scientific Bureau of the Socialist Party, is now prominent in expressing doubts about the effectiveness of the current framework. Even more astonishing is the fact that the liberals, who because of their political philosophy ought to be adversaries of the present system, are now to be found among its staunchest apologists. The elaboration of this phenomenon, however, would embroil us in sociology and psychology. We devote our attention in this chapter to the changing system, its origins, its evolution, and its current objectives. Nevertheless, political and professional doubts flourish. Bearing witness of this fact are the 1980 and 1982 conferences attended by high-ranking professional planners drawn from the various levels of government and universities concerned with planning in the uncertain atmosphere of the 1980s. An atmosphere resulting from changing conditions in the physical, economic, and social realms of the Netherlands.

THE CHARACTER OF PHYSICAL PLANNING

Physical planning in the Netherlands is, factually speaking, *spatial* planning. This means that a specific region, a specific part of the territory of the country, is taken as a regional and spatial basis for the planning process. The plans derived from this planning process are, as in most European countries, territorial plans—not just single project plans—made and approved by provinces and municipalities for a particular area of their territory. The most important of these plans are

(a) regional plans formulated and approved by provinces;
(b) allocations plans or land-use plans, formulated by municipalities and approved by the province in which the municipality is located.

A point worth noting is that there is no spatial plan at the national level. Spatial, or in a sense regional, planning is the geographic expression of the economic, social, cultural, and ecological policies of society. It denotes the spatial projection of human activities in a given region and must be governed by a purposeful policy ensuring the balanced development of various components.

Physical planning in the Netherlands is looked upon as a *coordinating discipline*. Coordination of competing demands for land is predicated on the basis of the spatial repercussions of all human activity that can be carried out in a given region. The different sectors of society, the different sectors of public and private life, and the different sectors of the responsibilities of the three levels of administration all have their spatial translation, that becomes visible in claims for a specific place in the region concerned. Housing, work, recreation, transport, and traffic all need and demand their functional space. Regional planning policy has a profound influence upon the development of our society. By planning living conditions and organizing the human habitat, regional planning is, in effect, tantamount to the planning of society. The prospective dimension of regional planning is, therefore, the key to harmonious development in the economic, social, cultural, and ecological fields, or so champions of a regional planning system would argue.

The aim of physical planning in the Netherlands is to bring about *the* most desirable development of a specific region. Both society, with its spatial demands and the region, the specific area in which that society lives, must be prepared in principle to adapt themselves towards the desired result, the appropriate development, not of one or two sectors of society, but of society as a whole. The development of society has its limitations, not only financially, but also ecologically and geographically. Thus, the consequences of new developments have to be carefully evaluated. When negative effects can be avoided or eliminated by using the best technical means, *carte blanche* should be accorded to the planners concerned. Physical planning should aim at high quality construction, layout, and design, as far as this is financially possible.

In its *national* dimension, regional planning must contribute to a balanced development of the various regions according to the specific characteristics and capacities of each of them. It must also contribute to the overcoming of obstacles affecting the internal development of regions as well as promote a general awareness among the general public of the need for balanced development. Physical planning as a coordinative discipline has two dimensions, namely the horizontal and the vertical. Horizontally, coordination is sought between different responsible authorities at a certain level. For instance, between ministries at the national level by means of a national physical-planning committee. Vertically, coordination is striven for between authorities of different levels, between state, province, and municipality. The coordinative instruments here are those given in the National Physical Planning Act of 1965;[2] there are also experimental new developments such as the construction of sectoral structural schemes or structural outline plans for water supply, land used by the military, transport and traffic, etc.

The classic instrument of regional planning execution is the allocation plan, the only spatial plan that is binding upon people, in which every new development must be inserted. This plan must be adopted by the local (municipal) council and approved by the regional (provincial) government.

At the national level, reports are prepared containing national guidelines and the national policy to which regional and local authorities should conform when making their plans.

Both structural schemes and national reports set forth the procedures for making a crucial physical-planning decision, ensuring both coordination and public participation (direct democracy as well as parliamentary treatment, or representative democracy).

The nature of physical planning has undergone substantial change over the years. At first, the main aim of physical planning was to draw up a fairly static, conservationist national plan in order to mark out built-up and non-built-up areas, to guide the location of industry so as not to obstruct residential development, and to conserve areas of great natural beauty and valuable farmland. Popular ideas on physical planning were greatly affected by rapid industrialization and the population boom of the 1950s. Planning turned into something akin to programming, the objective being the distribution of population and employment more evenly over the country. This more positive approach has subsequently been reflected in the attitudes adopted by the government of the Netherlands.

The positive policy is most evident in the *Second Report on Physical Planning* (1966),[3] in which the government describes the aim of physical planning as being the promotion of the establishment of a physical stucture that provides optimum living conditions for the people. The principles enunciated in the report have been adopted by successive governments, though a *Third Report* appearing in three volumes was issued during the 1970s and early 1980s.

A remarkable occurrence has been the shift in emphasis from a 'recording' approach to planning to imaginative planning, that is, from static to dynamic planning. The *Second Report* included a structural plan for major road arteries and for outdoor recreation, a structural organization scheme, and guidelines for the administrative organization of the country. These are, of course, subject to continual revision as new developments take place and more knowledge is gained; and it is left to the provinces and municipalities to work out the details of their implementation.

The Legal Basis of Planning

When we survey the whole edifice of physical-planning regulations we are struck by the fact that since the early 1970s only part of the structure can be called legally sound. This part covers the items dealt with in the National Physical Planning Act, in which physical planning finds its statutory base. The roots of this Act lay in legislation regarding public housing, specifically, the 1901 Housing Act.[4] The National Physical Planning Act itself and the accompanying decree only came into force in 1965. They cover the procedures for the preparation of regional and municipal land-use plans and the rules of the 'game' to be played among the three levels of government. The act and decree do not provide for what has become practice ever since: ruling by national report. This phenomenon will be described later in this chapter.

The National Physical Planning Act is a form of 'framework legislation.' This means that in the first place it contains only procedures and institutions. No policy elements whatsoever are given. Views on urbanization, land-use control, urban renewal and revitalization, the development of rural areas or population, and job distribution are laid down in national policy reports, such as the *Third Report on Physical Planning*, consisting of the *Orientation Report*,[5] the *Report on Urban Areas*,[6] and the *Rural Areas Report*.[7]

The National Physical Planning Act contains many procedural rules and guidelines which provide some basis of continuity for weighing what are often opposing interests.

The act also regulates democratic decision-making procedures and legal protection in matters of physical planning. Planning procedures are recognized as part of the Dutch administrative system and the Physical Planning Act ties in with this. Briefly, there are three levels of government, the state, the provinces, and the municipalities, each with its own political bodies: the government and the Lower and Upper Houses of Parliament; the Provincial Council and Executive; and the Municipal Council and Executive, the latter comprising the burgomaster and aldermen. Decisions in the field of physical planning are the responsibility of these general governing bodies (Fig. 6-1).

The government decides on physical planning policy at the national level, the Ministry of Housing, Physical Planning and Environment being responsible for the preparatory arrangements. Preparations are made at interdepartmental level by the National Physical Planning Committee whose views are accorded importance. Alongside the latter committee, which is largely made up of civil servants, there exists the Advisory Council on Physical Planning which is reponsible for advising ministers upon request, or even on its own initiative. The council is made up of representatives from a variety of organizations in the country.

Both the committee and the Council are served by the National Physical Planning Agency which also advises the Minister for Housing, Physical Planning and Environment in his capacity of coordinating minister for physical planning. Thus the Agency is a planning bureau as well as a policy department. (See Fig. 6-5 for a description of the Agency's structure and organization.)

The provincial executive is empowered to draw up regional development plans for the entire province or parts of it and it is prescribed that consultations be held with the municipal executive and the Provincial Planning Committee. The regional development plan outlines the most desirable developments foreseen, and if possible, it specifies means of implementation and gives time schedules; it is the major instrument of provincial land-use policy.

The municipal executive is the body that draws up local development plans which are legally binding on all citizens. The Physical Planning Act allows the municipal executive a large measure of freedom when it comes to the content of the plans. The general principle is that the intended purpose for the land area concerned should be indicated in the plan if this is deemed necessary for the purposes of sound physical planning and that, if need be, regulations should be prescribed for the use of this land.

The burgomaster and aldermen may use their discretion in implementing and formulating the plans while taking steps to safeguard the interests of all individuals concerned.

A sound physical planning policy requires a nexus between state, provincial and municipal plans. Certain procedures have been incorporated into the Physical Planning Act to bring about functional relationships between various plans and even to compel the authorities concerned to create some. The objective is to achieve a properly coordinated physical-planning policy while allowing the different levels of government to retain their autonomy.

Regional and local development plans differ in their legal ramifications, municipally adopted local development plans being the only binding ones. National guidelines and provincial plans are programs for the future. The provincial executive may indicate what modifications should be made to a local development plan to bring it into line with a regional development plan; this enables ideas emanating from higher levels of government to be reflected in local development plans. The Minister of Housing, Physical Planning and Environment enjoys similar powers concerning provincial physical-planning policy.

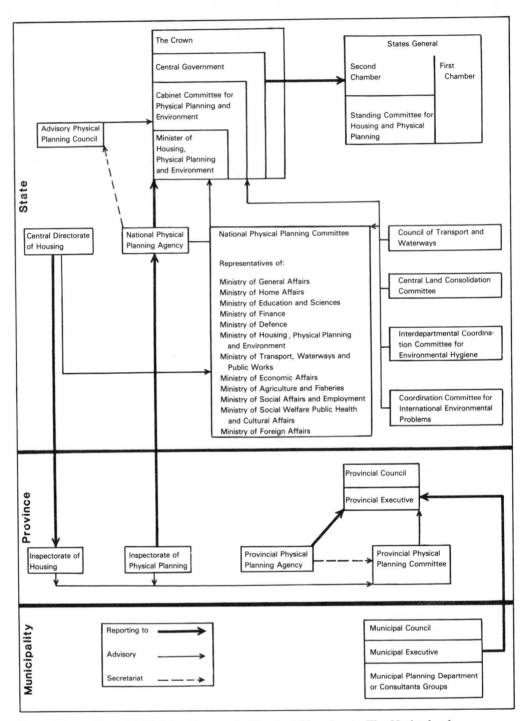

Fig. 6-1   Decision-Making Process in Physical Planning in The Netherlands

Meanwhile, a number of changes, both minor and major, to the Physical Planning Act have been proposed to Parliament. These amendments relate, *inter alia*, to the role, particularly in legal terms, of planning decision-making as a procedure for discussing documents of national importance; scope is allowed for participation, interdepartmental consultation, advice and decision-making by Parliament, and possible appeals to the Crown. In practice the appeals procedure, which is the legal avenue for lodging appeals with the highest judicial body against land-use plans, proves extremely time-consuming. Consequently, a more efficient procedure is being sought which will offer individuals the same legal protection as before.

National Policy Guidelines

These are laid down in National Reports, especially the *Third Report on National Physical Planning*, consisting of the *Orientation Report*, the *Urbanization Report*, and the *Report on Rural Areas*. The *Orientation Report* gives the general philosophy and is a kind of general introduction, although it is hardly cited anymore. But national policy guidelines are laid down in structural schemes and sketches for a couple of the most relevant sectors of society.

The Urbanization Report

This report deals intensively with the social and physical developments manifesting themselves in modern society and which must be considered in the process of formulating public policy. The most important social and physical developments at the regional level are:

the growing population pressure and congestion phenomenon in the large urban areas;
the invasion of open spaces and of ecologically valuable and traditional landscapes by urban populations and land-uses;
regional deficiencies and inequalities in the sphere of socio-economic development;
regional inequalities in the standard of amenities;
increasing physical mobility.[8]

At the urban level they are:

the deterioration of the 'residential climate' in certain areas, more especially in the older residential areas;
the population spillover from the cities, partly owing to a shortage of housing in the cities and partly due to shortcomings in the residential environment;
the absence of a freedom of choice with respect to housing accommodation, especially among finanically poorer groups in older neighborhoods;
the development of employment in the urban areas and in connection therewith the increasing distances traveled by the work-force;
the development of city centers, especially with respect to housing, employment, civic amenities, and their accessibility;
increasing mobility as a result of the dissociation of residential, work, and recreation areas;
the shortcomings in recreation facilities, especially within the urban areas;
the invasion of open spaces and ecologically and environmentally valuable areas within the urban sphere of influence.[9]

In the light of these developments, the *Urbanization Report* puts forward five general courses to be followed by plannning and deconcentration policy at regional level:

(1) congestion and unbalanced urban construction must be avoided;

(2) open areas and areas valuable from an ecological or landscape point of view must be protected;

(3) regional deficiencies and inequalities in the sphere of socio-economic development must be reduced;

(4) regional deficiencies and inequalities in the standard of amenities must be reduced;

(5) the growth of mobility must be retarded.[10]

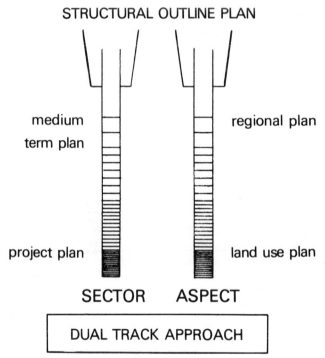

Fig. 6-2   Structural Outline Plan or Structural Scheme Translated into both Sectoral and Aspect Components from the National Level Down to the Local Level

Rural Areas Report

By far the greatest part of the land in the Netherlands is taken up by rural areas, consisting of a wide range of different landscapes, with grassland and arable land, forests and moorland, dunes, lake districts, and river landscapes. However, the landscape is steadily losing its variety and attractiveness. The principal reasons for this are the following:

Urbanization has a growing and generally disturbing effect on rural areas. More and more space is needed for housing, work, transport, and recreation at the expense of agriculture, nature, and the landscape.

Modern farming methods threaten to encroach upon areas of natural beauty. Methods such as intensive cattle-farming, for example, are not exactly compatible with certain characteristic landscapes.[11]

In brief, man is to a growing extent interfering with the often beautiful landscape, which he himself has played a part in creating over the course of centuries. Urbanization and—to a lesser extent—agriculture develop rapidly, so rapid in fact that nature and landscape conservation are incapable of keeping up with them. This threatens to create an aesthetically monotonous landscape.

In addition, the living conditions of the rural population are becoming increasingly difficult. In a number of villages there is insufficient employment. The younger population, especially, tends to migrate from villages. Those remaining behind are faced with inadequate amenities, with few shops, schools, and cultural facilities. Other villages simultaneously attract an increasing number of people fleeing from the cities. As a result it becomes difficult for the original villagers to find housing accommodations at reasonable prices.

Developmental possibilities are derived both from the urban and the rural areas reports. It follows from the basic goals of physical-planning policy that the use made of available space should exhibit the greatest possible variety. This variety can be achieved by intermingling land uses for urbanization, agriculture, recreation, and natural landscaping. Such intermingling is only possible, however, if the various uses do not interfere with each other.

Zoning of Areas

In dividing up available space it is possible, in principle, to choose between the segregation of and intermingling of different land uses. This possibility gives us three models; with urbanization, agriculture, and natural landscaping as the three component land use variables.

(1) Intermingling urbanization with agriculture and nature.
(2) Segregating urbanization from the other two.
(3) Effecting a strict segregation between the three kinds of land use.

In practice, however, it is rather a matter of achieving a sound combination of these three possibilities. It is not just a question of making a single choice from these models and then applying the model to the entire physical space of the country. There are, after all, considerable differences between the various regions of the country. In its policy the government usually decides to aim for a variety of land uses. The divergent forms of land use exhibiting a high degree of compatibility may be, and must remain, intermingled. Forms of land use which have a disturbing effect on or even displace each other must be segregated. If segregation is necessary, there should nevertheless be endeavors to ensure the greatest possible variety of land use within a delimited area. Planning policy in the Netherlands would therefore distinguish five kinds of areas:

(a) areas with a mainly agricultural function;
(b) areas with agricultural and other functions, each function in a large physical unit;
(c) areas with agriculture, natural landscaping, and other functions, in small physical units;
(d) areas mainly with natural landscaping;
(e) areas within the urban sphere of influence.[12]

Regional Policies

Besides provinces, which are administrative entities, Dutch physical planning distinguishes some regions as supersets of provinces. These regions of the country, such as the northern provinces of Groningen, Friesland, and Drenthe, are fairly distinct socio-economic and functional entities. Directed at these kinds of regions, national or social planning policy contains policy elements concerned with both development and distribution or deconcentration. Deconcentration policy supports the prime objective of development policy. This means that for the Randstad area in the West of the country policy is to reduce the migration of people towards the South and the East to avoid long-distance commuting and possible congestion in the future. Continued steady population growth is the goal for the North. Finally, in the *Urbanization Report*, some specific 'growth cities' and 'growth centers' are designated that enjoy certain facilities as well as preferential treatment in the queue for house building and the development of amenities and infrastructure. Besides traditional measures of financial support and economic stimulation this is one of the most effective policy instruments for directing people towards specific parts of urbanized areas, and is thus useful for enabling urban renewal as well.

COORDINATIVE ASPECTS OF PHYSICAL PLANNING

Physical planning takes place on the basis of the Physical Planning Act. It is adjusted to the administrative organization of the Netherlands. As far as it is applicable in this context, there exist three levels of administration: central government level, provincial level, and municipal level (See Fig. 6-1). General administrative bodies at all three levels are responsible for making decisions in the sphere of physical planning. Thus politics plays a very important role in physical planning. The relations existing between these three levels of administration are determined by the decentralized organization of government:[13] in principle, each level of administation is free to conduct a policy of its own and to lay down its own regulations, provided that, in doing so, it does not come into conflict with the policy or regulations of a higher authority. This decentralized set-up is also reflected in the physical planning policy and the Physical Planning Act. The decentralization of planning and decision-making is one of the reasons why physical plans exhibit a diminishing measure of abstraction and a growing measure of elaboration as one looks down the line of the levels of administration. Hence, it is especially in the municipalities that various policies are translated into regulations directly binding upon the citizen. Formally, the plans of a lower authority need not necessarily be in agreement with the policy of a higher authority. The latter authority, however, possesses the means to make modifications if the lower authority's policy is likely to conflict with its policy path. In the vertical line of coordination, one of the main tasks of the national administrative body is to ensure that each level keeps within its own, legally fixed limits.

Decisions relevant to physical planning are made within each of the administrative levels by different 'departments' or sectors, which are responsible for looking after specific interests entrusted to them. Experience has shown that many decisions taken at different levels of administration and in different 'departments' have physical aspects and physical effects, and that each level and each 'department' may hold different views on the most desirable development. These views are, generally, based on the jurisdictional responsibilities of the different levels and departments.

At the central government level, for instance, various ministers look after interests having a direct bearing on physical planning. Consequently, physical planning is not treated as a matter for the Minister of Physical Planning alone, but as a joint responsibility in which the said minister has a coordinating role. Examples of fields which have a bearing on physical planning are: building and urban renewal; administrative division of the Netherlands; the planning of schools and universities; traffic and transport; employment; and the struggle against pollution of the air, soil, and water. In all these fields, departmental or 'sectoral' ministers have a first responsibility, but where these subjects directly or indirectly affect physical planning, physical-planning interests are consulted at various levels of administration and in different policy sectors. It is of course unavoidable that, at times, these interests conflict. This brings us

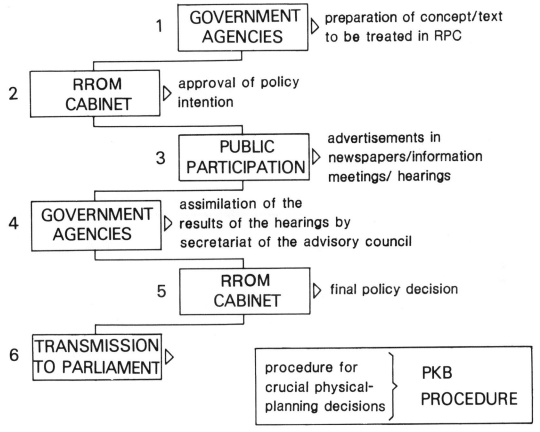

Fig. 6-3   Public Participation Process in Planning at National Level

RPC=Rijksplanologische Commissie (National Physical Planning Committee)

RROM=Road voor Ruimtelijke Ordening en Milieuhygiene (Cabinet Committee for National Physical Planning and Environment)

PKB=Planologische Kernbeslissing (Crucial Physical Planning Decision)

back to one of the most important aspects of national physical-planning policy; it is the responsibility of the government to foresee the consequences of various developments and to prevent conflict as far as possible.

To achieve this aim, coordination is essential, both vertically (between the different levels of administration) and horizontally (at each specific level of administration). The government attempts, though not always successfully, to fit various decisions into a coordinated physical-planning policy which has the support of different administrative levels and departments.

Coordination of physical planning, and the development of a national policy, take place in different administrative and political bodies. These obey certain rules and use instruments which only partly find their formal basis in the Physical Planning Act and the regulations derived from that. The bodies which are entrusted with a coordinating role form the units of the ensuing discussion. The most important administrative body in the field of physical planning in the Netherlands is the National Physical Planning Committee. In this committee the highest ranking officials (director-generals) of all those departments which may have a specific interest in physical planning are brought together. The committee has an independent chairman, and the National Physical Planning Agency houses the secretariat. Its main function is to advise the coordinating Minister for Physical Planning about policy matters of national importance and about regional plans of the provincial authorities. Thus this committee has an important horizontal as well as vertical coordinative role.

The Cabinet Committee for Physical Planning and Environment is another coordinating committee. It is partly political and partly administrative in function. Its membership consists of a number of ministers, state secretaries, and high-ranking officials from those ministries which have the largest interest in physical planning. The Minister for Physical Planning has the coordinating power in this committee, of which the Prime Minister is chairman. This committee is the main preparatory committee for the cabinet in matters concerning physical planning. Deliberations within this cabinet committee are prepared by the aforementioned National Physical Planning Committee (through advisory reports). Finally, mention must be made of the cabinet, in which the Minister for Physical Planning has the coordinating power for those matters which are directly relevant to physical planning. In practice, this generally means that proposals of relevance to physical planning have to bear the signature of the coordinating minister before they are placed on the agenda.

To summarize, it is obvious that in the Netherlands physical planning is a field where decisions are often taken on the initiative of the Minister for Physical Planning. These decisions are prepared in many widely diversified committees. When the initiative lies with one of the other departments or ministries, or with provincial bodies, the Minister for Physical Planning has the main coordinating role.

STRUCTURE SCHEMES—OR STRUCTURAL OUTLINE PLANS—AND THE PROCEDURE FOR CRUCIAL PHYSICAL-PLANNING DECISIONS

In the 1970s experiments were begun which later became standard practice, using tools and procedures that still lack the legal basis. They are called 'structural schemes' or structural outline plans and are the procedure for 'crucial physical-planning decisions' (Fig. 6-2). It became the practice for the central government as well as provincial and local governments to issue policy reports on every issue that would interest peo-

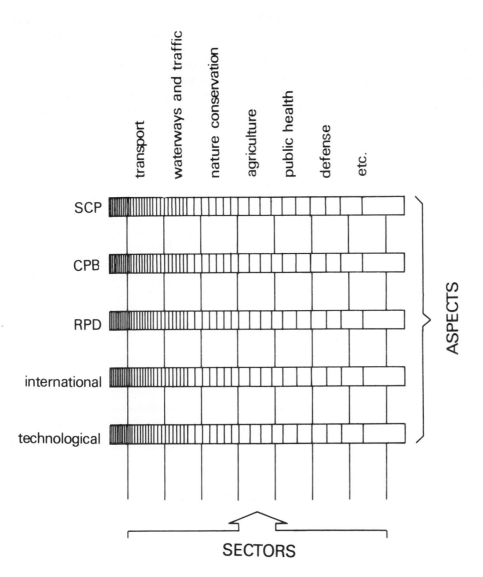

Fig. 6-4 Impacts of Policy Planning on Specific Sectors of Dutch Environment: Relationships between Sectoral Planning and Policy-Creating Agencies. The Physical Planning Loom: The Aspects (woof) cut across the Sectors (warp). Every Sector of Society has Social and Cultural Aspects (SCP), Economic Aspects (CPB), Spatial Aspects (RPD), and International and Technological Aspects. The Co-ordinating Role of Physical Planning (RPD) on Space Consumption by the Various Sectors is achieved through the Development of Structural Schemes.

SCP=Social and Cultural Planning Bureau
CPB=Central Planning Bureau
RPD=National Physical Planning Agency

ple. In the field of national physical planning these were the reports previously discussed. Produced by relevant departments of the administration, they were presented to national, provincial, and municipal parliaments for their consideration. Only after parliamentary review did executives feel free to use them. Before review by the various parliaments, public participation was sought (Fig. 6-3), thus ensuring direct as well as representative democracy. Information meetings and hearings were organized, information material was produced, and then the views of the public had to be digested and texts changed and amended time and again. There was a tremendous demand at that time for popular participation, with almost every issue politicized. But as the years passed, the real spirit of participation faded away. Nevertheless, the system kept a turbulent society relatively 'quiet'. Thus, physical planning procedures, both the ones laid down in the National Physical Planning Act and those born in the 1960s and 1970s, are in fact instruments of home rule or internal management rather than an attempt to seek the best intellectual, academic, or businesslike solutions. The main question is whether this procedure for crucial physical-planning decision-making is going to be legalized, as could be done through the still-pending 1977 amendments to the National Physical Planning Act of 1965. Structural schemes are sectoral mid-term plans that enumerate, for a period of five years, the spatial consequences of possi-

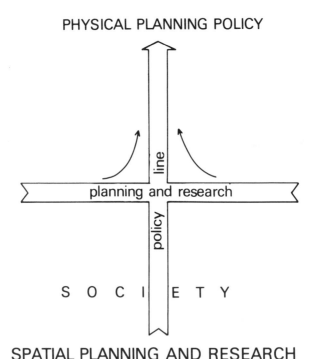

PHYSICAL PLANNING POLICY

line

planning and research

policy

S O C I E T Y

SPATIAL PLANNING AND RESEARCH

national physical planning agency
matrix organization

Fig. 6-5   The Process of Policy Development for the
National Physical Planning Agency

ble developments in a number of important fields of governmental jurisdiction. To date, twelve structure schemes have been published and find themselves in different stages of implementation. The schemes are concerned with: (1) pipelines, (2) civil aviation airfields, (3) drinking and industrial water, (4) electricity, (5) (re)construction of land, (6) land used by the military, (7) nature and landscape conservation, (8) open-air recreation, (9) waterways, (10) traffic and transport, (11) housing, and (12) seaports.[14]

Each structural scheme is prepared by a number of different ministries concerned with the field under consideration, in close cooperation with the National Physical Planning Agency, which is part of the Ministry of Housing, Physical Planning and Environment. This type of horizontal coordination at the national level between several ministries belongs to a framework that can perhaps best be explained through comparison with a weaving loom. Human activities require space. Houses, schools and hospitals are needed to sustain human life; work space includes offices, farmland and factories; recreation requires playfields, parks and natural areas; traffic and utilities require roads, rails, waterways and easements for transmission lines. Physical planning as a coordinative discipline operates on the basis of calculations concerning the spatial requirements of various sector developments. Structural schemes result from negotiations between a particular sectoral demand for space and the public body authorized to allocate space for development. Following the terminology of a 1979 government advisory committee, specialists prefer to bracket all government activities and responsibilities, into specific *sectors* and *aspects*. Sectors stand for different specific responsibilities, such as traffic, housing, defense, water supply, etc. (see list of twelve structural schemes), whereas an aspect or facet is a broader element applicable to or even existing as an element of each separate sector. So, using the image of the loom, the sectors are the warp, and the aspects the woof that cuts across the warp. Besides the aspect of space, some further aspects were distinguished such as social, cultural, economic, and financial aspects. Fig. 6-4 provides a picture of what Dutch theoretical planners had in mind when building up the planning edifice in the sixties and seventies, a time when they still believed that they knew exactly which 'cake they were baking'.

In theory the system is genuinely commendable, but life always turns out to be harsher than the planners imagine. Serious thought has always been given to coordinating all sectors along the lines of different facets, using the National Physical Planning Agency, which has existed since the 1940s, the Social and Cultural Planning Bureau, and the Central (economic) Planning Bureau. An even higher level of coordination was sought by integration of the work of different fields through the established Scientific Council for Government Policy. At the same time this council might function as a government think tank as well. It has provided some very good prognostic studies indeed, but has not performed any coordinating task. However, the structural schemes, and more precisely the procedures that have to be followed in carrying them out, are part of the proposed 1977 amendments to the existing National Physical Planning Act that have been presented to Parliament for consideration and will be debated in 1984.

FINAL REMARKS

Readers of the foregoing text may involuntarily try to compare the Dutch planning system to the American approach. It is necessary to recall what has been said about the character of the Dutch system earlier in this chapter: physical planning is *spatial* planning, taking a specific, well-defined, and sharply circumscribed area, and planning the most desirable development of that area, often on the basis of a politically approved policy. The desires, needs, and possibilities of different sectors are compared and then a rigid plan is constructed. Of course, there are, fortunately, ways of escaping the plan, but in essence any development required by sudden new needs or initiatives has to be cross-checked against the existing plan and usually does not receive permission if it does not conform with it. These ideas of comprehensive planning, or rather this collectivistic philosophy behind the Dutch planning edifice, is quite different from American thinking.

Apart from large-scale projects such as the Delta Project or the creation of a new polder in the former Zuiderzee, Dutch initiatives are not, in the first place, judged on their own rights and merits, but are instead checked with a plan that may not have foreseen the need for such developments. This sets the political process in motion all over again. The introduction of environmental assessment procedures some years ago has not fundamentally changed the planning system. The system has tried to incorporate these new procedures into the existing mechanism. Yet these were regarded as a threat and could have meant a fundamental change of the planning system in the Netherlands. Under a fundamentally new system every project would be examined and analyzed individually against the background of politically set norms and standards using an extensive interpretation of the notion of 'environment'. This would mean an essentially different approach and would make the traditional, spatial, comprehensive 'expectation' plans superfluous, at least as a legal basis for delivering building permits and thus realizing projects. This in turn would cause the situation with which we began our discussion—rumor in *casa*.

NOTES

1. Theo Quené, 'Persoonlijk heb ik graag kontank met mensen' in *Open Huis*, vol. II, no. 3, 1978, pp. 3–6
2. 'Wet op de Ruimtelijke Ordening', in *Nederlandse Staatswetten*, no. 64, Zwolle, Schuurman and Jordens, 1979.
3. *Tweede Nota over de Ruimtelijke Ordening in Nederland*, The Hague, Staatsuitgeverij, 1966; *Second Report on Physical Planning in the Netherlands*, Condensed Edition, the Hague, Government Printing Office of the Netherlands, 1966.
4. 'Woningwet', in *Nederlandse Staatswetten*, no. 19, pts. I and II, Zwolle, Schuurman and Jordens, 1982.
5. *Derde Nota over de Ruimtelijke Ordening*, vol. 1, *Orienteringsnota Ruimtelijke Ordening*, The Hague, Staatsuitgeverij, 1974.
6. *Derde Nota over de Ruimtelijke Ordening*, vol. 2, *Verstedelijkingsnota (regeringsbeslissing)*, The Hague, Staatsuitgeverij, 1979.
7. *Derde Nota over de Ruimtelijke Ordening*, vol. 3, *Verstedelijkingsnota (regeringsbeslissing)*, The Hague, Staatsuitgeverij, 1979.
8. *Verstedelijkingsnota*, p. 5, n. 6.
9. Ibid., p. 6.
10. Ibid., pp. 5–6.
11. *Nota Landelijke Gebieden*, A (*Beleidsvoornemen*), pp. 14–15, n. 7.
12. Ibid., pp. 4–6 and 16.
13. Wim Brussaard, *The Rules of Physical Planning*, The Hague, Ministry of Housing and Physical Planning, 1979.
14. See monthly PKB, Reports on crucial physical-planning decisions, nr. 19, February 1983, Ministry of Housing, Physical Planning and Environment, the Hague.

7
Social Planning in The Netherlands: Organization and Practice

J.M. Timmermans and J.W. Becker

Planning for the social and cultural aspects of life in the Netherlands is a comparatively recent phenomenon; more recent, for example, than in countries with which the Dutch welfare system is often compared, such as the Scandinavian countries. This relatively late start and the form which social planning eventually assumed can to a great extent be ascribed to the peculiar structure of Dutch society and in particular to the dominant role so long played by private initiative.

This chapter begins with a historical survey. Following this is a description of the first efforts in social and cultural planning in the 1960s and 1970s, with special emphasis on planning for the elderly and the changing popular opinion of the welfare state.

THE WAY TO THE WELFARE STATE:
THE SUPREMACY OF PRIVATE INITIATIVE

There is some justification for giving the starting date of social and cultural planning in the Netherlands as the end of the eighteenth century and the beginning of the nineteenth. At that time groups of Dutch citizens took the initiative in creating a more comprehensive system of poor relief. The role of the govenment was limited to that of financier, since responsibility for poor relief rested with religious or private institutions. Round about 1900 there was increased pressure on the authorities to play a more active role, partly under the influence of the labor movement, one of the emancipatory movements which grew up in the Netherlands in the nineteenth century.[1] Thus around 1900 various statutory provisions came into being concerning education, housing, and health care, a development which was in part made possible by economic growth before and around the turn of the century. The religious and private charity organizations, which had a statutory responsibility for poor relief, could not, however, in the long run meet the demand for services, even though in 1899 there were in the Netherlands 7,476 institutions engaged in social and charitable work for a population of five million people. Where the government, for various reasons, failed to meet the need for services, it was the charitable movements of the Catholics, Protestants, and labor which set up a variety of self-help organizations.

Each group strove to contain its own followers within institutions and services of its own school of thought. Smaller ideological or religious groups, such as the Baptists, Jews, and Humanists also followed the same method, which has become known in the

Netherlands as *verzuiling* (literally pillarization). In the pre-World II period this type of organization, based on a particular religious or ideological creed, came into being in charity activities, child care and protection, prisoners' aftercare, hospital and district nursing, health insurance, funeral expenses insurance, secondary (vocational) education, broadcasting, housing, sport, and amateur art activities. During this period local initiatives were bundled into national umbrella organizations and in this way the foundation was laid before the Second World War for the structure of the present system of services.

By that time the part played by the religious and private institutions in the fight against poverty had dwindled considerably. Their role declined after World War I when union pressure resulted in social security measures which provided support for the unemployed. In 1938 only 12.5 percent of income benefits were paid out by charitable institutions while in 1910 they were responsible for 41 percent.

After the Second World War the 'pillars' or denominational and political groups were soon resuscitated and the activities which had been organized along general lines during the German occupation were for the most part reclaimed and reserved for the individual group. Nevertheless, a start was soon made on setting up a system of social security. This represented the implementation of the recommendations of the van Rhijn committee, set up by the Dutch government in 1943, which were mainly based on the British Beveridge report.[2] This social security system was completed for the most part with the introduction of the National Assistance Act in 1969. This act guarantees a minimum income to every Dutchman who is unable to provide for his own means of livelihood. Thus an important element in social care was withdrawn from the sphere of private initiative, namely: the provision of financial means. Private initiative in the form of the denominational and political groups retains the management of the other welfare services, even where the government finances these services from public funds.

In the sixties, when the structure of the welfare state had reached considerable proportions, the denominational and political 'pillars' were being hollowed out. The main reason for this was the rapid secularization of the Dutch population. In any case, by this time the services provided by a group were no longer for the exclusive use of that group's own following. The greater the extent to which services are paid for from public funds, the more use can be made of these facilities by all citizens.[3]

The establishment of a collective system of services means that the continuity of services is guaranteed and that services are systematically distributed throughout the country. With the establishment of this system the government also makes certain qualitative demands in that it expects that those who provide the help should be experts who conform to specialist training requirements. It was inevitable that this widely supported pursuit of organization, continuity, and a reasonable qualitative level, should lead to a very considerable degree of professionalization of the care system. The private organizations also changed since they became managed increasingly by professional staff, although officially they still retained their own label. Table 7-1 gives a picture of the situation in 1977.

From the description given above it is apparent that when the welfare state started in the Netherlands it was private groups that provided the services. This remained the case when the traditional civil and religious initiative was superceded by initiatives from ideological groups which had developed from the emancipatory movements. Nor has the picture changed yet in the post-war years with professional staff taking over

Table 7-1 Number of organizations in education, residential health care, and the social services grouped by denomination, 1977

	1	2	3	4	5	6
	Roman Catholic Number	Protestant Number	Percentage for columns 1 and 2	Non-denominational Number	Non-denominational Percent	Total Number
Education						
Primary[a]	5,730	5,050	65	5,900	35	16,680
Secondary[b]	1,355	981	60	1,541	40	3,877
Residential health care[c]	174	135	57	257	43	592
Social Services						
Home help	29	47	29	196	71	275
Old peoples' homes[d]	599	420	60	690	40	1,709

[a]Compromises full-time nursery, primary, and special education.
[b]Comprises full-time MAVO, HAVO, VWO schools (intermediate secondary, higher secondary, pre-university), and junior, senior, and higher vocational education.
[c]Comprises general special, and teaching hospitals, psychiatric hospitals, nursing homes (excluding nursing homes exclusively for somatic mental homes).
[d]Figure refers to 1975.

Source: P. van Wersch, *Demokratisering van het bestuur van non-profit-instellingen*, Alphen, 1979, p. 36.

the work within the private institutions. As will be seen in the following sections, discussion is still in progress on the question of who has the prime responsibility for welfare and welfare policy, the state or professionalized private initiative. Over the years, however, the role of the private organizations had diminished. Finance and the supervision of quality have become the responsibility of the state or of the social security system.

These developments have been treated here in some detail, because the fact that priority was always given to private initiative explains why the Dutch government, compared for example with Scandinavian governments, started to concern itself at a later stage with the organization, scope, and supply of welfare services. Moreover, it explains the particular form taken by Dutch social and cultural planning in the last fifteen years.

THE BEGINNING OF SOCIAL AND CULTURAL PLANNING

The Dutch government's involvement with social and cultural planning is comparatively recent. Various reasons are to be given for the fact that in the 1960s the government increasingly began to occupy itself with this subject. The secularization of Dutch society, the complexity of the care system, and the belief in the scientific preparation of policy concerning social issues are three of the more important of these reasons.

Secularization in the Netherlands is removing the foundations from which the 'pillars' or denominational and political groups operated. The services provided by a group used to be naturally attuned to its members. The leaders of the groups represented their members in all fields of social life.[4] The structure of the groups today, dominated as it is by professional workers, and cast in a scientific mold, cannot offer such an ideological framework. It is in this situation that the concept of *welzijn* (well-being/welfare) has developed. In the first place, the notion is used to distinguish the provision of immaterial goods from that of the strictly material. Secondly, the notion is used to provide an ideological basis for a coherent package of services—a basis which should be guaranteed by the government. The demarcation of the fields covered by this notion is a question of political choice. There is, however, agreement that the following areas are covered:

(a) education and training, health care, child care and protection, prisoners' aftercare, penal institutions, cultural affairs, social developments, complementary social provisions, and certain aspects of employment policy;

(b) matters concerning emancipation, participation, and leisure activities;

(c) forms of policy for specific groups, such as policy for youth, and housing for special groups, cultural minorities, the elderly, the disabled, and so on.

Another development during the sixties, which forced the government to play a more active part, was the increased complexity in the socio-economic field. The supply of services increased in scope and diversity to such an extent during that period that planning and harmonization became increasingly necessary. Where care changes from being a favor to a right guaranteed by the government, it is natural that the government should take the initiative in planning and harmonization. Moreover, this same period saw the growth of important democratizing movements, such as the New Left, the student movement, the women's liberation movement, and a more active trade union movement, which tried to enforce their right of codetermination in the social and cultural fields, and thus stimulated the authorities into taking action.

A third important stimulus for the government to play a greater role was the growing belief in the possibilities of scientific policy preparation in planning generally and, in particular, socio-cultural planning. In the fifties it was already felt that socio-scientific research should make a greater contribution towards the preparation of policy. In 1968 a committee was set up to carry out a preparatory inquiry into the future structure of society. In 1970 this committee produced a report on planning as scientific policy preparation.[5] The committee noted that the instruments at the government's disposal both for the integration of planning activities and for proper operation in the field of 'social and cultural welfare' were inadequate. It was recommended that a Planning Council (which later became the Advisory Council for Government Policy—WRR) and a Social Planning Office be set up. At about the same time the report of the Committee on Interdepartmental Coordination and Allocation of Responsibilities (van Veen Committee) was published. This contained proposals for the systematization and expansion of the existing coordinative structure.[6]

The present system, as devised by the van Veen Committee, ensures the coordination of major aspects of government policy through Cabinet standing committees, which prepare the ground for Cabinet decisions. A coordinating minister is appointed for each of these committees; however, he has little power and few instruments to help him achieve a coordinated policy.

At the official level there are a number of interdepartmental coordinating committees. These act as 'official portals' for Cabinet committees and their task is to prepare for meetings of their particular committee and make recommendations on plans and measures which fall under the competency of more than one minister or of the Cabinet as a whole. The secretariats of these committees are run by the planning offices or coordinating units of the ministries concerned. In this way a link is established between the planning and coordinating structure.

Thus it appears that before the government had taken significant steps to give substance to planning in the social and cultural field, it had already created a structure for scientific policy preparation. At that point the notion of planning started on its social and cultural career. However, theorizing about the general objectives which society should try to achieve, a form of planning to which Jantsch gave the name normative, has been going on in the Netherlands for a long time.[7]

During the post-war period of economic growth the government seldom had cause to worry about the choice or evaluation of policy objectives and instruments (sometimes also known as strategic planning). Nor at that time did the government pay much attention to programming activities, whereby a desired quantitative output could be produced within a set time (so-called operational planning). If the output was found to be inadequate or the instruments proved unsatifactory, the government could permit itself the luxury of financing new provisions or instruments, often actually carried out by private groups. However, the combination of the hollowing out of the 'pillars', the increasingly complex nature of society, the growth of democratizing movements, and a belief in the possibilities offered by planning compelled the government to become involved in the social and cultural field.

In view of the developments mentioned above it is not surprising that during the seventies the government made several forceful efforts to promote social and cultural planning. First evidence of this was a number of important government memoranda concerning health care, education, and recreation.[8]

The memoranda on education and health care concentrated mainly on organizational problems. The report of the consultative committee on constraints in the harmonization of welfare policy and welfare legislation, known as the 'bottlenecks memorandum', went further than this. As the name suggests, the report indicated a number of constraints or 'bottlenecks' in the welfare field. These 'bottlenecks' are ascribed to the following causes.

(1) The social situation, which has given rise to a multiplicity of difficult welfare problems: society has become extremely complex, disconnected and contradictory in various aspects. This is explained by swift economic growth, the exponential growth of the population, the rapid development of science, the uncontrolled growth of education and training, the inhospitable social climate of the cities, etc. All this has resulted in cultural malaise and fundamental criticism of the technological industrial society.

(2) The situation in welfare work, which shows signs of being over-organized, over-professionalized and over-specialized.

(3) Shortcomings on the part of the government, which has developed too many incoherent schemes and provisions; there is rivalry between and within different government levels, unchecked political power over welfare work.[9]

The conclusion of the memorandum was that a new policy system is required, which complies with criteria of cohesion, accessibility, democracy, flexibility, and legal security. This policy system should be based on two administrative principles: decentralization and the coupling of financing to policy.

In 1977 a Specific Welfare Provisions Bill was proposed in the Second Chamber. The bill includes some of the principal recommendations of the 'bottlenecks memorandum'.[10] In 1976 a bill had appeared which was of vital importance in the field of health care, the Health Care Provisions Bill (WVG), which embodied the most important elements of the memorandum on the structure of health care.[11]

The main aim of the Specific Welfare Provisions Bill is to bring about coherence between various welfare provisions, both those contained in the bill itself and provisions for specific welfare contained in other acts of Parliament. In the Specific Welfare Provisions Bill responsibility for planning lies with the government. The provisions covered by the bill are distributed over three administrative layers, municipal, provincial, and central government. Policy preparation is in the hands of an advisory body, which is intended to be representative of citizens' interests. This advisory body has given rise to a certain amount of controversy, which is still not resolved. It is as yet uncertain whether the task of this body should be restricted to making recommendations or whether it should be extended to actually preparing plans. The old question of whether the primary responsibility for welfare work and welfare policy should lie with private organizations or with the government is at the root of this ambiguity. The overall plan for the field of welfare is to be drawn up for a period of four years and a program is drawn up each year on the basis of that plan. The idea is that funds for the implementation of the plan and the program will be transferred from the central government to the local authorities.

During the parliamentary debates the bill's scope was gradually restricted. The ultimate result bears more resemblance to an act concerned with one particular sector than an all-embracing welfare act. In 1982 this bill as well as the Health Care Provisions bill were passed by Parliament. In 1983, however, the government indicated that the Specific Welfare Provisions Act would probably be rescinded.

The Health Care Provisions Act is primarily concerned, as was the Memorandum on the Structure of Health Care, with the organizational aspect of health care; as a result of the act plans must be developed which clearly establish the nature, scope, distribution, coherence, and quality of health care provisions. The initiative for planning is vested in the provincial authorities, while policy preparation is entrusted to a committee consisting of politicians, representatives of the provisions in question, insurers, and representatives of the patients/consumers. Just as with the advisory body proposed in the Specific Welfare Provisions Bill, it is not clear exactly what this policy preparation committee is supposed to do. Also, although the responsibility for planning rests with the provinces, the planning areas under the Act do not correspond with the provincial divisions, so there must be interprovincial negotiations.

Both acts cover a part of the field of care. In view of the relationship between the provisions in these two aspects of care, it is desirable that planning under them should be integrated. From the description given above it is obvious that there are significant differences between the bills, which form an impediment to integration. It is unlikely that a unified operational planning system will be put into effect in the care sector before the end of the century. There are some important reasons for this. In the first place the initiative for planning legislation developed partly in order to meet the wish for the right of codetermination expressed by the democratizing movements. And this right of codetermination is something which cannot but conflict with the dominant role of the professionalized private groups. Thus, there is opposition to planning legislation from private organizations and allied politicians. In the second place the organization of the government forms an impediment. The duties and interests of the separate departments, and sometimes subdepartments, are so interwoven with those of the private organizations in their own policy field, that separate lines of policy have developed in total disregard of one another. This phenomenon, which is known as compartmentalization, is very difficult to combat.[12]

Thirdly, the pressure of economic developments has led to a shift in government exertions. Planning for the sake of democratization, increased coherence, or simply belief in planning is slowly but surely becoming planning for the sake of control and economy. As a result the original plans are now serving purposes for which they were not drawn up and to which they are not suited.[13] Nevertheless, progress *has* been made in social and cultural planning in the Netherlands. The following sections of this chapter describe the structure of intersectoral planning and in particular the role of the Social and Cultural Planning Bureau and provide a discussion of sectoral planning for hospital services.

COORDINATING SOCIAL AND CULTURAL PLANNING POLICY

Fig. 7–1 offers a description of the position of the Social and Cultural Planning Bureau (SCP) within the administrative structure of the national government. The SCP was established in March of 1973. Its functions include: (a) researching into the existing

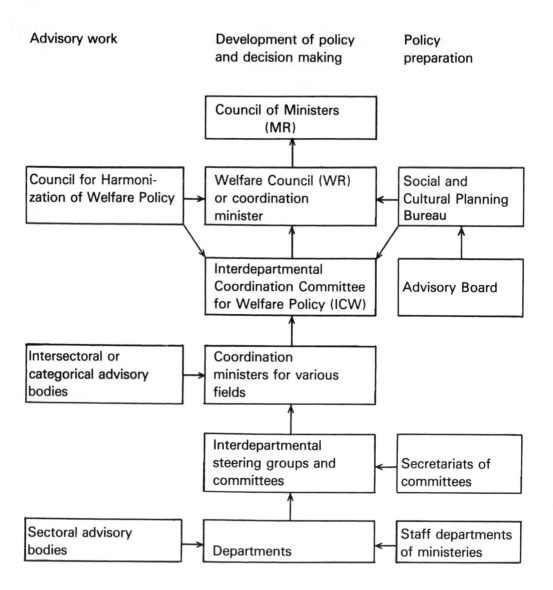

Fig. 7–1   Structure of Policy Implementation in
the Social and Cultural Fields

social and cultural conditions of the Netherlands and projecting anticipated changes in these conditions; (b) contributing to an informal choice of policy objectives by identifying the advantages and disadvantages associated with different objectives; and (c) gathering information concerning the implementation of interdepartmental policy. The office pays particular attention to issues where the policy of more than one ministry is involved.

The SCP is firmly embedded within the bureaucratic policy and decision-making system outlined in Fig. 7-1. Its position is analogous to that of the other planning offices. Its budget and daily activities come under the jurisdiction of the Minister for Welfare Policy. However, its biennial working program has to have the approval of the interministerial Welfare Council. The separate ministers can, after joint consultation, give specific tasks or assignments to the SCP staff which have an intersectoral nature and a medium- or long-term planning horizon.

Apart from this formal framework for joint consultations there is regular contact between senior civil servants, government ministers, and the directorate of the office. Other members of the staff are also in contact with the ministries and other government services.

The office maintains frequent, varied, and sometimes intensive contact with bodies other than the official ones, though these relations are not as a rule of a permanent nature. Contacts with the scientific world are particularly significant.

The outlines of its activities are laid down in the two-year brief referred to above. The office spends considerable time on data collection, the preparation of extensive studies concerning the objectives of its scientific investigation, and policy development. It also carries out specific studies and provides information for government ministries, and very occasionally carries out research for external bodies or groups.

Intersectoral Planning: Provisions of
Manpower in the Quaternary Sector

To give an impression of the SCP's contribution to policy preparation it is useful to go more closely into one of the office's projects. The project chosen is the study of manpower trends in the noncommercial services, known as the quaternary sector.[14] The choice of this subject was made in part because it gives at the same time an example of intersectoral planning. The core of the study is formed by the forecasts of future use of some fifty services provided by the government. The development of the demand for services was assumed to correspond to past trends. In determining trends, account was taken of the differences in the demand for services between various age groups in the population and also demographic developments which can be expected in the Netherlands. Estimates of this kind are, of course, subject to all sorts of limitations. This is not the place to go into these. It must, however, be emphasized that no account has been taken of possible effects of changes in government policy. The results should only be seen as a guide. If it is assumed that the present manpower/services ratio will remain unchanged, it is possible to estimate the amount of manpower needed at some point in the future. The forecasts for the fields of care, education, recreation, justice, public transport, and public administration are summarized in Table 7–2. The picture given is extremely important because it is the first time that data on different sectors have been assembled in this way.

Table 7–2 Forecast of manpower needed in the quaternary sector, 1990 (000 man-years)

	1980	1990	Increase
Institutional health care	219	239	+ 20
Other health care	55	65	+ 10
Social services	107	125	+ 18
Social and cultural work, culture and recreation	18	21	+ 3
Other social and cultural work etc.	25	33	+ 8
Education and research	264	238	− 26
Judicial sphere	17	16	− 1
Public transport	40	46	+ 6
Public administration etc.	430	441	+ 11
Total	1,175	1,224	+ 49

Source: *Social and Cultural Report 1980*, The Hague, Staatsuitgererij, 1980, p. 199 (English edition).

The results indicate that certain policy choices appear to be inevitable in light of certain demographic developments. A drop in the birthrate and an increase in the expectation of life lead to an ageing population. This will result in an increasing demand for care facilities and a decreasing demand for educational facilities. It stands to reason that a shift of this kind in demand should be matched by a shift in the supply of facilities. However, this means considerable change, not only in vocational training but also in the system of finance. In view of the government's limited planning control over training and finance it will be obvious that this shift in demand constitutes a considerable problem for the Dutch authorities. Thanks to the SCP's intersectoral survey, this problem has at least been revealed to its full extent. In the meantime the government has set up an interdepartmental working group whose task, in cooperation with the SCP and on the basis of the inquiry described above, is to arrive at a coherent plan for the provision of manpower in the quaternary sector.

SOCIAL AND CULTURAL PLANNING IN PRACTICE

Planning of Hospital Services

A previous section described the way in which systematic planning has been developed for health care in the Netherlands and has been laid down in the Health Care Provisions Act (WVG). As far as residential health care is concerned, such a planning system was already in place. Provincial authorities produce four-year plans for these services. These plans are made on the basis of detailed instructions with regard to the nature and scope of the supply, as laid down in the Hospital Provisions Act. The latter act constitutes only part of the planning instruments; it is linked to another act regulating quality and supervision (the Health Care Tariffs Act) and one covering admission and financing (General Act on Exceptional Medical Expenses). To elucidate this point a summary is given below of the instructions which have been laid down for the residential psychiatric services.

According to the provisions of Article 3 of the Hospital Provisions Act, 1.5 places in a residential psychiatric institution must be available for each thousand inhabitants in a health region.[15] This norm is in turn subdivided into six subnorms, which vary from 1.1 place per thousand inhabitants in general psychiatric hospitals to 0.07 places per thousand inhabitants in clinics for drug addicts. The provisions of the act also include instructions with regard to separate services, the basic package of services, and special facilities. Thus every psychiatric hospital must, apart from separate departments for short- or long-term treatment, provide opportunities for day-patient and outpatient treatment. Departments for drug addicts or psychiatric patients in the criminal law system are not included in the basic package, but can at the direction of the central government be attached to certain institutions.

In addition to this planning act there is, as has been mentioned above, the Health Care Tariffs Act dealing with quality and supervision. The provisions of this act contain precise instructions for the manpower allowable per occupied place or bed and for the amount of chargeable running costs.[16] Table 7–3 gives an example of such precise instructions, again relating to psychiatric services. The financing of psychiatric services is laid down in the Exceptional Medical Expenses (Compensation) Act. This act defines the conditions for financing a service and for allowing an insured person to make use of the service after the service is approved by one of the bodies which administer the law. Finally, the annual Financial Survey of Health Care determines the basis upon which future changes in the guidelines for supply and quality may be made.[17] When the entire system is in operation, it will be possible to know exactly what will be offered in the future in the way of services and manpower.

Some comments on the system of residential health care are called for at this point. In the first place this system fails to provide for full cost control. What the various employees in the institutions may or may not do has not been specified, which means that expansion of functions and activities can take place without any control. In 1982 the cost for all hospitals rose by 120 million guilders as a result of the autonomous growth of functions and activities.[18] It will only be possible to control cost increases of this kind if both the regions and the institutions keep within the margins of allocated budgets. At the moment experiments are in progress with this budgeting system and its gradual introduction is under consideration.[19] Were it to be introduced, however, detailed planning systems, such as those described here, would be more or less superfluous.

There are also other disadvantages attached to such detailed planning. The system is so rigid that it leaves the local authorities who are responsible for planning scarcely any decision-making authority. Only limited adjustments are possible, provided that the total norms are not exceeded and provided that no extra costs accrue from the adjustments. Finally, such a rigid set of regulations leaves little room for the involvement of citizen or client in planning. The desirability of increasing that involvement was after all one of the reasons for the government's concern with planning.

Table 7–3 Number of staff in wards of psychiatric hospitals (intended for admission, observation, and short-term treatment (up to three months), 1981 (in 000's)

State registered nurses	14.5
Student nurses and other nursing staff	27.7
Therapists	6.3
Other paramedical staff	5.5
Medical and social-scientific staff	7.86
Total	61.86

Source: see n. 16.

POLICY FOR THE ELDERLY: A STUDY IN SOCIAL PLANNING

A somewhat fragmentary picture of social and cultural planning emerges from the preceding sections of this chapter. This is inevitable since the nature of social and cultural planning in the Netherlands is indeed fragmentary. This is clearly evident from a closer examination of the policy for the elderly pursued by government departments. The departments responsible for policy for the elderly are: (a) Culture, Recreation and Social Work, (b) Public Health and Environmental Hygiene, (c) Social Affairs, and (d) Housing and Physical Planning. In the course of the years, this policy-making has resulted in an impressive level of services, but with the economic recession and the ageing of the Dutch population both the level of the services and also the policy itself are under considerable pressure.

Policy for the Elderly: The 'Closed Circuit'

The living conditions of the elderly compare unfavorably with those of other population groups in the Netherlands. As regards income, housing, health, and domestic help, they are in a worse position than other members of the Dutch population.[20] They have also been found to have less knowledge, less influence in society, and fewer social contacts.

In Dutch policy for the elderly great emphasis is, therefore, placed on the elimination of this underprivileged situation through the provision of facilities. The 1975 *Memorandum on Policy for the Elderly* states that: 'the elderly should be enabled to go on living independently in their own familiar surroundings as long as possible and should be able to continue participating fully in social life to the extent that they wish and are (still) able to do so.'[21]

One of the mainstays of policy for the elderly is the so-called 'closed circuit' in the provision of services. By this is meant: 'a system of facilities, the elements of which are logically and organizationally linked in such a way that it is possible to provide an integral approach to the welfare and health demands of old people, or at any rate insofar as that can reasonably be effected via institutions and services.'[22] If such a system works properly, then it is possible for each needy old person to receive assistance adequate and necessary for the maintenance of independence. The following provisions are reckoned to form the parts of a 'closed circuit': (a) residential and nonresidential health care, (b) housing facilities for the elderly, (c) social services, and (d) socio-cultural and recreational facilities.

The majority of old people in the Netherlands live in ordinary dwellings and can manage there perfectly well. However, there are a number of elderly people who sometimes cannot, or will not, stay in an ordinary dwelling because this has become too large or too difficult to run. In cases such as these a move to a dwelling purposely built for the elderly can provide a solution to the problem, especially as a varied supply of such housing has become available during the last few years. In 1975, it was anticipated that by 1985, 25 percent of the elderly would be living in dwellings of this kind. This objective will not be achieved, however, because the building of this type of dwelling does not appeal to the financiers of the Dutch housing industry and many elderly people find the rent of such housing too high.

When maintaining an independent household, even with help from relatives or home-help services, is no longer possible, then housing in an old people's home is required. About 9 percent of the elderly in the Netherlands live in an old people's home.[23] The government aims at reducing this percentage to 7 percent, since the services in old people's homes are more expensive and are not necessary in all cases. Where the income of an elderly person is insufficient to cover the cost of residence in an old people's home, government help is available through the Supplementary Benefits Act. Some 80 percent of the places in old people's homes are financed in this way.[24] In 1981 over two billion guilders were spent for this purpose.

In order to allocate the available places in old people's homes as fairly as possible, a national system for admission has been in effect since 1977. All elderly people who wish to be considered for admission to an old people's home have to submit a written request to an 'indication committee', which checks whether there are indeed reasons for admitting the person in question. The inquiry covers: (a) vital daily functions (for example, whether the person in question can dress and undress him/herself), (b) sight, (c) difficulties in performing domestic chores, (d) psychosocial circumstances (for example social contact difficulties), and (e) social circumstances.

The committee's recommendation does not guarantee admission since old people's homes are free to operate their own admission policy. They are even permitted to accept old people who have received a negative recommendation. But a certain amount of useful information and experience has been gained from the indication committees. If the conclusions of the indication committees were to form the basis for the planning of old people's homes (this was the underlying idea when the committees were set up), then a place in an old people's home should be available to 11 percent of the elderly.[25]

Thus, many more old people may require admission to an old people's home than the government is prepared to accomodate. One of the reasons for this high figure, one often put forward by the indication committees themselves, is the inadequate supply of facilities such as purpose-built housing and domestic help from the home-help service. Home-help organizations providing help for the elderly do form an important link in the circuit. In the past few years an increasing number of old people have made use of this facility. The number of cases of help provided per thousand persons living independently rose between 1973 and 1978 from 63.6 to 75.0,[26] but has since remained at the same level. Since 1976, a charge system has been in operation. Every client must make a contribution to the costs according to his or her financial means.

Many old people need help in caring for themselves or are bedridden. In order to restrict the necessity for institutional care as far as possible, use has been made of the district nursing organizations. In 1977 district nursing organizations had some 283,000 elderly people in their care for general and nursing help, preventive care, and information and advice.[27]

The facilities mentioned above all contribute to the circuit of services for the elderly. When so many organizations, all with their own traditions and responsibilities, are involved in providing care for the elderly, it is important that their services be conveniently arranged and accessible. Because of the relative autonomy of private organizations, coordination cannot be required by the government even though a general lack of cooperation is admitted by all parties.

A typical welfare state solution was proposed by government for this situation. This was the creation of a new organization responsible for the coordination of care for the elderly. These new coordinating agencies, however, have no control over the services which they are supposed to be coordinating. As a result, recent developments point more toward the growth of new kinds of services rather than toward coordination. Among these are information services and services in the sphere of recreation. Competition with existing service providers in these fields is possible.

There is another reason why coordination in this field has failed. For coordination to be successful it is necessary to have criteria on the basis of which the provision of the best possible services can be set in motion. At the moment efforts are being made to develop criteria for all forms of help. The criteria for admission to old people's homes have already been discussed. Criteria are similarly being developed for care in nursing homes.

In the field of home help, no one has yet succeeded in developing such criteria. In practice, certain norms are in use; but these have not been standardized. In view of the fact that need often varies, it is not always easy to adhere to strict criteria. Added to which, the individual wishes of elderly people will not always be in agreement with certain criteria.

Finally, the closed-circuit principle presupposes that all the services relevant to the circuit come within the sphere of influence of coordinating bodies or of the administrative authorities. Nothing is, however, further from the truth. The care of the elderly by their children and by commercial organizations (for example through service flats), is as large in scope as the care provided in old people's homes. There is a far greater volume of domestic help provided privately and by relatives and neighbors, etc., than by the home-help organizations. Changes in the subsidized sector affect the private sector and vice versa.[28]

CHANGING ATTITUDES TOWARD THE WELFARE STATE

The organization and planning of welfare policy is not an art which is practiced for its own sake. Perhaps more than in other policy fields government action in the welfare realm is in the service of people and is directed toward solving their problems and increasing their potential for personal growth. What do the people concerned think about this welfare policy? And do their opinions reflect a willingness to make sacrifices which are necessary to continue financing the welfare state? The SCP's project 'Cultural Changes in the Netherlands', which was begun in 1975, makes it possible to give a partial answer to this question. This project consists of data on opinions, continually updated.[29] The government does not always base its policy on what people want. Indeed, policy and opinion are often diametrically opposite. Compulsory schooling, for instance, was introduced in 1900 in the face of considerable opposition; but it is now fully accepted. Data on opinions do give indications as to where the obstacles to policy exist. Such indications are particularly important when policy-makers are thinking of asking the public to make sacrifices.

Some Important Changes of Opinion about the Welfare State

Though the project 'Cultural Changes in the Netherlands' was only initiated in 1974, the Steinmetz Archief in Amsterdam, an important data bank, made data available from inquiries held before 1975. The same questions were asked anew so that a chronological series of data on opinions was built up, and the series has been maintained since 1975. Many of the changes in public opinion are connected with aspects of the welfare state, welfare policy, and welfare planning. The following trends are of importance.

Public expenditure on a number of social and cultural provisions is not fundamentally rejected, but the backing for these measures showed a consistent downward curve during the seventies.

From another series of opinions it is obvious that people's willingness to pay for the facilities is *not* on the increase. Thus there is a certain tendency for people to want social and cultural facilities only if the authorities provide them free.

The data on public expenditure in general and the payment of taxes in particular also lead to the conclusion that the public is not very keen to make sacrifices in aid of government services. The opinion that public expenditure should go down is increasingly prevalent. People increasingly desire that taxation should remain at the same level. (Table 7–4 and 7–5)

Democratization plays an important part in welfare policy, as was apparent with the introduction of the Specific Welfare Provisions Act. However, a number of forms of participation became less popular during the seventies.

Social security benefits do not really belong to welfare policy in the narrow sense, but they nevertheless determine to a great extent the actual well-being of a very large number of Dutchmen. Project results show that the public willingness to pay more for these benefits is decidedly limited. (Table 7–6)

All in all the project data indicate a certain growth of indifference towards important elements of welfare policy. This indifference is accompanied by diminishing approval, which is strongly marked in the case of social security.

Table 7-4 Opinions on public expenditure (percentages)

	1967	1970	1975	1979	1980	1981
(a) Do you think the government should have more or less money with which to pay for services?						
[ ] A lot more		44.5	26.1	22.0	22.3	21.3
[ ] A little more		31.9	31.7	33.4	34.6	33.7
[ ] The same as at present		16.5	26.1	30.7	29.5	27.5
[ ] A little/a lot less		7.1	16.1	13.9	13.6	17.5
Total sample		(1,811)	(1,641)	(1,694)	(1,724)	(1,689)
(b) Should public expenditure rise, fall, or stay as it is?						
[ ] Rise	10.5		8.3	12.4	7.3	8.5
[ ] Stay as it is	67.7		58.0	47.1	41.5	33.1
[ ] Fall	21.8		33.7	40.5	51.2	58.4
Total sample	(605)		(1,251)	(1,223)	(1,280)	(1,248)

Source: *Sociaal en Cultureel Rapport*, The Hague, Staatsuitgeverij, 1983, p. 231.

Table 7-5 Opinions on taxation and introduction of maximum income (percentages)

	1967	1970	1975	1979	1980	1981
(a) Taxation should:						
[ ] Be raised	2.5		2.9	2.3	1.8	2.5
[ ] Remain as it is	23.9		29.6	46.5	47.2	45.8
[ ] Be reduced	73.6		67.5	51.2	51.0	51.7
Total sample	(1,013)		(1,430)	(1,335)	(1,340)	(1,304)
(b) People's opinions on the level of taxation on their own incomes:						
[ ] Too high		76.4	63.6	50.6	54.1	50.6
[ ] Reasonable		23.1	34.1	48.1	45.4	48.4
[ ] Too low		0.5	2.3	1.3	0.5	1.0
Total sample		(642)	(1,438)	(1,442)	(1,457)	(1,393)
(c) Opinions on the introduction of a maximum income:						
[ ] A good idea		33.6	56.6	48.7	56.7	
[ ] Not a good idea		66.4	43.4	51.3	43.3	
Total sample		(595)	(1,372)	(1,365)	(1,428)	

Source: *Sociaal en Cultureel Rapport*, 1982, p. 238.

Table 7-6 Opinion on certain social security benefits (percentage)

Type of benefit	Reply	1966	1970	1975	1978	1979	1980	1981
Sickness benefit	Too high				7.0	10.6	11.1	13.2
	Adequate				83.3	83.8	83.0	79.9
	Adequate/ Too high				90.3	94.4	94.1	93.1
General old-age pension	Too high			1.0	1.0	1.4	1.0	1.2
	Adequate			63.7	68.5	70.1	73.8	73.0
	Adequate/ Too high	36.8	32.1	64.7	69.5	71.5	74.8	74.2
National assistance	Too high			20.0	16.0	17.0	13.4	16.8
	Adequate			59.2	62.8	64.0	61.5	59.3
	Adequate/ Too high	60.5	54.7	79.2	78.8	81.0	74.9	76.1
Unemployment benefit	Too high			26.8	31.5	29.1	25.4	26.6
	Adequate			60.5	57.3	59.7	62.4	61.5
	Adequate/ Too high	74.4	73.4	87.3	88.8	88.8	87.8	88.1
General widows and orphans benefits	Too high					1.7	0.9	2.0
	Adequate					64.4	59.1	61.4
	Adequate/ Too high	37.2	33.3			66.1	60.0	63.4
Disablement insurance	Too high				6.3	12.1	13.0	13.0
	Adequate				63.5	65.3	64.4	65.2
	Adequate/ Too high				69.8	77.4	77.4	78.2
Total sample		(1217)	(1925)	(1681)	(1015)	(1700)	(1600)	(1600)

Source: *Sociaal en Cultureel Rapport*, 1982, p. 235.

Important Groups in the Dutch Population and their Opinions

Opinion changes in the Netherlands occur at more or less the same pace among the different segments of the Dutch population. The differences in lifestyle between groups of Dutchmen are very slight. Dutch society is characterized by its homogeneity. Moreover, there is intensive provision of information in the Netherlands and this information can easily reach the Dutch population, above all because of television and a high average level of education. However, the fact that change in opinions is not very highly differentiated need not necessarily indicate a consensus of opinion. People with a high level of education and people with a low level of education, for example, may well have different opinions on an issue and yet change their views at roughly the same pace and in the same direction. The result will be that the original differences are maintained. However, looking at the views expressed on various aspects of the welfare state there does appear to be a high level of consensus. Regarding public expenditure in general, expenditure on specific social and cultural provisions, and taxes, there are very few subgroups of opinion which diverge from the general picture. Younger people and students want more money spent on public facilities. This same group, together with people in receipt of benefits and those in the lower income brackets, more often consider that public expenditure should go up. The lower income groups and city dwellers are especially in favor of public housing construction. Finally, younger people support citizen participation in decision-making more than other groups.[30]

CONCLUSIONS

Social and cultural planning in the Netherlands has developed rapidly during the post-war period. Much of this development came about as a result of increasing government involvement in social issues. Originally social and cultural programs were carried out by private organizations which were primarily religious in nature. With the growing secular orientation of Dutch society and the increasing demand for standardized provision of social services, the role of private organizations diminished.

The rapid development of welfare state legislation in the 1950s and 1960s firmly committed the national government to assuming the central role in social and cultural planning. To coordinate and evaluate the efforts of the various ministries in social and cultural planning, the Social and Cultural Planning Bureau was established in 1973. However, the SCP's role is primarily advisory to the ministries and departments and integration of national policy in the social and cultural area has not been achieved.

A case in point concerns the services for the elderly population of the Netherlands. An extensive system of facilities has been built up in the Netherlands, whereby it is possible to guard against elderly people getting into situations with which they cannot cope. This system came into being above all thanks to the useful work done by private groups in close cooperation with the authorities. The harmonization of the policy of departments most closely concerned with policy for the elderly has been a continual problem and the 'closed circuit' was introduced as a framework for integration. However, the government has done no more than pronounce that such a framework is desirable. A statutory framework was not considered necessary, since preparations had already been made for general social and cultural planning and also since economic growth made it possible to combat problems with new facilities. For the same reason not much progress has been made on in coordinating the planning and financing of any other range of services.

In the meantime a radical change has occured in a number of aspects concerning welfare policies in the Netherlands. It seems that social and cultural planning in the Netherlands will only take definite form after many more years of discussion. A statutory basis for the 'closed circuit', and, thus, for the harmonization of interrelated facilities is not expected in the near future. Also, by the early seventies it was apparent that the greater range of services was leading to enormous increases in public expenditure. The economic recession of the last few years makes this uncontrollable rise in costs all the more of a problem. Finally, the Dutch population is ageing and at a much faster rate than was expected. According to the last population forecast, the Dutch population aged seventy-five and over will increase by 52 percent between 1900 and 2000.[31] There will be a greatly increasing demand for facilities for old people.

Planning in general and control in particular instances are only possible if the necessary instruments are available. Good instruments are lacking and, owing to the influence of various factors, the very need for the instruments has greatly increased.

The growth of provisions and facilities and of their accompanying costs is the result of this lack of instruments for planning and control.

An appeal to the generosity of the Dutch taxpayer cannot provide a solution to this problem. The result is that the departments concerned with policy for the elderly effect the necessary economies in the facilities whose cost are easy to control and do not pay much attention to the results of these measures on the facilities whose costs are more difficult to control. Apart from the fact that the economies might turn out to be minimal, this course of action leads to a very unbalanced system of services, which is often contrary to policy wishes previously expressed. Thus a desirable shift from the care in old people's homes to care at home by home-help services is halted becaused the first facility is still subject to little control, while the second can easily be subjected to economies.

This unbalanced state of affairs need not have arisen if the Netherlands had had a broad comprehensive planning system which would have made it possible to weigh various measure against each other. The division into departmental sectors with accompanying private organizations did not permit such a planning system to develop and thus the danger arises that what was once a stimulating force behind the growth of the Dutch welfare state may now become the cause of its downfall.

NOTES

1. W. P. Knulst, *Memorandum on Volunteer Workers Policy: Ministry of Culture, Recreation and Social Work, Vrijwilligersbeleid*, vol. 1, The Hague, Ministry of Culture, Recreation and Social Work, 1980. Also, see H. Nijenhuis, *Volksopvoeding tussen elite en massa: een geschiedenis van volwasseneducatie in Nederland* (Popular education: a history of adult education in the Netherlands), Meppel, Boom, 1981.
2. *Cei. van Rhijn*, (Inaugurated by the Minister of Social Affairs, 26 March 1943), Part 1, The Hague, 1945.
3. J. J. A. van Doorn and J. C. M. Schuyt, *De stagnerende verzorgingsstaat* (The stagnant welfare state), Meppel, Boom, 1978.
4. Th. Quené, 'Grenzen aan beleidsvoering' (Limits to the pursuit of policy), *Acta Politica*, vol. 17, no. 1 (1982), p. 5.
5. *Rapport van de commissie voorbereiding orderzoek toekomstige maatschappij structuur* (Report of the committee for the preparatory survey of the future structure of society), The Hague, Staatsuitgeverij, 1970.
6. *Commissie van Veen: Bestuursorganizatie bij de kabinetsformatie 1971* (Cabinet formation and administrative organization 1971), The Hague, Staatsuitgeverij, 1971.
7. E. Jantsch, *Perspectives of Planning*, Organization for Economic Cooperation and Development, Paris, 1969.
8. These Memoranda were: Ministry of Health and Environmental Hygiene, *Structuurnota gezondheidszorg* (Memorandum on the Structure of health care), The Hague, Staatsuitgeverij, 1974; Consultative committee on bottlenecks in the harmonization of welfare policy and welfare legislation, *Knelpuntennota* (Bottlenecks Memorandum), The Hague, Staatsuitgeverij, 1974; and Ministry of Education, Discussion document on *Contouren van een toekomstig onderwijsbestel* (Memorandum on contours of a future education system–Contours Memorandum), Ministry of Education, The Hague, 1975.

9. H. M. Jolles and J. A. Stalpers, *Welzinjnsbeleid en sociale wetenschappen* (Welfare policy and social science), Deventer, Van Loghum Slaterus, 1978, p. 19.
10. Ministry of Culture, Recreation and Social Work, *Ontwerp Kaderwet Specifiek Welzijn* (Specific Welfare Provisions Bill), Second Chamber, 1976 Session, no. 14493.
11. Ministry of Health and Environmental Hygiene, *Wetsontwerp Wet Voorzieningen Gezondheidszorg* (Health Care Provisions Bill), Second Chamber, 1976–77 Session, no. 14181.
12. For a description of this problem see: Social and Cultural Planning Bureau, *Social and Cultural Report 1980*, The Hague, Staatsuitgeverij, 1980, ch. 13, pp. 275–310 (English edition).
13. An evaluation of this legislation appears in: Social and Cultural Planning Bureau, *Sociaal en Cultureel Rapport 1982*, The Hague, Staatsuitgeverij, 1982, ch. 12, pp. 263–306.
14. Social and Cultural Planning Bureau and Central Planning Bureau, *De kwartaire sector in de jaren tachtig* (The quaternary sector in the eighties), The Hague, Staatsuitgeverij, Bulletin 2.
15. Ministry of Health and Environmental Hygiene, *Guidelines under Article 3 of Hospital Provisions Act, The Hague, Staatsuitgeverij, 1981.*
16. *COZ-vademecum* (COZ is the Central Council on Hospital Tariffs), Alphen aan de Rijn, Samson, 1978.
17. Ministry of Health and Environmental Hygiene, *Fifth financial survey of health care*, Second Chamber, 1981–2 Session, no. 17100, ch. XVII, p. 14.
18. Ibid., p. 32.
19. Social and Cultural Planning Bureau, *Sociaal en Cultureel Rapport 1982*, pp. 42–3.
20. M. Mootz and J. M. Timmermans, *Zorgen voor later* (Care for the future), The Hague, Staatsuitgeverij, 1981, p. 14.
21. Ministry of Culture, Recreation and Social Work, *Memorandum on Policy for Care of the Elderly 1975*, Second Chamber, 1974–75 Session, no. 13463, vols. 1 and 2, p. 71
22. Ibid., p. 86. The notion in this form was introduced by F. J. G. Oostvogel and described in depth in his thesis *Verzorgingsbehoefte van bejaarden* (The elderly's need of care) in 1968, Utrecht University.
23. Central Bureau of Statistics, *Statistiek Bejaardenoorden* (Statistics of Homes for the Elderly), The Hague, Staatsuitgeverij, 1980.
24. Central Bureau of Statistics, *Sociaal Cultureel Kwartaalschrift* (Social and Cultural Quarterly), The Hague, Staatsuitgeverij, 1982–3.
25. Mootz and Timmermans, op. cit., p. 36.
26. Central Bureau of Statistics, *Statistiek Gezinsversorging 1977* (Statistics of Home Help 1977), The Hague, Staatsuitgeverij, 1979.
27. Mootz and Timmermans, op. cit., pp. 123–4.
28. Ibid., chs. 6 and 7.
29. The most important results of the surveys are to be found in the *Social and Cultural Report*. These are available in an English translation and can be ordered from the Social and Cultural Planning Bureau (Postbus 37, 2280 AA, Rijswijk, The Netherlands).
30. Younger=18–34 years of age; low income=in the lowest 20 percent of income recipients; low level of education=primary school only; city dwellers=in the urban category of the urbanization scale prepared by the Central Bureau of Statistics.
31. Central Bureau of Statistics, *Statistisch Bulletin*, Central Bureau of Statistics, Voorburg, vol. 37, 1981, p. 106.

8
National Development and Economic Policy in the Netherlands since 1945 with Special Reference to Regional Economic Policy

A. van Delft and A. Kwaak*

In studying the evolution of economic policy in the Netherlands since the Second World War several changes in the manner in which governments have tried to influence economic development can be identified. These changes relate not only to the intensity and detailed nature of government intervention, but also to the choice of the sectors of the economy which were to be subject to such intervention. The basic philosophy of economic policy, however, did not change: government should be concerned with economic development in a restrained manner. Also the basic goals of economic policy have not changed since the beginning of the 1950s. These goals concern: (1) maintenance of economic growth, (2) full employment, (3) equilibrium on the balance of payments, (4) a just income distribution, and (5) the abatement of inflation. Since the beginning of the 1970s, a sixth goal has been added, which involves the concept of selective economic growth. Economic development should be assessed as to its impact upon physical planning and the use of energy.

The intensity and character of economic policy has been determined mainly by economic development itself. Broadly speaking, since 1945 three periods of economic development in the Netherlands can be identified. The first period encompassed the reconstruction era after the Second World War and lasted until 1963. The second period (1963–73) was one of fast and constant economic growth together with a high level of employment. The third and current period beginning in 1973 has seen gradual economic stagnation and high unemployment.

RECONSTRUCTION: 1945–1963

Economic policy during the period of reconstruction after the Second World War was characterized by detailed government intervention in many sectors of the economy in the first half of this period, and a gradual liberalization of government control afterwards.

By the end of the Second World War the economy had come to a complete standstill. Initially, it was necessary to use all scarce means to set the economy going again. This

*The views expressed in this paper are those of the authors and not necessarily those of the organizations they represent.

had to be done in a situation in which trade relations with other countries were seriously disturbed. In these years, a system of rationing was implemented because of a shortage of foodstuffs and other goods.

Because of the scarcity of raw materials, foreign currency, and energy, economic policy exhibited a high degree of central planning. High priority was given to agriculture and manufacturing, especially the steel and the chemical industry. Aid under the Marshall Plan further strengthened the influence of the government on economic development. This plan created financial opportunities to set up large industrial projects in which the government often actively participated. However, after the first years of reconstruction, the government gradually decreased its direct influence on economic life.

Another important feature of economic policy during the period of reconstruction was the restrictive wages-policy. Until 1963 wage rises were controlled by central government. The consequent small wage rises resulted in a high degree of competitiveness of Dutch enterprises in international markets. The abandoning of this restrictive wages-policy can be viewed as the end of the period of economic reconstruction.

PERIOD OF ECONOMIC GROWTH: 1963–1973

The years between 1963 and 1973 constitute a period of restricted government intervention in the economy. Because of fast economic growth, the five basic goals of macroeconomic policy as listed above were fulfilled. The attention of economic policy was turned towards extension of the system of social security and other services which enhance individual well-being (for example housing, education, etc.).

Despite general economic prosperity the development of some sectors of industry was rather slow. Because of a tight labor-market there was a sharp increase in wages which put Dutch industries at a disadvantage in international markets. Thus, more attention was paid to the long-term development of the structure of the Dutch economy in order to ensure that economic growth was maintained.

The attention to the long-term aspects of economic growth was strengthened by the consideration given to the adverse consequences of unrestrained growth (for example exhaustion of raw materials, deterioration of the environment, etc.). This led to the adoption of selective growth as a goal of economic policy. However, a systematic policy aiming at a desirable industrial structure was never set up. The government restricted its activities to incidental financial support for the reorganization of various sectors of industry. But, regulations concerning the environmental consequences of economic activity were strengthened.

THE POST-OIL-CRISIS ERA

The sharp increase in oil prices in 1973 was the beginning of the third period of economic development and policy in the Netherlands. In the first years of this period, economic growth was still at a reasonable level but the rising costs of energy and labor caused many problems for a growing number of enterprises. Economic policy in this period is, thus, characterized by growing financial support for individual companies from central government.

The policy of selective economic growth was reformulated according to this new economic situation. Its main instrument at present is a highly differentiated system of investment premiums (Investment Account Act, Wet investeringsrekening, WIR). The policy objective is to stimulate those activities which are desirable from the national point of view.

To improve the international competitive position it was necessary to bring down labor costs. The government intervened in negotiations between employers and trade unions in order to keep down wage rises. In this wage-containment policy special concern was given to the position of low-income groups.

As the level of public expenditure increased, the gap between government income and public expenditure widened. To prevent a further increase in government debt a program to slow down the growth of public expenditure was designed and partly carried out.

As the last element of economic policy in this period the abatement of inflation should be mentioned. Slowing down wage rises is an important part of this policy, as is reducing the rate of growth of government expenditure. In addition, the government has imposed some direct price controls, especially in the field of energy prices.

INSTITUTIONAL ASPECTS OF ECONOMIC POLICY

Some consideration should be given to the institutional aspects of economic policy in the Netherlands. Firstly, it should be mentioned that, traditionally, economic policy has been strongly centralized. Although in other areas, especially in physical planning, municipal and provincial authorities play a strong part in the process of decision-making as well as the execution of policies, the responsibility for economic policy lies primarily with the central administration. Three ministries are involved: the Ministry of Finance, the Ministry of Social Affairs and Employment, and the Ministry of Economic Affairs.

Concerning the preparation of economic policy, much work is done by the Central Bureau of Statistics (CBS, founded in 1899) and the Central Planning Bureau (CPB, founded in 1945). The task of the CBS is to prepare statistical information about the economy. The CPB is expected to analyze the functioning of the Dutch economy and to make forecasts of future economic development. Furthermore, the CPB evaluates the effects of certain policy measures. This is usually done with the aid of econometric models, a tradition started by the first Director of the CPB, Professor Jan Tinbergen.[1] It should be noted that the role of the CPB is only advisory; decisions about economic policy are made at the ministries mentioned above.

Finally, the Social Economic Council should be mentioned. This is a consultative board consisting of equal numbers of employers and trade-union representatives, as well as independent experts nominated by the government.

REGIONAL PATTERNS OF LABOR-MARKET DEVELOPMENTS 1955–1980

To present only the essential outline of regional developments in the Netherlands, the country has been divided into four regions (Fig. 8-1). First of all, attention is paid to the pattern of population and labor-force development. Then, regional employment developments are described, and finally, the regional distribution of unemployment is discussed. The analysis in this section confines itself to the labor market due to the lack of reliable time series data on regional production and income.

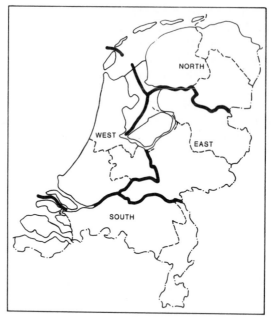

Fig. 8–1 Four Regions for Economic
Planning in The Netherlands

Population and Labor Force

With respect to population size, the four parts of the Netherlands differ greatly. In 1980 the number of inhabitants varied between 6.3 million in the West and 1.6 million in the North.[2] Between 1955 and 1980 the average yearly population growth in the North was 1.0 percent (compared with a national figure of 1.1 percent). In the fifties and sixties the North experienced negative migration balance, while in the seventies the reverse occurred. The West held a decreasing share of the total population throughout the period between 1955 and 1980 (average yearly growth of 0.8 percent), especially after 1970. In the seventies the big cities even had a population loss. The declining share of the West was absorbed by growth in the East and the South (with average yearly growth rates of 1.5 percent and 1.4 percent respectively).

The pattern of labor-force development has, of course, some correlation with that of population growth. The two are related by the development of labor-force participation. This has been especially important for the West, since in this region the decrease in the participation rate was much smaller than in the other regions. In the West over the whole period the increase in the labor force (on average, 0.8 percent a year) equalled the national growth rate even though population growth in the West was less than the national average. For the other regions, the pattern of labor-force development is comparable with the regional pattern of population growth: the North below, and the East and South above the national growth rate. On average, the North experienced a decline in its share of the national labor force while the South increased its share. Labor-force growth in the East was of the same magnitude as the national figure (0.9 percent a year).

Employment

Before describing the regional pattern of employment growth, the differences concerning the regional industrial structures should be mentioned. Traditionally the North has had a large agro-industrial complex while other industries and the service sector are of less importance. In the East and South agriculture and manufacturing are the main sources of employment, while some emphasis on textile manufacturing is also important.

These differences should be taken into account when assessing the regional pattern of employment development. Since the Second World War there has been a continuing decrease in employment in agriculture. After an increase in the fifties and the beginning of the sixties, manufacturing employment has also declined. Only in the service sector has there been an almost continuous growth of employment. These national trends, together with the industrial structure of employment, partly explain the regional pattern of employment growth.

The regional pattern of employment growth since the beginning of the sixties can be characterized by an increasing trend towards decentralization from the West. Since the beginning of this period the South has benefitted from this trend, and since the beginning of the seventies, the East has also. With a few exceptions, the North showed a below-average employment growth between 1955 and 1980.

Developments in the northern region have been dominated by the sharp decline of employment in the agro-industrial complex. This decline has only partly been offset by the development of manufacturing, stimulated by the abundant supply of labor and by regional economic policy. In the seventies, the service-sector also showed an above-average growth in the North.

The growth of employment in the East has been influenced by the favorable development of the service sector. However, the substantial decline over the 1955–80 period of the initially large share of agricultural employment in total employment explains the relatively moderate increase in employment for this area throughout the period.

The decentralization of employment from the West can be observed in the manufacturing as well as the service sector. The main reasons were the presence of a tight labor-market, which is especially unattractive to manufacturing industry, and the relatively small population growth, which affected the service sector.

The South owes its employment growth to the industrial as well as to the service sector. Availability of labor and rapid population growth have been the main causes of this growth. Also, in the seventies, employment growth resulted from regional economic policy intended to offset the severe impact of coal-mine closures in the province of Limburg between 1965 and 1970.

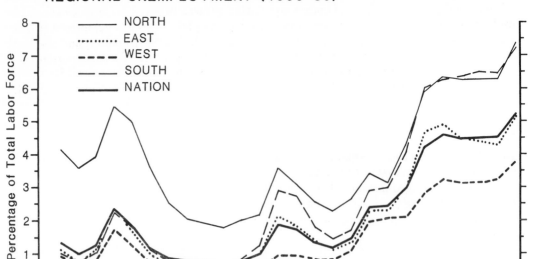

Fig. 8-2   Unemployment by Regions

Unemployment

From the foregoing it can be concluded that the pattern of growth of the labor-force and of employment did not vary greatly between the regions except in the case of the South. As a result the regional distribution of unemployment did not change much, except, again, for in the South (Fig. 8-2). However, some developments are worth mentioning.

In the North, unemployment has been significantly above average since 1955. However, the unemployment rate declined (relatively) from more than three times the national average in 1955 to about one-and-a-half times the national average in the second half of the seventies. The difference between the northern and the national unemployment rate widened during the seventies.

Up to 1965 the difference between unemployment in the South and the national unemployment rate was very small. However, in the second half of the sixties and the beginning of the seventies the rise of unemployment in the South was much greater than for the Netherlands as a whole, due to the closing down of the coal mines in Limburg. In the former mining region, unemployment is still extremely high.

REGIONAL ECONOMIC POLICY IN THE NETHERLANDS

One of the basic goals of economic policy in the Netherlands has always been the maintenance of economic growth. However, even in the sixties, when economic growth was considerable, the regional distribution of economic prosperity has been rather uneven, as indicated in the previous discussion of the regional differences in unemployment rates.

Regional differences have been partly reduced by the impact of national economic policies. For example, policies designed to improve the performance of certain sectors of industry have had a regional impact. Regional growth has also originated from government financial support given to individual companies, since in many instances this support was only granted to firms in regions experiencing high unemployment rates. Furthermore, a specific regional impact arose from the business-cycle policy when government expenditures were directed towards sectors strongly concentrated in specific regions. However, the persistence of regional differences in prosperity gave rise to a specific regional economic policy, which will be dealt with in this section.

General Characteristics of Regional Economic Policy

Regional economic policy in the Netherlands is pursued by central government, as indeed is all economic policy. As a result, regional authorities have only very limited budgets with which to pursue economic policies. However, there is a trend towards more participation of provincial and municipal authorities.

Regional economic policy in the Netherlands has always striven towards two interrelated goals: equity and efficiency of regional economic development. The equity goal is related to the improvement of the opportunities for work and income in the regions that are lagging behind (mainly the northern and southern parts of the country). The efficiency goal pertains to the contribution to total national economic development that can be made by each region exploiting its locational advantages.

Because of the interrelatedness of the two goals, it is quite difficult to discover changes pertaining to emphasis put on just one of the goals, especially because implementation of the goals is always sought with the same kind of instruments. Thus, the construction of harbors in the western part of the country is undoubtedly related to the efficiency goal of regional economic policy, while in the North it would relate to equity. However, in the latter case, making better use of available resources (especially manpower), in seaport-related industries, will enable the North to increase its contribution to national production. Thus there are elements of efficiency here as well. In some cases the equity goal may come into conflict with the efficiency goal, for example, when capital is allocated to regions where it is less productive. Some gradual changes concerning the emphasis on either equity or efficiency can be observed. During the period of reconstruction of the national economy (1945–63), emphasis was placed on the efficiency goals, while in the next decade, regional economic policy focused somewhat more on equity. In recent years there has been a tendency towards more efficiency, at least partly caused by the gradual stagnation of economic growth.

Traditionally, the northern part of the country has been the subject of regional economic policy because of a decline in employment in the agro-industrial complex in this region which resulted in high unemployment.

After 1965 the southern part of the Netherlands also came under the influence of regional economic policy because of the closing down of coal mines (especially in the southern part of the province of Limburg). To varying degrees, other regions (mainly outside the West) have benefitted from regional economic policy as well, but not to the extent of the North and South.

In the beginning of the seventies, regional economic policy was set into a broader context. This can be concluded from the *Report on the Northern Part of the Country*, published in 1972,[3] and the fact that in 1974 the Selective Investments Regulations Act (SIR) came into force. In the report, the economic development of the northern region is put into a framework of physical planning and social and cultural development.

With the introduction of the SIR the link between regional economic policy and physical planning was strengthened. Among other things the SIR seeks to reduce congestion in the western part of the country by a system of levies and allowances for industrial investment in that region.[4] Together with the Investment Account Act (WIR), the Selective Investments Regulations Act seeks to achieve a maximal differentiation of investment premiums in favor of the regions outside the western part of the country.

In 1978, the economic development of the North was placed into a broader context of social, physical, and cultural planning through the *Integrated Structure Plan (ISP) for the Northern Part of the Country*. (Refer to Chapter 9 of this book for further discussion of the *ISP*.) This plan became operational as a result of cooperation between central government and provincial authorities.

The *Report on the Perspectives of South Limburg* is another example of mutual agreement. Thus, there is a trend developing towards the participation of regional authorities in the preparation of regional economic policy.[5]

This trend is enforced by the publication of the *Report on Regional Socio-Economic Policy 1977–1980*.[6] In this Report provincial authorities are invited to report periodically about economic developments in their regions and to present their views on existing and expected constraints on regional development. In this way it is hoped to remove such constraints in regional economic development and to allow for a better tradeoff between economic development and , for example, environmental protection and physical planning. Furthermore, experiments to involve provincial authorities in the execution of regional economic policy are also under consideration.

In recent years more attention is being paid to the economic problems of the large cities. Not only the cities in regions with a traditionally weak economic structure, but also those in the more prosperous areas are confronted with a relatively sharp rise in unemployment, frictions in the labor market, stagnation or even decline in the level of population, and other aspects of urban decay. The unemployment problem in these cities has a strong social dimension since unemployment is concentrated within the older districts with a rate sometimes more than three times the national average. From the *Report on Regional Socio-Economic Policy 1981–1985* it is apparent that the central government intends to address these problems. There is still another reason why in regional economic policy more attention is given to the urbanized western part of the country. To attack the economic recession, regional economic policy should aim to stimulate the contribution of every region to national prosperity. It is stressed that the large cities in the West have the potential to develop the high technological industries of the future.

Instruments of Regional Economic Policy

The instruments of regional economic policy mainly try to influence, directly or indirectly, the locational choice of individual enterprises, to the benefit of certain areas.

The main instruments of regional economic policy can be divided into four groups: investment-premium schemes, infrastructure policy and direct job-creation, regional development corporations, and the relocation of government offices. In some respects, the instruments of labor-market policy can be viewed as complementary to these. This

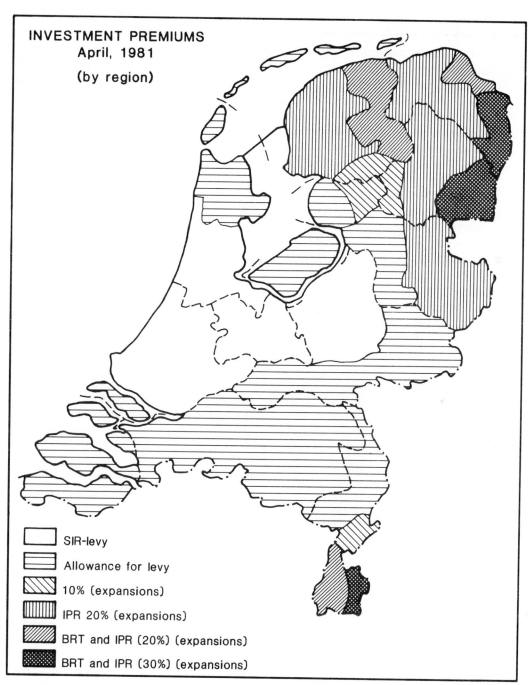

INVESTMENT PREMIUMS
April, 1981

(by region)

SIR-levy

Allowance for levy

10% (expansions)

IPR 20% (expansions)

BRT and IPR (20%) (expansions)

BRT and IPR (30%) (expansions)

Fig. 8–3   Investment Premiums by Regions

section is devoted to a description of these instruments of regional economic policy, and in the next section some attention will be paid to their effectiveness.

Investment-Premium Schemes

Regional investment-premium schemes have always constituted the core of regional economic policy, although they have been subject to drastic change. In the fifties and the beginning of the sixties, these schemes were exclusively aimed at the industrialization of selected areas and should, therefore, be viewed as part of a national industrialization policy. In the second half of the sixties two important changes in the investment-premium instrument gradually took place. Firstly, besides industry, basic services also became eligible for investment premiums. Secondly, because of the adoption of the concept of selective growth, the schemes became related to the goals of physical planning. As a consequence of this, it was decided to regionalize a hitherto nationally operative fiscal investment-subsidy scheme (accelerated depreciation). In this scheme, an extra fiscal depreciation on capital goods during the first years of their fiscal life (at the expense of depreciation in later years) is allowed for. This has the effect of increasing the rentability of the investment projects concerned. Thus, in the urbanized areas in the western part of the country, to counteract congestion, investments were not allowed this kind of subsidy. At the beginning of the seventies, this policy was put into operation through the already mentioned Selective Investments Regulations Act (SIR).

In 1978 a general system of fiscal investment-incentives was introduced, namely the Investment Accounts Act (WIR). This system offers the government the opportunity to stimulate investment selectively. This selectivity concerns both the type of investment and the region for which the investment project is intended. Regional selectivity is attained on the one hand by an extra premium on investment in certain areas in the North and the South (Special Regional Allowance, BRT), and on the other by temporarily reactivating the system of levies of the SIR. Furthermore, a special economic benefit is given to investors in certain municipalities in which development is desirable from the point of view of physical planning (Physical Planning Allowance, ROT).

The Investment Premium Regulations Act (IPR) has been operative since 1968.[7] It aims to diminish regional differences in unemployment rates by stimulating investments in the North and the South. Fig. 8-3 shows the present-day distribution of regionally differentiated investment premiums. However it should be noted that central government has stopped the BRT and ROT premiums, and lowered IPR premiums from January 1, 1984.

Infrastructure Policy and Direct Job-Creation

Another important instrument of regional economic policy is the construction of infrastructure. The government aims at improving the physical conditions for economic development and emphasis is put on increasing the accessibility of the assisted areas. Central government gives financial support to provincial and local authorities for the construction of roads, railroads, bridges, canals, harbor facilities, and so on, and these schemes have been in force since the end of the fifties. In recent years, financial support is also given to construction work in important industrial districts.

In the first instance, infrastructure policy was proposed as an indirect way of

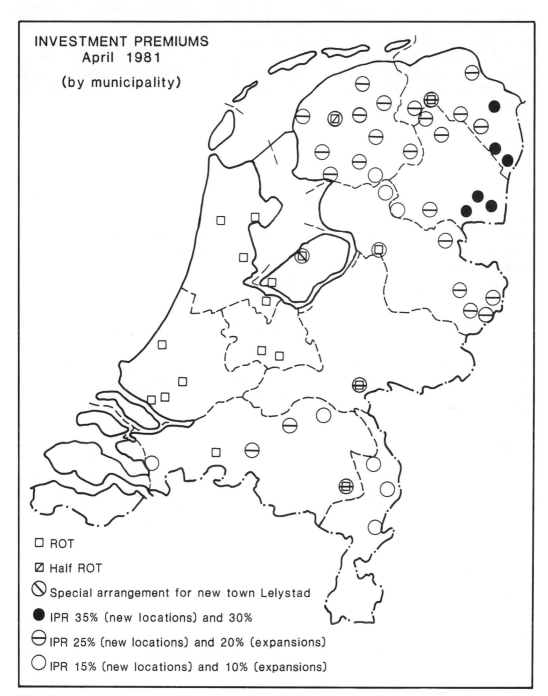

Fig. 8-4   Investment Premiums by Municipalities

stimulating regional economic development. In the second half of the seventies, however, emphasis was also placed on the direct effects of job creation in the construction sector. In this way, infrastructure policy is related to another instrument of regional economic policy namely, direct job-creation in special areas.

This instrument increases employment in the building sector by providing funds for the construction of socio-cultural facilities such as sports halls, swimming pools, and the like. An indirect effect may be that through the improvement of amenities, the regions concerned may become more attractive locations for other economic activities. Inevitably, the direct effects of these job-creation programs are temporary.

Regional Development Corporations

Recently a new instrument of regional economic policy has been introduced. This is the regional development corporation. These corporations are created by central government, though occasionally also by provincial authorities. Their principal aim is the promotion of regional economic activity. One way in which this is accomplished is to give financial support to enterprises. This financial support was meant to establish new economic activity but it has proved necessary to use some of the finance to preserve already existing activity, too.

Regional development corporations also act as consultative bodies. They help in the management of individual firms and also transfer technological knowledge. Furthermore, they are involved in the acqusition of new enterprises, often from abroad.

The intensity with which the above-mentioned tasks are executed differs among the individual corporations. The northern and Limburg development corporations are primarily involved in giving financial assistance, while the others (in the provinces of Overijssel and Gelderland) primarily restrict themselves to their advisory and acquisition tasks. The foundation of another regional development corporation, in the province of North Brabant, is partly completed.

Relocation of Government Offices

In contrast to the instruments of regional economic policy mentioned so far, the relocation of government offices has had a permanent direct influence in regional employment. Originally this policy arose from the physical-planning view which saw as undesirable the concentration of government offices in the western part of the country, especially in the Hague. It was decided to relocate government offices to less congested areas. Later, this instrument was incorporated into regional economic policy. Nowadays, the relocation of government offices is seen more as a way of creating jobs in the assisted areas, than as a method of relieving congestion in the West. Emphasis is, therefore, placed on the location of new or fast growing government services in the special areas.

Between 1970 and 1980, the relocation of government offices involved about 5,100 jobs (including new offices); 20 percent of these were located in the North, 59 percent in the South, and 21 percent in the East. The growing importance of the arguments concerning regional economic policy in the decisions about this instrument can be seen by the fact that in recent years all relocation of government offices has been to assist areas in the North and the South.

Labor-Market Policy

The instruments of regional economic policy discussed so far all aim at stimulating regional economic activity and employment, as a means of eliminating or arresting any worsening of regional differences in unemployment rates. Labor-market policy is complementary to regional economic policy in that it tries to diminish the frictions between supply and demand in regional labor markets. In contrast to the other instruments, labor-market policy finds its momentum on the supply side of the labor market.

Labor-market policy consists of three types of measures. Firstly, some of the unemployed are given training, either on-the-job training, or training in government-established institutes. Secondly, the rehiring of unemployed people is encouraged through placement-promotion schemes that give temporary labor-cost subsidies. Finally, job-creation schemes for special groups of unemployed (for example the long-term unemployed) help to preserve their skills. The job-creation schemes for construction workers have already been mentioned.

The regional dimension of labor-market policy differs from that of the other instruments of regional economic policy. This is because its instruments are not regionally differentiated; a regional dimension is derived from the intensity with which these instruments are applied, an intensity which varies with the intensity of regional unemployment. This is illustrated in Table 8-1.

In 1980 the number of applicants for labor-market policy measures in each region was more than proportional to the number of unemployed, if the regional unemployment rate was above average. This held particularly for job-creation measures. The relatively high proportion of applicants for the training schemes from the West, reflects the fact that in the West, especially in the urbanized areas, the qualitative discrepancies between supply and demand are considerable. In other regions the absolute shortage of jobs is more important so in these regions the emphasis is less on training schemes and temporary labor-cost subsidies and more on direct job-creation (Table 8-1).

Table 8-1 Regional distribution of applicants for labor-market policy provisions, 1980

	training schemes (a)	placement promotion (a)	job creation (a)	unemployment level (a)	unemployment rate (b)
North	12.9	12.8	18.1	14.1	7.4
East	18.2	23.4	16.4	18.5	5.1
West	34.3	24.3	25.6	33.9	3.8
South	34.6	39.5	39.9	33.4	7.2
(Neth)c	(13,355)	(5,825)	(12,626)	(261,934)	(5.2)

(a) percentage of national total
(b) percentage of labor force
c between brackets, national levels are presented

Source: Ministry of Social Affairs and Employment and Central Planning Bureau.

Effectiveness of Regional Economic Policy

Research into the effects of regional economic policy is difficult from a methodological as well as a statistical perspective. The main part of research in the Netherlands was begun in the second half of the seventies, and at present, only little can be said about the effects of regional economic policy.

The effectiveness of regional economic policy is strongly dependent on the general level of economic development. This is because most instruments of regional economic policy focus on the development of new activity in assisted areas. When economic growth slows down, as it did in the seventies, so will the pace of this development, and hence regional economic policy will be less effective.

As has been stated already, the effects of regional economic policy are hard to assess. However, some research in this field has been conducted, particularly in relation to two instruments of regional economic policy, namely, the investment-premium schemes, and the relocation of government offices. In 1961, Vanhove concluded that regional economic policy in general, had exerted a favorable influence on the regional allocation of employment.[8] The *Report on Regional Socio-Economic Policy 1981–85* provides information from the Central Planning Bureau on the effects of investment-premium schemes in the seventies. This report asserts that the gross redistributive effect of investment premiums on industrial employment was 9,5000 man-years between 1973 and 1979. Taking into account all relevant side effects, investment premiums probably relocated only some 5,000 man-years from the West to the other regions during this period.[9] However, some experts express doubt as to whether the investment-premium schemes exerted any significant influence on the regional distribution of employment.[10]

Concerning the effects of the relocation of government offices, employment multipliers between 1.25 and 1.50 have been reported.[11] Between 1970 and 1980 some 5,100 jobs were relocated in this program, so that total relocation effects can be estimated to be about 7,000 man-years. It should be noted, however, that the decrease in unemployment was smaller, because about one-third of the civil servants involved moved with their jobs to the new locations.

CONCLUSION

Economic policy in the Netherlands in the post-war period has been described in relation to the general economic situation. Three periods have been distinguished: post-war reconstruction, economic growth, and the period after the oil crisis of 1973. In regional economic policy, however, these periods cannot be distinguished because with, essentially, the same set of instruments, two different goals, namely efficiency and equity of regional economic development, have been sought. A discussion of future national and regional economic policy in the Netherlands would be the obvious conclusion to our chapter. However, it has not yet become clear how economic policy will deal with an economy which has been stagnant for quite a long period of time. Political and scientific discussions have not yet been conclusive. Nevertheless, some elements of these discussions can be mentioned.

First of all, consensus seems to have been reached on the basic goal of future economic policy: economic growth. The main question is how best to set about achieving this goal. On the one hand, it is put forward that the government should produce a climate more conducive to private enterprise; by cutting public expenditure, lowering taxes, and by the deregulation of business activity. On the other hand, it is argued that the government should stimulate growth in a more active and selective way. Public investment, government participation in important private projects, and the maintenance of demand for goods and services are elements of such an economic policy.

In the discussions about future regional economic policy more emphasis is placed on the goal of efficiency: the efficient contribution of regions to national economic growth. The efficiency of present regional policy instruments is being studied. Moreover, the wish to diminish government regulation of business may result in the conditions of the Selective Investment Regulation Act being lifted for the western part of the country. Nevertheless, the stimulation of economically depressed areas is still accepted as a basic element of regional economic policy in the Netherlands.

NOTES

1. These models usually relate to the development of the whole economy. Forecasting may be carried out by constructing macroeconomic models for the short, medium, or long term, or by building multi-sectoral or multi-regional models. More information about the work of the CPB is contained in Varii Auctores, *25 Jaar Centraal Planbureau* (25 Years of the Central Planning Bureau), The Hague, 1970. For more information about the current models, see Central Planning Bureau, *Een macro-model voor de Nederlandse economie op middellange termijn* (A medium-term macroeconomic model for the Dutch Economy), The Hague, 1977; and A. van Delft and W. B. C. Suyker, *Regional Investment Subsidies. An Estimation of the Labor-Market Effects for the Dutch Regions*, Papers of the Regional Science Association, no. 49, 1983.
2. For the other regions, the corresponding figures are East, 2.8 million, and South, 3.5 million.
3. Ministry of Economic Affairs, *Report on the Northern Part of the Country*, The Hague, 1972.
4. The system of levies was deferred soon after its introduction. It came into force again in 1978 with the implementation of the Investment Account Act and was deferred again in 1981.
5. See also *Report on Regional Socio-Economic Policy 1981-1985*, The Hague, 1981, produced by the Ministries of Economic Affairs, of Social Affairs and Employment, and of Housing and Physical Planning.
6. *Report on Regional Socio-Economic Policy 1977-1980*, The Hague, 1977 produced by the Ministries of Economic Affairs and of Social Affairs and Employment.
7. Systems of regional investment premiums already existed before 1968, but they were not so well formulated as this new scheme.
8. N. D. Vanhove, *De doelmatigheid van het regionaal-economisch beleid in Nederland* (The efficiency of regional economic policy in the Netherlands), Eeklo, 1961.
9. See also A. van Delft and W. B. C. Suyker, *op. cit.*
10. H. Folder and J. Ooterhaven, *Measurement of Employment Effects on Dutch Regional Socio-economic Policy*, Groningen, 1980.
11. See National Physical Planning Agency, *Evaluatie van de spreiding van rijksdiensten* (Evaluation of the relocation of government offices), The Hague, 1982. In an annex to this publication, the Central Planning Bureau estimates the employment multiplier to be about 1.5. See also C. van der Vegt, *Spreiding Rijksdiensten: regionaal economische effecten* (Relocation of government offices: regional economic effects), Amsterdam, 1982.

9

An Integrated Structure Plan for the Northern Netherlands: A Test of Integrated Regional Planning

Marc de Smidt

INTRODUCTION

Public intervention in the market economy and the allocation of collective expenditures through the welfare state are both courses that can be pursued to decrease interregional and intraregional disparities. When looking at the interdependencies between the socio-economic, socio-cultural, and socio-spatial facets of a national society, an argument for integrated planning on a regional level can be made. The *Integrated Structure Plan for the Northern Netherlands (ISP)* is an attempt to pursue comprehensive regional planning for a specific area; it has been in operation since the early 1970s. Experience of two decades of regional planning in the three fields or facets mentioned above contributed to this integrated approach. This test of integrated regional planning has been instructive from the viewpoint of both the horizontal and vertical coordination of regional policies. In this chapter a profile of the region concerned is given, with an interregional as well as an intraregional comparison, and the four key issues addressed by the *ISP* are discussed in order to understand better the basic problems underlying the aims of the integrated structure plan for this region. The issues are: (a) labor and employment, (b) land use and natural environment, (c) rural areas and towns, and (d) individual development. An evaluation of the *ISP* is also provided which attempts to assess integrated regional planning and the quest for crisis management in an era of economic stagnation.

INTEGRATED REGIONAL PLANNING

The growth of a welfare state in the Netherlands reinforced government intervention designed to allocate collective expenditures according to principles of equity. Regional socio-economic planning was introduced in the early fifties and is controlled primarily by the national government. In the socio-cultural realm, a broad spectrum of denominational and non-profit organizations are active at different geographic levels in the field of education, health, leisure, and housing. Facilities and authorization for their work have been provided by the national and local governments. Socio-spatial planning is closely linked to physical planning, the oldest part of the planning triptych. At the local and regional levels, government intervention in the built environment is very strong. Recently there has been public intervention to save the natural environment.

These differences in the scope, intensity, and spatial level of public intervention in the three main fields of planning do not alter the fact that human welfare is tied to the interdependencies of these elements since they provide opportunities for work as well as for housing and leisure facilities. In retrospect, *regional planning* can be seen as coordinated action to stimulate activities in underprivileged areas and to curb activities in overdeveloped regions (Fig. 9-1). In the fifties, the regional backwash effects of a growing national economy, expressed in high regional unemployment figures, had to be addressed. In the sixties, congestion problems in the Randstad urban areas created the need for coordination of socio-economic and spatial policies in order to both direct new growth and relocate existing activity to the northern periphery by stimulating migration of both economic activities and population. In the seventies, economic recession required a more intensive socio-economic program to ensure employment opportunities in peripheral regions, but also in the main urban areas of the Randstad. In the eighties, greater attention will have to be paid to the problems of housing and physical planning in the Randstad. Socio-cultural policies in these urban areas are becoming more and more important because of the issues associated with minority groups, urban 'squatters', and the need for urban renewal. Even in the area of socio-economic policies, the Randstad region will receive some funds during the 1981–5 period, although 75 percent of these funds have been set aside for the traditionally depressed regions of the North and South Limburg.

The three main fields of planning exhibit different patterns of control and execution. Socio-economic policies are the concern of the national government, spatial or physical planning policies of local or provincial government, and socio-cultural policies of local or national governments. A decentralization of socio-cultural policies has been carried out, but in the socio-economic field this has been allowed only to a limited extent. The contents of integrated regional planning are not arranged in an institutional framework of horizontal and vertical coordination that is suitable for the handling of interdependent sets of problems. Since integrated regional planning is not possible, an *ad hoc* or project approach must be utilized. The *ISP* is an example of that kind.

ISP—A NEW PLANNING STRATEGY

In a government statement in 1971, Prime Minister Biesheuvel launched the proposal for a new kind of regional planning. This new approach was to be combined with a relocation scheme for government services (intended to move 16,000 jobs in two phases from the Hague to five centers outside the Randstad) and a selective location policy for the West (Selective Investment Regulation Act, operational in 1975).

The *ISP* became a cornerstone in this new regional policy consisting of long-term goals for economic, social, and spatial developments as well as population distribution. At first, short-term programs for the late seventies had to be worked out and suggestions for new instruments to realize these programs proposed. Regional planning for the northern region concerns the function of the region within the framework of national economic and social development and national population distribution policies.

Preparations for the *ISP* began in 1973. A steering committee of high level representatives from different ministries and planning bureaus, headed by the Minister of Economic Affairs, and of governors and deputies of four provinces (Groningen, Friesland, Drenthe, and Overijssel) and their advisors, was constituted. Working

Period/Phase	KEY PROBLEMS	SOCIO-ECONOMIC POLICIES	SOCIO-CULTURAL POLICIES	SPATIAL POLICIES
I 1952-8	Population growth far above European level, transformation from agriculture and commerce into manufacturing, regional unemployment	Regional economic policy for regions with high unemployment (funds for infrastructure, industrial estates, premiums)	Improvement of living standards in peripheral rural areas (housing, welfare, education) and looking after social impacts of industrialization	Development of a national plan as a framework for regional planning. Redistribution of population on a macro-level
II 1958-68	Increasing congestion in the Randstad urban areas. Growing interregional imbalances of population and economy (offices, rush to the coast of basic manufacturing)	Integrated development of peripheral regions (growth points), fostering deconcentration of light manufacturing and port activities. Labor-intensive premiums	Backing integrated regional development by concentrating facilities in central places of the peripheral urban network. Making up of arrears in education, health, etc.	Decongestion policies in the Green Heart of the Randstad. Counter-balance policy for urban areas in periphery. (First Report on Physical Planning 1960, Second Report 1966)
III 1968-72	Climax of urban congestion and economic growth, suburbanization of economic activities and population, shift of frontiers to the intermediary regions. Restructuring of some economic subsectors	Continuance of integrated development of peripheral regions. Restructuring regions new elements in regional policy. Capital-intensive premiums. More careful selection of growth points	Continuance of policies for increasing quality of life in peripheral rural areas. New programs for old workers and youth in restructuring areas (education, leisure)	Intensifying of redistribution policies at macro-level, fighting suburbanization and growing attention to conservation of inner cities and natural environment
IV 1972-8	Economic recession. Increasing unemployment. Urban renewal. Decreasing suburbanization. Diminishing long-distance migration of firms	Selective (regional) growth policies. Limiting regional aid to the North and South-Limburg. Restricting locational opportunities in the West (SIR)	Increasing attention to social problems in the old urban quarters and restructuring areas. Selective aid for some peripheral regions	Urban renewal campaign. Containment of urban areas (new towns). Growth centers outside the Randstad. (Urbanization Report (1976))
V 1978-81	Economic depression. High rates of regional unemployment in both traditional regions and Randstad cities. Stabilization of population. Energy crisis. Environmental laws	Differentiated, intensified program of regional economic aid in more regions. New investment fund (WIR). New town premium. Start of I.S.P. and P.N.L. (Limburg)	Social problems of urban renewal (marginal groups). Small villages action groups. Socio-cultural programs of I.S.P. and P.N.L. (restructuring areas). Institutional decentralization.	Elaborating new urbanization policy in regional plans. Severe housing shortages in Randstad. Conservation of rural areas with high natural qualities.
VI 1981-5	Continuing economic depression. Crisis in building construction. High unemployment nationwide	Continuance of regional aid program. New ideas for economic recovery of main cities. Innovation-oriented policy	Attention to minority problems in cities. Education facilities for labor-market re-entry Small villages fund	Concentration policy in main urban areas. Restricting new town development. De-creasing selective location policy.

Fig. 9-1   A Matrix of Post-War Dutch Planning

groups for the three fields involved (economic, socio-cultural, spatial), together with representatives from different government levels and private organizations, began their work. A specialized working group on integrated regional models was established as well as a coordination center for citizen participation.[2]

The *ISP*, as an integrated regional plan encompassing the three fields mentioned above, was intended to identify both qualitative and quantitative interdependencies within and outside the region, and also to provide an institutional framework for influencing the sectors and interest groups concerned. The quantitative revolution in economics, geography, and planning held out a splendid prospect for integrated regional models, basic to comprehensive planning. The broad scope of the *ISP*, reflected in its complex organization and high expectations, was challenged in 1976 by a report on socio-economic policy for the northern region.[3] This report emphasized short term socio-economic goals rather than the broad, integrated and long range planning goals of the *ISP*. It was intended as a contribution to the *Nota regionaal sociaal-economisch beleid 1977 tot en met 1981*, (the *Regional Socio-economic Policy Report 1977–1981*), but because it was viewed as a progress report and issued separately, it received greater attention. The central theme of the 1976 report concerns the socio-economic backwardness of the northern region compared to the nation as a whole. Because of its early release, the results of working groups and citizen participation could not be included in this report. These, however, were summarized in the final *ISP* report of 1979. The result of quantitative research were published without a proposal for an integrated planning policy.[4] In the final report a broader scope of issues was treated, although the analytic part of that study is very limited. To understand the basic problems of the northern region in greater depth, the following analysis attempts to describe these problems with the help of more recent data. This provides a background for a discussion of the four major issues of the final *ISP* report and an evaluation of the *ISP*.

THE NORTHERN NETHERLANDS: INTERREGIONAL COMPARISON

The northern Netherlands has been characterized by Tamsma as a 'large problem area in a small country, and a small problem area in a large economic community'.[5] In international terms, regional disparities in the Netherlands are minor problems, although the northern provinces do still stand out. Interregional comparisons conceal intraregional contrasts which are in some respects striking. The themes dealt with have to be carefully selected, because a change of scale means a shift in crucial problems. Three central elements of regional structure and development have been chosen: (a) population, (b) employment and production, and (c) residential patterns and environmental conditions. A short account of these elements is given in order to consider some problems in greater detail in relation to several selected key issues.

The northern region is part of the periphery of the Amsterdam–Dortmund–Calais triangle. It has few international contacts, lying outside the European megalopolitan heart and not being situated in between two or more centers of gravity. As Tamsma stated: 'the economic development of the North depends on its own intrinsic resources and its interaction with the rest of the Netherlands.'[6]

From the standpoint of the *population*, the northern region has tripled in size between 1850 (500,000) and 1980 (1,560,000), but its share of national population declined until 1960, from then onwards its share stabilized (17 percent of the national population in 1850, 13 percent in 1930, 11 percent in 1960 and 1980). The process of industrialization and urbanization meant a concentration of population in the Randstad and in some manufacturing regions in the southern and eastern provinces. An extensive and selective migration took place. The autonomous deconcentration of manufacturing industry in the sixties changed this picture, although in some sections of the province of Groningen this shift to an immigration surplus occurred only in the second half of the seventies (Fig. 9-2). From the mid-sixties on, migration from the urbanized western provinces to all northern provinces became an established pattern. The industrial expansion of the North had been based primarily upon local blue-collar workers with white-collar workers coming from other regions. The local labor force, showing the effects of selective migration, exhibits a lower level of training when compared to the national average (31.2 to 33.5 percent); those with secondary or higher education are also underrepresented (24.2 to 26.9 percent). Moreover, in some areas of Drenthe and Friesland a surplus of pensioners attracted by cheap housing indicates that economic perspectives are just one explanation for the age structure of the region.

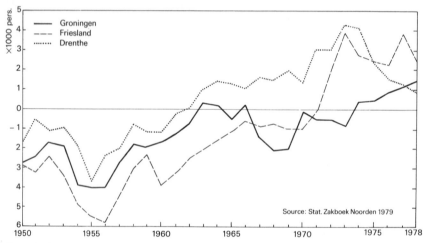

Fig. 9–2   Internal Migration Patterns (1950–78) (Source: Stat. Zakboek Noorden 1979)

From a viewpoint of *employment* and *production* the northern region strengthened its position, both in absolute and relative terms, in the 1963–73 period. Differences in income between the North and the nation as a whole decreased in this period. In the recession period the proportions of the work force employed in the different economic sectors did not change much (Table 9-1). The northern region became relatively more manufacturing oriented than other regions, although jobs were lost in the restructuring processes in the agro-industrial complex of the Peat Colonies. Social services (including government) with a local or regional orientation have been the main source of employment growth next to the growth of commercial activities on a local and regional level (especially banking). Externally oriented services grew at a slower rate

Table 9–1 Employment by non-agricultural sector, 1963–1979 (percentage)

Sector	North			Other regions			Netherlands		
	1963	1973	1979	1963	1973	1979	1963	1973	1979
Manufacturing	40.9	35.4	30.2	39.2	32.6	27.1	39.3	32.8	27.4
Construction	12.7	12.4	11.7	11.5	10.3	9.8	11.6	10.4	10.0
Commerce	14.4	13.5	14.5	16.0	16.5	17.4	15.8	16.3	17.0
Transport	6.8	5.3	5.3	8.1	6.7	6.7	8.0	6.6	6.9
Banking, Insurance	3.8	5.5	7.5	5.3	7.7	10.0	5.2	7.5	9.7
Social Service*	21.4	27.9	30.8	19.9	26.2	29.0	20.1	26.4	29.0
Total	100.0	100.0	100.0	100.0	100.0	100.0	100.0	100.0	100.0

*Includes government employment and non-governmental socio-cultural services.

Source: Central Bureau of Statistics (CBS)/Geographical Information System, Department of Geography, University of Utrecht.

(transport, business services, etc.). Manufacturing industry and agriculture are two basic sectors for the North. In some areas these are interconnected by large cooperative agri-businesses with a strong export orientation. Manufacturing plants in the Netherlands are frequently branches of large national or international firms with headquarters elsewhere. Thus the basic features of a 'branch plant economy' are present.

Looking at Gross Regional Product by economic sector (Table 9-2), the dominance of agri-business in the North is quite clear as is the weakness of the petrochemicals and public utilities sectors. (This is despite the fact that the large quantities of natural gas found in this region represents about 40 percent of GRP before correction.) Basic business services including offices are also underrepresented in the North.

A crucial yardstick for regional disparities had always been the rate of registered unemployed. In the last two decades interregional differences have decreased. In the Randstad core areas and in some eastern and southern cities, unemployment increased tremendously (Fig. 9-3).

From a perspective of *residential patterns* and *environmental conditions*, just two indicators are available to illustrate the position of the northern region. Looking at the degree of urbanization, the North is predominantly a rural region with small cities, only partly industrialized. The underrepresentation of large cities and the lack of suburban regions, except for the Groningen urban region, is striking (Fig. 9-4). As regards land use, commercial building sites and industrial estates take up a proportion of land nearly equal to the national proportion (10–12 percent). Land use for recreational facilities and housing, however, is a much higher proportion than the national average (15–16 percent for each). The low density of population (11 percent of national population on 25 percent of the national territory) allows an ample (according to Dutch standards) allocation of space to inhabitants.

On the socio-cultural scene, there are few comparative indicators, although the *Socio-Cultural Report of 1980* indicated that educational and cultural facilities are not used in the North to the same degree as in the other regions, especially the Randstad.

Table 9-2   Gross regional product by economic sector, 1977 (percentages excluding taxes, interest, premiums and natural gas)

Sector	North	Other regions
Agriculture, food, beverages	16.2	8.3
Natural resources, petrochemicals, public utilities	4.5	8.4
Manufacturing industries	12.5	14.8
Construction, transport	14.0	14.0
Commerce, banking, real estate	24.9	28.6
Social services	11.2	10.3
Public services	16.7	15.6
Total	100.0	100.0

Source: Central Bureau of Statistics (CBS)/Geographical Information System, Department of Geography, University of Utrecht.

Housing, social welfare, and health conditions are more or less comparable to national (average) standards, the North being better off in these areas than the Randstad.

To summarize, the most important problems of the North, when compared with other regions, are higher umemployment, lower income, and sparsely populated areas. The last factor contributes to the creation of service deficiencies because threshold populations are not sufficient for many services to be economic. Human welfare conditions are not so much different from those prevailing throughout the country.

THE NORTHERN NETHERLANDS: INTRAREGIONAL COMPARISONS

The subregions of the North do have common problems, but at the same time they also display different patterns of population growth and distribution, economic base and residential development, as well as environmental conditions.

Looking at *population*, the population increase during the sixties in the northern region as a whole was followed by a smaller increase in the seventies. The decline in the national growth rate over the same period was much greater, however (Fig. 9-4). In the Groningen urbanized area, the process of suburbanization toward the north of Drenthe intensified. In the traditional manufacturing subregions of the Peat Colonies (East Groningen, South-West Drenthe) restructuring caused a decrease in the growth rate, indicated by negative migration. Even the modern industrial port of Delfzijl was affected by an economic slowdown. In contrast with the slackening of the growth of the eastern subregions within the North, the rural or industrialized rural areas of Friesland and Drenthe showed continued high growth (Figs. 9-4 and 9-2). A more detailed analysis indicates that these areas were affected by the regional multiplier of earlier manufacturing growth and the location of welfare institutions resulting from the strong growth of government spending in deprived regions. Moreover the settlement of senior citizens (fifty-five plus), returning in part from the Randstad, and the

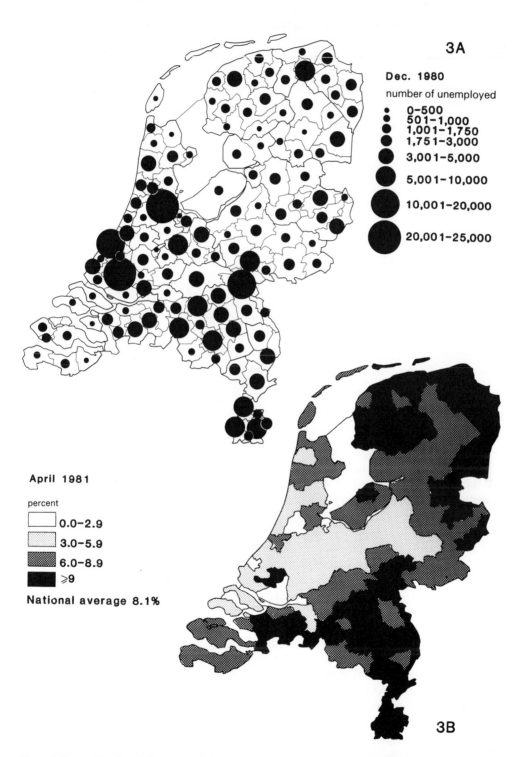

Fig. 9-3   Regional Unemployment (Source: Min. of Social Affairs)

immigration of long-distance commuters or independent (business) travellers had some effect on population growth in the southern Frisian and Drenthian subregions.

From a viewpoint of *economic development* the two indicators of the level of employment and Gross Regional Product are used at the intraregional level. A classification has been made based on both sets of data (Table 9-3). Three types of subregions could be discerned:

(a) rural-industrial subregions (southern and south-western),
(b) manufacturing subregions (eastern border: Peat Colonies, Delfzijl),
(c) subregions oriented to urban services (around the three provincial capitals).

Table 9-3 Socio-economic classification of subregions of the Northern Netherlands

Type of subregion	Gross regional product (1977)	Employment/nonagrarian (1979)	Subregions
(a) Rural-industrial	Agriculture >20percent Manufacturing[a] 12–15 percent	Manufacturing[b] 30–33 percent Services[c] 48–53 percent	SW and SE Friesland SW Drenthe
(b)Manufacturing	Agriculture 12–16 percent Manufacturing[a] >18 percent	Manufacturing[b] 37–42 percent Services[c] 43–4 percent	Delfzijl, peat colonies E. Groningen, SE Drenthe
(c) Urban services	Agriculture 13–15 percent Manufacturing[a] 8–12 percent	Manufacturing 23–8 percent Services[c] 51-8 percent	Cities of Groningen, Leeuwarden, Assen, and their rural/suburban hinterlands

[a]Excluding petrochemicals, mining, public utilities, and construction.
[b]Including petrochemicals, mining, and public utilities.
[c]Excluding construction and transportation.

Source: Central Bureau of Statistics/Geographical Information System, Department of Geography, University of Utrecht.

The development path of employment has been traced in Fig. 9-5. The figure provides data from the period of economic growth (1963–73) in the Netherlands, supplemented with recently collected statistical material (1979) from the recession period. In broad outline, a subregional division was already present at the beginning of the sixties.

The three *rural–industrial subregions* had an employment profile which showed a relative decrease in the share of manufacturing in the period from 1963–79 (from over 40 percent to 30 percent approximately). The growth of social (public) services and some of the economic services apparently resulted from the rapid development of welfare state activities.

The *manufacturing subregions* do not show a uniform pattern of development. The Peat Colonies of East Groningen and South-East Drenthe have been extremely dependent on the traditional agro-industrial complex producing farina derivatives, strawboard, etc., on the one hand, and post-war established plants of large Dutch industrial companies (Philips, Akzo) on the other. The share of manufacturing in these subregions decreased from 55 percent (North 41) in 1963 to 40 percent (North 30) in 1979. The Delfzijl port-industrialized subregion, however, retained a high proportion of manufacturing employment (37–8 percent). The relative growth of the service sector took place at the expense of the important construction and transportation sectors in this subregion.

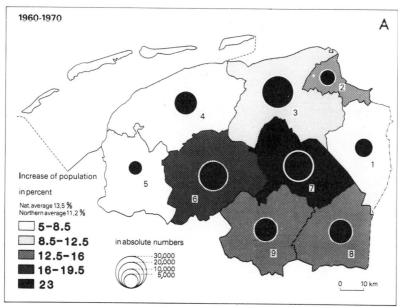

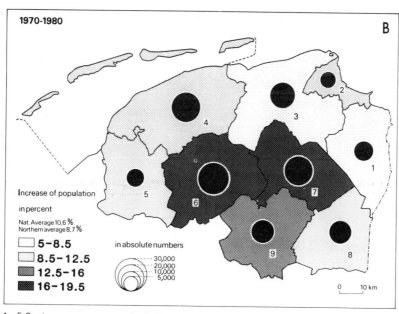

Fig. 9–4   Population Change

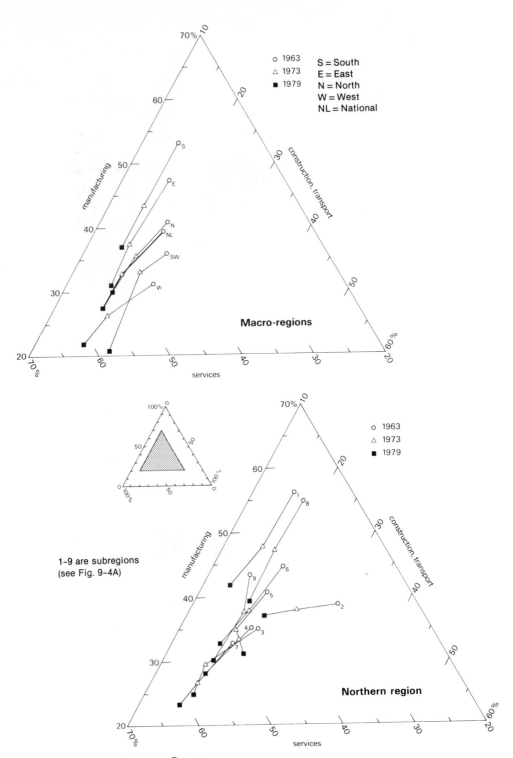

Fig. 9-5   Employment Structure

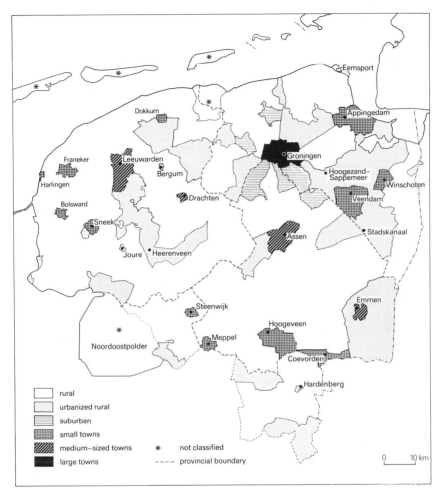

Fig. 9-6   Levels of Urbanization in the Northern Region (Source: ISP 1975
             and M. de Smidt 1981)

In 1963 the three *predominantly urban subregions* already displayed a relatively low
degree of industrialization. The three northern provincial capitals of Groningen,
Leeuwarden (Friesland), and Assen (Drenthe) strengthened their positions as centers
for (regional) services with the expansion of the welfare state.

Does this spatial differentiation in the structure and development of population and
economic activity correspond to the mosaic of *residential patterns*? The map of
municipalities (and towns) (according to the degree of urbanization) indicates that this
parallel is quite clear (Fig. 9-6). The industrial rural municipalities form part of the
Peat Colonies industrial area of East Groningen.

Some new cities emerged from the industrialization process resulting from foreign
and domestic investment in manufacturing plants (Emmen, Drachten) as well as port
industrialization (Delfzijl). Suburbanization is of some importance only around the city of Groningen (165,000 inhabitants, metropolitan area 250,000). As already stated,
the process of urbanization on a large scale, including a vast suburbanization, is not a

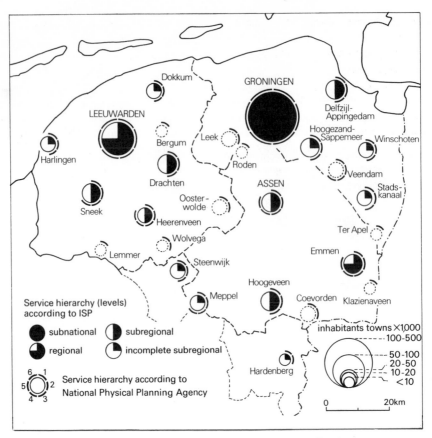

Fig. 9–7   Service Center Hierarchy in the Northern Region
               (Source: ISP 1975 and M. de Smidt 1981)

characteristic feature of the North. The problem of low density of population in some
subregions (100–150 per square kilometer) along the western and northern fringe of
the Northern Netherlands became an issue in *ISP* discussions. Thus, the levels of service functions in relation to the spatial range of the service center concerned are important elements of regional socio-cultural and physical-planning policies for rural areas
(Fig. 9-7). In the discussion that surrounds the hierarchical levels of urban places proposed by an *ISP* working group, the National Physical Planning Agency (RPD), there
is general agreement concerning the top level (Groningen followed by Leeuwarden and
Emmen), but problems arise in dealing with the intermediate level of the service-center
hierarchy. At this level the emerging manufacturing towns, recently evolved into more
complete service towns as well, compete with older and smaller towns that possess
some traditional institutional functions. At the intermediate level, the spectrum of
services available is satisfactory on the whole but problems concerning the provision
of human welfare services arise at the bottom of the service hierarchy.

    Quality of life is partly dependent on the type of subregion or settlement in which
people live; areas differ as to their employment opportunities, services, recreational
space, and natural beauty. Environmental conditions are attractive in most of the

towns and villages in Friesland and Drenthe, as retirement-related migration figures indicate. Poor employment prospects prohibit vast immigration and local politicians do not always like to stimulate immigration because the housing stock would diminish and house prices would rise. The relation between the different levels of human welfare and quality of life is found in the level of income earned by people in the subregions discussed. Data collected for 1974 showed that the gap between the North and the national average (the North's figure being the lower) had decreased from 14 percent in 1960 to 9 percent (per inhabitant). Intraregional differences are present and have not changed fundamentally. The industrialized rural areas showed the lowest levels of income (10–15 percent under the national average) while the suburban area had higher incomes (1–6 percent under this level). Nevertheless intraregional and interregional disparities are not as significant as in other European countries. Some southern and eastern regions in the Netherlands show the same low levels of income.

KEY ISSUES OF THE *INTEGRATED STRUCTURE PLAN*

The *ISP* progress report of 1976 presented the relative socio-economic backwardness of the North as the central issue and gave little attention to the region's role in a national context. In the *ISP* final report of 1979 the central issue was labor and employment, but, in addition, three other issues were dealt with: (a) land use and natural environment, (b) rural areas and towns, and (c) individual development. In each field a set of policy measures were proposed and are to be carried out over a seven-year period (1979–85). Relations between the issues are not made explicit in the final report.

Labor and Unemployment: The Major Policy Issue

The economic–geographical profile of the Northern Netherlands brought out the fact that the two pillars of demand for labor, the agro-industrial complex and the manufacturing plants of large corporations, are beginning to weaken. Technological innovations and environmental concerns require agro-industrial companies to spend vast sums on restructuring their plants. Competition from low-wage countries threatens the operations of large corporations in the North. The quality of the labor supply in the North is below national standards because of the lower educational level of school-leavers and the migration of skilled staff to urban areas elsewhere. An improvement in quality is best achieved in a coordinated long-range program.

   In the short term, however, the goal of the *ISP* is to reduce the number of unemployed in the North, at least bringing the unemployment rate down to the national average. The 'extra' unemployment, that amount which pushes the North above the national average, was estimated for 1980 to be 10,000 jobs (full-time). In fact, this regional component was much higher in 1982: 15,000 jobs. Government actions within the framework of the *ISP* are threefold: (a) stimulating the private sector, (b) increasing the supply of jobs in the public sector (or jobs in private, non-profit organizations paid for with public funds), and (c) temporary labor-market measures.

   Stimulating the private sector is the most crucial, but at the same time the most risky, step. Instruments for fostering private investment are provided under regional socio-economic policies, but they cannot necessarily guarantee success. The Northern

Development Corporation (NOM), financed by the national government, has funds at its disposal to participate in new or existing enterprises and to initiate innovative projects in order to create new jobs or to renew obsolete factories. These projects might offer new products or alternative paths to a particular product market. Large projects connected with state-owned companies (for example the Natural Gas Corporation plan to receive liquified natural gas in the Delfzijl-Eemsport) can be planned with some degree of certainty.

Government money can create jobs either by stimulating building construction (highways, schools, touristic infrastructure) and the reconstruction of rural areas (Peat Colonies Plan), or by initiating new projects for the preservation of the natural environment, monuments, and landmarks, or by stimulating socio-cultural activities. Besides these elements, the relocation scheme for government services (Table 9-1), which is being carried out despite strong political pressure, is another way of stimulating development. An example of this is the relocation of the post office headquarters. In the 1980–5 period, 3,000 jobs will have been relocated from the Hague to Groningen, Leeuwarden, and Emmen.

Temporary labor-market measures include earlier retirement, temporary jobs for school-leavers, and the expansion of some socio-cultural and medical services in the short run. Each year an evaluation of the *ISP* is made.[7] The results of the first phase of the *ISP* (1979–81) indicated that the private sector did not reach the targets set for it. The public sector did achieve its stated goal, but on the basis of a disproportionately high number of temporary jobs in the quaternary or noncommercial services sector. In reshaping the short-run program for 1981–2, more investment in building construction was included. The relocation of government services will accelerate over the first half of the eighties. Decreasing the regional component of unemployment and strengthening the structure of the northern industries remain the dominant elements in the *ISP*. Taking Gross Regional Product per capita, the northern region is at the top of the European Economic Community's list of subnational units. Correcting for natural gas yields, however, reduces the figure for the northern region to moderate levels by European standards and to 20 percent below the national average.[8]

Land Use and Natural Environment

In areas where agriculture is the main function, the problems of large-scale farming require that there should be more planning control (zoning). In areas with a mixture of functions more attention in physical planning will be given to capacity constraints for recreation (for example aquatics), and intensive agriculture. Direct measures will not be taken because regional plans offer ample opportunities for intervention.

Rural Areas and Towns

This is the policy issue that is particularly connected with problems of efficiency and equity. A well planned hierarchy of service centers can be an efficient distribution network providing accessibility to services for people in sparsely populated areas. As far as small villages are concerned, provincial funds have been established, which are financed through the *ISP* by the national government, in order to protect some basic services in sparsely populated areas (for example primary schools, general stores, community centers, and medical centers). Experiments with alternatives to the traditional regional bus system have been carried out. These have been generally quite successful. Mobile commercial services have been introduced (grocery, bank, etc.). Small projects to remove and reconstruct bad housing in villages is part of reshaping living conditions in rural areas. How best to preserve small communities is a human welfare problem, but it has not been solved in a satisfactory manner thus far.

Individual Development

This is a policy issue that cannot be isolated from other issues concerning the conditions of human welfare. Removing socio-cultural backwardness requires the stimulation of indigenous regional cultural (for example the Frisian language and identity) as well as the establishment of educational facilities and programs for adults and specific groups. In fact both the expenses for social work by volunteers and specific projects for unemployed persons are paid for by the national government. Special funds are available for these different projects within the framework of the *ISP*. Special attention is given to people who want to participate (for example housewives) and others who want to retrain themselves for the labor market.

EVALUATION OF *ISP*: INTEGRATED PLANNING AND CRISIS MANAGEMENT

An evaluation of the *ISP* is now given, looking at three aspects: (1) planning fields and styles, (2) planning methods, and (3) planning scales.

From Indicative to Communicative Planning—*ISP* Planning Fields and Styles

During the first phase of the preparation of the *ISP*, a variant of indicative planning was implicitly advocated. This planning style is traditionally linked with economic planning and is characterized by preconcerted action leading to written agreements between the public and private sectors in a mixed economy. The formulation of goals and consultation during the planning process is important. At the same time quantitative analysis and models are used.[9]

After the publication of the preliminary progress report of the *ISP*, the indicative approach evolved into a form of *communicative planning*, a process of decision-making based on frequent consultation and negotiation between the different levels of government and on contacts with private interest groups. When one sorts out the different elements in these forms of planning in order to identify the fields and styles of planning distinguished by Kreukels,[10] strategic planning and equivalent policy planning are not found. In fact some elements of these planning styles should have been used when reviewing the original instruction by the Secretary of Economic Affairs.

Elements of strategic planning, including such dichotomies as short- and long-term perspectives, and search processes for internal strengths/weakness and external constraints/opportunities, were not used. Equivalent policy planning, characterized by the phasing, adaptation, and flexibility of plans within an uncertain environment, receives some implicit attention in the period after 1978. This is found in the call for two phases in executing the *ISP* (1979–81, 1982–5). Each phase includes provisions for annual reports and meetings of participants in order to adapt or modify plans on a short-term basis. This pragmatic course is quite a contrast with the original approach mentioned. Not only were some planning styles changed and others not even applied, but some planning fields did not receive equal attention. From the first progress report (1976) onwards, socio-economic affairs played a central role in the preparation and policies of the *ISP*. Socio-cultural aspects had not been neglected, however, and were summarized in a separate report. In the physical-planning field a preliminary report, but not a final report, was issued.[11] However, a study on the qualities of the natural environment was published in 1979. Thus, the interdependencies of the three planning fields mentioned did not receive full attention, although that they should do so is considered crucial for integrated planning.

Management of Uncertainty calls for Alternative Scenarios—
A Review of *ISP* Planning Methods

In his evaluation of *ISP* planning methods, Drewe[12] utilized the strategic choice approach and the AIDA technique as yardsticks. In strategic planning, policy is made clear after a formulation and comparison of possibilities over a wide field of anticipated as well as actual situations. Choices are repeatedly made between alternative courses of action while possessing an inadequate picture of their future implications.[13] The Analysis of Interconnected Decision Areas (AIDA) formulates alternative programs after structuring the decision areas and their interrelations, looking in particular at impediments of or constraints on the different options involved.[14]

Alternatives are not generated and evaluated in the *ISP* approach, although alternative population distribution models were presented in the first volume of the *Third Report on Urbanization*, the *Orientation Report*, in 1973. Changing economic conditions during the 1970s required the development of alternative scenarios. These, however, were not prepared. Nor was there a well-developed citizen participation or consultation program developed for the region. Different views on the prospects of the North should have been solicited from government institutions at the national and regional levels and from interested groups as well.

As Drewe suggested, a strategic choice approach could have shown the interrelatedness of issues involved, both in terms of time and space. Choosing as the central issue the relative socio-economic backwardness of the northern region at a time when the results of the different reports on facets of planning were not available, made it difficult to work out alternative scenarios regarding the non-socio-economic planning fields. But even within the socio-economic planning realm alternatives were not given. The working group on integrated planning (WIP) concluded that a linkage between policy fields was not made. In addition, the long-term outcomes of the policies of the ministries concerned were not predicted on either a national or a regional level. This does not imply that proper planning methods were totally absent in the preparation of the *ISP*. The use of 'COBA policy' (Committee for the Development of Policy Analysis) analysis is an example of one method used.[15] The number of indicators in this matrix of relationships of goals, instruments, and interests was reduced and then they were extrapolated to 1990 using the 1950–70 period as a basis for trend development. In this context a regional employment model was used. However, it is not clear how these exercises have been coupled to the contents of the final *ISP* report, especially the four main issues or themes mentioned earlier.[16] The change in approach from rational comprehensive planning at the beginning of the *ISP* preparation period to incremental planning, which tries to relate goals and instruments in specific fields, should be noted.[17]

The final report avoids the exclusively socio-economic policy approach of the 1976 progress report, but the basic criticism of the earlier stages of planning for the *ISP* has not been answered in a satisfactory way. Even within the limited scope of a trend scenario, a cross-impact analysis which interrelates trends and changing relationships among the elements of the planning program would have given more insights.[18].

SPATIAL SCALES, DECENTRALIZATION AND INTEGRATED REGIONAL PLANNING

A prerequisite of accomplishing the goals formulated for the four main planning issues is integrated policy planning at the provincial level. Such planning, however, does not exist.

The regional physical plan, meant as a framework for integration of spatially relevant actions, plays the role of a 'pseudo' integrated regional plan. However, experience in regional physical planning regarding citizen participation and negotiation with local authorities at several stages of planning, is of great help in carrying out integrated planning of a wider scope. In a market economy, physical planning is used to arrange the spatial elements of society. The *ISP* was an attempt to follow a different path, but the inclusion of provincial plans in the final report reaffirmed the institutional restrictions of planning in a market economy, quite apart from the limits to decentralization set by the Ministry of Economic Affairs.

Evaluating the *ISP* as a specimen of integrated regional planning, leads to the conclusion that the alternative of incremental or partial planning may give better results in a changing society with a restricted time horizon.

Interrelations between planning fields can be improved, through selective, partial planning. This selective approach is necessary in the different planning phases, including analysis and monitoring, and in the review of interconnections, between analyses and policies. The projects selected through this approach will be the main elements in negotiations within government circles as well as between government and private interests.

Thus in the future, the Integrated Structure Plan can be reformed into a type of selective planning, interconnecting carefully chosen key issues.

NOTES

1. Marc de Smidt, 'La politique régionale et l'aménagement du territoire aux Pays-Bas', *L'Espace géographique*, vol. 8, no. 3, 1979, pp. 161–72.
2. For more information on the institutional structure of *ISP* see Paul Drewe, 'Integrated Regional Planning as Applied to the Northern Netherlands', in H. Folmer and J. Oosterhaven, eds., *Spatial Inequalities and Regional Development*, The Hague, Martinus Nijhoff, 1979, pp. 219–54; D. Cools, 'Het Integraal Structuurplan Noorden des Lands', *Intermediair*, vol. 16, no. 16, 1980, pp. 43–57; and J. H. Zoon, 'Komt er wel een ISP?', *Beleid en Maatschappij*, vol. 4, 1977, pp. 241–7.
3. *ISP*, Het sociaal-economisch beleid van het Noorden des lands, 's-Gravenhage, Staatsuitgeverij, 1976.

4. *ISP*, Het Noorden in nationaal perspectief, Rapport 11, 's-Gravenhage, Staats-uitgeverij, 1977.

5. R. Tamsma, 'The Northern Netherlands, Large Problem Area in a Small Country, Small Problem Area in a Large Economic Community', *Tijdschrift voor Economische en Sociale Geografie*, vol. 63, no. 3, pp. 162–79; M. de Smidt, 'Het Noorden: balans van een stimuleringsgebied', in J. G. Borchert, G. J. J. Egbers, and M. de Smidt, *Ruimtelijk beleid in Nederland*, Haarlem, Romen, 1981 (4th edn.), pp. 190–230.

6. R. Tamsma, *Three Decades of Regional Policy in the Netherlands 1950–1980*, Series in Human Geography, no. 18, Groningen, Department of Geography, University of Groningen.

7. The direct employment effects of the *ISP* expected for 1981–2 (as compared with 1979–81) are: private sector 25 (4,500 to 6,000) jobs, and public sector 4,250 (2,150 to 2,350) jobs. In the 1979–81 period within the private sector 1,500–2,500 new jobs were created, 1,000–1,500 jobs were retained, and 2,000 jobs for a LNG (Liquified Natural Gas) project were created. The relocation of government services created 100–300 jobs in the 1979–1981 period and another 400 jobs during 1981–2. Temporary labor-market measures were responsible for 2,500 jobs in the first period and 1,250 in the last period. Altogether in the 1979–81 period, 9,150–10,850 jobs were created, and in the 1981–2 period 5,525 jobs. Source: *Noordelijk Bulletin*, Bestuurscommissie Noorden des Lands, Groningen, 1978–82.

8. G. Cardol and R. F. C. van Engelenburg, *Development of the Regional Imbalance in the European Community 1970–1977*, Strasburg, European Parliament, Research and Documentation Papers, Regional Policy and Transport Series, no. 11, 1980.

9. George Dalton, *Economic Systems and Society*, Harmondsworth, Penguin, 1974, p. 155.

10. A. M. J. Kreukels, *Planning en planningproces*, 's-Gravenhage, VUGA, 1980, p. 82.

11. ISP, *Ruimtelijke ontwikkeling*, Rapport 6, 's-Gravenhage, Staatsuitgeverij, 1975.

12. Drewe, op. cit.

13. J. K. Friend and W. N. Jessop, *Local Government and Strategic Choice*, London, Tavistock, 1969, pp. 79–110.

14. M. Roberts, *An Introduction to Town Planning Techniques*, London, Hutchinson, 1974.

15. Cools, op. cit.

16. *ISP, Integraal Structuurplan Noorden des Lands*, 's-Gravenhage, Staatsuitgeverij, 1979.

17. Cools, op. cit.

18. Rijksplanologische Dienst (R.P.D.), 'Betekenis van toekomstverkenning voor de ruimtelijke ordening', *Jaarverslag Rijksplanologische Dienst*, 's-Gravenhage, Staatsuitgeverij, 1981, pp. 11–47.

10
Government Housing Policies in The Netherlands since 1945

Otto J. Hetzel

AN OVERVIEW OF SIGNIFICANT TRENDS AND ELEMENTS IN DUTCH HOUSING POLICIES

Since World War II there have been several significant trends in Dutch housing policies. Overall these policies are distinguished by a high degree of government intervention in housing markets by means of a number of mechanisms.

The Dutch government has invested heavily in extensive housing production in order to help serve the needs of the country's highly dense population. While originally efforts were concentrated on renting housing to particular social or low-income groups, the data reveal an increasing trend, peaking in the late 1970s, towards support for homeownership.

The most significant form of government intervention has been a variety of housing subsidies. These subsidies have influenced much of the housing production since World War II. The national government channeled these subsidies through municipalities and then later through housing associations. These funds generated substantial levels of construction of Housing Act Dwellings, the units given the most substantial level of subsidy.

Other subsidies were applied under the Rent Price law that has aimed at a more efficient and less costly use of government funds to support and spur construction. As a result, a good deal of rental construction was carried out by the private sector, including housing associations. In addition, 'premiums' constituting 'front-end' grants, have also been given for private rental construction and even for housing to be sold. Interest-rate subsidies and government insurance for development loans have also been provided. Additionally, the tax deductibility of mortgage interest constitutes a major indirect form of subsidy, directly related to the taxpayer's income, i.e. the higher the income the greater the subsidy.

Subsidies have been made available not only for the construction of new dwellings but also in the form of direct subsidies to individuals and families in order to help them meet housing costs. These rent allowances have been used to try to keep the rent paid by those Dutch families in the lower portion of the income range under a national limit of about one-sixth of income.

As a result of initial shortages (and partially as a corollary of the extensive range of subsidies provided), control of rents and even of the allocation of dwellings in crowded cities has been imposed. Given the extensive government involvement in construction activity and housing markets, both sales and rentals, while a private sector continues to exist, it is small in scale and heavily influenced by government fiscal policies.

The Dutch have also been mindful of land use planning objectives, directing new development to growth areas capable of supporting the influx of population. Polders created from the sea have expanded the areas available for housing construction while providing the sites for a number of new towns.

Starting in the 1960s in older urban areas, a policy of rehabilitation was substituted for clearance and new construction. 'In-fill' housing has also been used in order to fill gaps in existing neighborhoods. These renovation policies and attendant subsidies have maintained the levels of residential land use in major cities. Commercial development has not significantly displaced residents in these older cities.

The task of delivering housing services in the social housing sector has been allocated by the national government primarily to housing associations rather than to municipalities. While dependent on government for funding and subject to monitoring of their activities, associations have combined the perspectives and energies of private construction and management with the extensive financial support of the national government. They have produced very significant amounts of housing within a relatively short, thirty-five year period. Associations have also served to implement government employment policies, financed through construction projects. As such, their activities have complemented housing development financed by private investment, helping to augment construction activity during slumps in private construction.

A Statistical Profile

The 14,200,000 people of the Netherlands live in almost 5,000,000 dwellings,[1] about 3,000,000 of which were constructed after World War II. Of the country's 41,160 square kilometers,[2] 24 percent is committed to residential use. Dwellings of owner-occupiers constitute about 43 percent[3] of the stock. In the rental sector, the other 57 percent of dwelling units, 74 percent is government supported, broken down as follows: 15 percent is operated by municipalities and 59 percent by non-profit housing associations. Fifty-eight percent of the 26 percent in private rentals is owned and managed by private institutional landlords.

Quality and Size of Housing Units

Housing produced since World War II has been of high technical quality. Over 80 percent of units constructed since then have central heating. Dutch government-supported dwelling units are also among the largest in Europe. In 1981 51 percent of the units averaged four or more rooms plus bathrooms. In the 1980 construction figures, the 66 square meters average for Housing Act Dwellings (36 percent) compared favorably with the 68 square meters average for subsidized dwellings (39 percent) and the 97 square meters average in the non-subsidized sector (25 percent) mostly owner-occupied . Such high quality has been justified by the anticipation that future maintenance costs in the social housing sector will be lessened.

Government's Historical Role in Housing

The Netherlands has a rich history of government concern with housing. All three levels of government—central, provincial, and municipal—have had a role in the evolution of housing policy. The central government determines general objectives and provides the subsidies for implementing local initiatives at the municipal level.[4] Provinces have a coordinating role and review and make recommendations on their municipalities' requests for funds as part of the submission process to central government.[5]

The government role in Dutch housing policy essentially originated with the enactment of an extremely enlightened piece of legislation—the 1901 Housing Act. This legislation was very advanced for its time. In addition to creating an extensive array of powers to enable municipalities to control the problems of poor housing and abysmal health conditions, the government committed itself to providing subsidies for development of housing in order to overcome extensive overcrowding in urban areas.

A major element of the 1901 Act was its policy of assisting in financing the construction of 'Housing Act Dwellings'. Municipalities and non-profit housing associations (some of which were created by private developers), upon approval by central government, could develop Housing Act Dwellings. Financial support for Housing Act Dwellings were the same for all developers. Long-term, fifty year loans for construction and land were provided by central government through the municipalities. The 1901 Act also established the concept of subsidies, but on a very small scale, where replacement housing was provided for very low income families living in dilapidated buildings. The long-term loans and subsidy policies emanating from the 1901 Act continue to this day to provide support for new housing construction as an essential element of Dutch housing policies.

Secondary Objectives for Housing Subsidies

Provision of housing subsidies, however, was also part of a deliberate government decision after World War II to reduce housing expenses for workers in order to restrain pressures on salaries, which would otherwise have occurred owing to shortages of dwellings and increases in housing costs. Rent controls were a corollary to this policy. One objective was to keep wages down in order to make Dutch products competitive in international markets.

Stimulation of building activity and employment in the housing industry have also been closely related to subsidy policies in the Netherlands. Building subsidies have been used to maintain construction activity. Rent controls applicable to most rental units are viewed by investors as preventing them from obtaining adequate returns on their investments. Thus, subsidies have been essential in helping to provide reasonable returns to investors in rental housing.

Housing Shortages

Shortage of housing has been a persistent problem in the Netherlands since the nineteenth century. The Netherlands has the heaviest population density (402 persons per square kilometer) of any country in Europe. Following the devastation of World War II, and the absence of construction activity during the war, substantial housing production was one of the country's top priorities. Immigration from former colonies and infusions of foreign workers have contributed to continuing housing shortages to this day.

One major element of housing shortages today is the trend towards a concentration of population in cities of over 20,000 in which over 64 percent of the population lives. This is particularly the case in the Randstad, an area that encompasses the major industrial complex in the west coast triangle between Rotterdam, Amsterdam, and

Utrecht. Government has found it difficult to provide the necessary housing for many of those who, drawn to this area's employment potential, wish to live there.

Various governmental controls on access to housing have evolved in the struggle to deal with the housing shortages. Restrictions were imposed in 1947, for instance, through a permit system to control the number of residents allowed into areas in which housing is in short supply. While this condition now exists primarily in the Randstad, some rural areas also have experienced shortages and are using the permit system to control the number of residents. Municipalities are thus given legal authority by central government to restrict access to existing housing by limiting approvals for permission to reside in the area. Where there are shortages, municipalities usually require employment ties or other links with the area to justify permission to move to areas in which housing availability is limited. Units are registered and allocation of those that become available are handled by the city on the basis of waiting lists.

Rent Control Policy

Rent controls also have been imposed on most of the rental housing stock since World War II.[6] In addition, security of tenure, by restricting the eviction of tenants except on limited grounds, has been provided.[7] Attempts at 'liberalization', or the elimination of rent controls on portions of the rental stock, have been frustrated to some degree by the continued shortage of housing.

Government controls in the light of the shortages have meant that housing markets in the Netherlands are essentially divided into two sectors: controlled and free. Exchanges of property above certain cost ceilings, whether for rental or for sale, are free of most government restrictions. In view of some planners, however, over 90 percent of the inhabitants can only afford housing in the controlled sector.

Delivery of Housing Services through Housing Associations

Owing to the substantial role of the non-profit, social housing sector, housing associations have become particularly important in Dutch housing policy.[8] Their role can be traced back to the 1901 Act which made them a significant source of housing development. Over the years, housing associations, rather than municipal government, have become the principal providers of subsidized housing.

Owner-Occupied Housing

The percentage of owner-occupiers as compared to those renting houses increased substantially in the 1970s: from 35 percent at the beginning to 43 percent by the end of the decade. Several factors account for this increase. To some extent homeownership had been perceived by many as an investment, given the escalating housing values of the 1970s. Also, since 1973, the numbers of units available for private rentals have contracted. In part this contraction was due to the fact that since 1975, 20,000 to 30,000 private rental dwellings have been converted annually into owner-occupied dwellings. This conversion has taken place primarily in the cities. The resultant 'gentrification' has meant a rapid reduction in the number of reasonably priced rental units. Moreover, during the same period, rent levels have been allowed to rise, thus making home-ownership more attractive.

Planning for Location of Housing

The system of physical planning has had a significant effect on the location of residential housing in the Netherlands. The planning powers provided to municipalities in the 1901 Housing Act have been substantially augmented by the 1965 Physical Planning Act enacted along with the new Housing Act of that same year. One objective of planning policies is to help make the best use of available land in the country with the highest population density in Europe.

SOME HISTORICAL BACKGROUND

In order to understand Dutch housing policies since World War II, the earlier Dutch experience with housing and with long-standing housing institutions and housing trends needs to be reviewed. The following brief description demonstrates the government's extensive concern with housing since the end of the nineteenth century, its continuing commitment to various forms of subsidies, its use of local government and private sector housing associations as delivery systems for the construction and management of social housing, and its imposition of rent controls in the face of housing shortages.

Housing conditions throughout Europe were extremely poor in the nineteenth century. The deplorable housing conditions in the Netherlands may be illustrated by the fact that even cellars were used in 1859, providing accommodation for over 23,000 persons in Amsterdam alone.[9] The movement of population into the cities had created intolerable overcrowding and serious public health problems. Unsatisfactory housing came to be recognized as an important contributor to social ills.

The 1901 Act: Landmark Social Legislation

The Dutch Parliament enacted a Housing Act and Health Law in 1901 which recognized the interrelationship of health and housing conditions. The Act was concerned primarily with improving housing conditions by granting various powers to the municipalities and by providing limited government funding for the construction of dwellings.

The Scope of the 1901 Act

The cities were given the authority under the Act to:

enact building ordinances to ensure the proper construction and maintenance of dwellings;

require registration (in cities of over 20,000 people) of all properties that were rented or available for rent or sale as dwelling units;

condemn properties for clearance and redevelopment when the units were unfit for habitation;

adopt simplified procedures for condemnation;

use government subsidies for slum clearance;

adopt building restrictions through a system of building permits and expand built-up areas under plans that designated future sites for the building of streets, canals, and squares; and, provide financial assistance for housing construction through funds provided by the local and central governments.

A major element of the new policies was the opportunity for either approved housing associations or municipalities to construct what were called 'Housing Act Dwellings'. The 1901 Act provided the same support for both.

Although the 1901 Act did not state it explicitly, the explanatory memorandum and the text indicate that priority in the construction and operation of Housing Act Dwellings was given to approved housing associations, companies, and foundations, rather than to municipalities.

Government loans, for up to fifty years, were made available for the financing of Housing Act Dwellings. Housing associations were made eligible for such financing because it was expected that the private sector would work better and more cheaply than municipalities.

The scope of the 1901 Act was quite broad. Its purpose was to improve housing conditions not only for the benefit of the working man but for all sectors of society. A reflection of this objective was the initiation of town-planning authority. Similarly, improvement by means of demolition and redevelopment was made easier by the relaxation and simplification of the earlier, rather unwieldy condemnation procedures.

Support for Housing Associations

Perhaps the most significant element of the 1901 Act was its provision of funding for housing associations. While some concern was expressed about the ultimate cost to the government of doing so, associations and municipalities were to provide housing for those with lower incomes.

The 1901 Housing Act established the basic framework for the housing association movement. Its original concepts are still followed. The essential provisions of the Act with respect to associations were:

approval(certification) of housing associations (including associations, companies, and foundations) by the central government;

restriction of an association's activities to promotion of housing and related functions; and,

making central governmental funds available to cover the cost of the municipal loans to approved housing associations for housing development.

Access to housing developed by associations, however, has not been limited to persons with lower incomes. Housing associations have at times been permitted to build dwellings for those who might 'move-up' to more expensive dwellings, freeing more modest units for other with lower incomes. Today, this is known as the 'filter-down' process. Financial aid was also given to housing associations for the construction of units for middle income families, as for instance, when the commercial construction market collapsed during World War I. Assistance for higher income families, however, was never meant to be a major activity of the associations; their primary objective was, and is, to provide housing for working people, although others may still benefit.

The basic thrust of the 1901 Act was the use of loans to finance investments in housing through which, over time, housing associations could accumulate interests in appreciated property while also realizing profits from the rents. Thus the initial intention was that housing associations should be financially sound. It was anticipated that, with relatively low governmental costs, a perpetually renewed housing fund would be created, fed by the redemption of the loans. While it was necessary to advance monies to associations to 'prime' their building programs so that activities could be initiated (within an acceptable time), the assumption was that housing associations would soon become financially sound and would themselves furnish the future financing of their building programs.

It took a few years for housing development to materialize under the provisions of the 1901 Act. The first two Housing Act Dwellings built by housing associations were not completed until 1906. Only six associations established before the 1901 Act applied for certification. By 1906, fourteen had been approved. Private developers and landlords thus continued to dominate housing construction and management. This situation prevailed until the economic crisis of 1907 dried up the capital funds market and, therefore, possible new construction.

It was not until 1910 that housing association became a major factor in social housing development (Fig. 10-1). In 1911 Ons Limburg, the first Regional Federation of Housing Associations, was organized by the Catholic diocese of Limburg to coordinate and deal with housing needs in the mining areas of that province. In 1913 the Nationale Woning Raad (NWR), a non-religious national federation of housing associations, was organized to provide technical and administrative support to housing associations. A church-related consortium, the National Catholic Institute for Social Housing (NCIV), was created by mergers in 1971 of Ons Limburg, the Catholic Institute for Social Housing (created in 1948), and the Union of Christian Housing Associations and Foundations (created in 1951).

Up to 1914 associations constructed very modest working-class dwellings with less than four rooms. One way of looking at this government support for housing was as a hidden form of relief for the poor. Soon, however, this changed.

The effects of World War I led to the escalation of construction costs and prices for building materials which were in short supply. As a result, the private construction sector nearly collapsed between 1913 and 1920. During this period, home building required government loans and was therefore carried out primarily by associations and municipalities.

It was during this period that new approaches towards subsidies were employed in order to stimulate housing production in addition to the loans available under the Housing Act. To insure greater continuity of housing production, interest-rates subsidies were initiated in 1914. These were followed in 1916 by subsidies for costly building materials. Both these subsidies were replaced in 1918 by the inclusive 'crisis' subsidies which were designed to meet deficits in operating accounts of social housing developers. These subsidies were particularly significant in assuring the continued strength of housing associations during this period.

These new subsidies reflected government's realization that associations could be a manageable instrument of policies to maintain housing production when private developers faltered. Thus the 'crisis' subsidy provided at first 50 percent, then 75 percent, of operating losses experienced by Housing Act developers. Social housing development became very attractive.

Typical of the growth of housing associations during this period was the fact that in 1913 there were slightly over 301 approved associations. Between 1918 and 1920, 743 associations were approved, and by 1922 the total had reached 1,341.[10]

These subsidies set a significant precedent for the role that government might play if it needed to intercede in the housing market—a lesson that was not forgotten in later years.

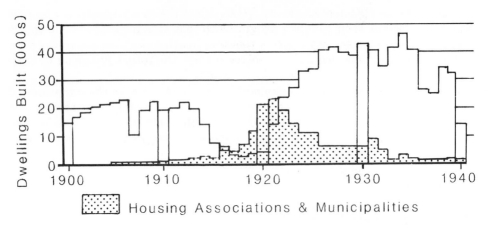

Fig. 10-1   Dwelling Units built Between 1900 and 1940 and Share of Housing
Associations and Municipalities in Relation to the Privately Constructed Units (Source: J. Nycolass, 1974, p. 157)

Rent Control Measures

One Dutch response to housing shortages and subsidy costs over the years has been
rent control. Thus, in order to offset the effects of increasing building costs on rent
levels, the government enacted the Lease Committee Act of 1917. This first form of
rent control provided for the establishment of rent committees to whom tenants or
landlords could submit their rent-related disputes, thereby allowing rents to reflect
more accurately prevailing levels of comparable dwellings.

Concurrently with these initial incursions into the area of rent control, government
policy was starting to develop standards for what would be generally acceptable
levels. About 15 percent of the family's income, before deductions for taxes and social
security contributions, became an accepted standard. Rents were not to exceed this
percentage of the average worker's income.

The 1918 Lease Termination Act was passed to protect tenants from unreasonable
lease terminations and acted as an initial form of security of tenure. The 1921 Lease
Announcement Act required public notice for all dwellings that were made available
for rent.

As the economy strengthened in the 1920s, in part due to Dutch neutrality in World
War I, the tenant protection laws and special subsidies became unnecessary and lost
their effectiveness by the end of the decade even before they were formally repealed.

As the war overtook the Netherlands in 1940, however, rent controls became a major, and essentially permanent, element of housing policy. From 1940 until the present, some form of rent controls have remained in effect. While there have been periods
of 'decontrol' of certain portions of the housing stock and attempts to regain a market
rental economy, the overall scheme in the Netherlands has involved control of rents in
all but a small segment of the highest priced portion of the rental housing stock.

The impact of rent control on housing subsidies has been formidable. Indeed, so
great has it been that rents are held below costs of development and operation on rental properties in the private or public sector and the gap has had to be bridged by a
subsidy. Without subsidy, the developer might forgo maintenance on existing units
and certainly would not construct new ones.

In order to prevent a sharp rise in rents during the occupation, the Germans promulgated a Rent Decree of 1940 and, in 1941, a Rent Protection Decree. Later that year, a Lease Execution Decree was also enacted. After liberation, these decrees were continued in effect by the 1947 Rent Law. Rents remained frozen at the May 9, 1940 level until 1951.

HOUSING POLICIES AFTER WORLD WAR II

1945-1960: An Active Government Role in Recovery

From the onset of the Great Depression and continuing through World War II, the production of housing essentially ceased for all sectors. The devastation of the war along with the moribund construction industry meant that major governmental intervention would be required to deal with the enormous housing shortage, estimated at 250,000 dwellings. There was also a tremendous shortage of building materials, which forced the government to ration the little that was available. Understandably, private initiative in housing construction developed slowly; rent controls had been fixed at levels too low to provide an adequate return on investment, and construction costs were skyrocketing.

The government was anxious to repair devastated dwellings and increase the production of new houses as quickly as possible. Loans were extended to stimulate the building of Housing Act Dwellings in order to meet the housing shortage and to maintain acceptable rent levels. The share of publicly-financed dwellings in the first few years after the war was greatly in excess of those produced by the private sector.

Most of the post World War II housing associations were still operated by non-professional staff and were relatively small. They were not prepared to take on building programs as they were asked to do after World War I. In addition, few of the associations were motivated to do so since any surpluses achieved had to go back to the government to repay earlier subsidies.

This time municipalities were selected to play a much more extensive and active role in the building program; perhaps this also reflected changed concepts of the function of government in the Dutch socio-economic system. The assumption of this role by municipalities was consistent with the greater responsibility over housing matters which they had generally been given. Cities became active participants along with housing associations in housing development.

Municipalities:

—either owned or could compel the sale of building sites and could prepare them for construction;

—had planning powers over the future use of various sites and thus were able to implement their decisions readily;

—were responsible for the issuance of building permits to control construction activity;

—received housing allocations for governmentally-assisted dwellings from the central government;

—were responsible for a fair distribution of the limited supply of dwellings in accordance with the 1947 House Distribution Act (residence in a dwelling required a permit from the city); and,

—could claim the use of vacant rental properties and take over all functions in the place of the owner except where the lease provisions conflicted.

During this post-war period, however, housing associations also became more active. As part of the revitalization of the housing sector, *operating cost* subsidies were initiated in 1947 to offset the effects of limited income from rents because of rent controls. These subsidies were borne by central government. Associations benefitted from this new subsidy. But, along with these funds came an increase in government regulations concerning the operation of associations. At the same time, however, the provision requiring associations to pay back 80 percent of surpluses to refund earlier subsidies was liberalized, to permit the creation of an operating reserve fund. Thus associations were given greater freedom in their operations and more of an incentive to sponsor new development.

In 1947, in response to the severe housing shortages, a Housing Distribution Act was enacted. It had significant impact on housing associations. Until then associations were more like unions of tenants, often with some shared interests. With municipal allocation of all vacancies, however, housing associations began building, not for their members, but for renters of different socio-economic classes, religions, and philosophies. This more heterogeneous tenant group, the increasing size of management portfolios, and the recruitment of professional managers made associations more impersonal. The concept of tenants joining together to manage their own housing was dying out.

The impact of housing subsidies on the national budget was quite severe. Thus, in 1948 the government required municipalities to secure loans on the private market for both housing associations and the municipalities own construction of Housing Act Dwellings. Interest rates, however, could not exceed levels specified by the government. To reduce costs further, allocations of subsidies to municipalities and associations could be exceeded where construction costs were kept below certain levels. This resulted in reduced sizes in social housing units constructed at this time.

By 1958, as the economy improved, the central government again started to make loans. The loan terms were extended, with 50 years for construction and 75 years on land costs, with a fixed interest of 4 percent.

The change in the relationship between municipalities and housing associations after World War II had several aspects. One was that many of the new associations which were established and certified took the legal form of foundations with outside, non-tenant directors; a number of these had strong municipal ties. Some municipalities set up foundations and controlled their decisions by appointing municipal officials to their boards. Such foundations were, in essence, disguised municipal housing departments, the creation of which evaded the original intention in the 1901 Act to give priority to private enterprise over local government.

In order to try to stimulate the private market, the government initiated a 'premium' housing subsidy that bridged the difference between rent returns and construction costs. The government, however, paid only 4 percent interest on the developer's investment. After 10 years, the operating expense gap was to be closed by rent increases. In 1953 this was changed to allow for annual premium payments. By 1955 a variation was introduced permitting half the normal premiums in return for freely established rents on these units. This policy applied to 75 percent of the premium supported construction that year.

One advantage of premiums was to avoid continuing government involvement in management. In 1960, the subsidy system was altered to give an initial small lump sum with decreasing annual payments reflecting depreciation write-offs. The effort was to try to bring private sector subsidies in line with those of the public sector. Between 1956-1960 the premium scheme was extended to owner-occupiers who, in addition, were provided with municipal guarantees on their private mortgages.

1960-1970: Housing Associations Become the Primary Vehicle for Social Housing and Rent Controls Were Modified

Housing associations became the recognized vehicle for social housing production and management by 1965. The Committee de Roos was appointed in 1958 to review the role of associations in housing policy. It completed its Report in 1962. The government, however, did not release the Report until 1964 because of objections from local government and because of the need to coordinate its recommendations with the 1965 Housing Act then being considered in Parliament. The Committee's recommendations had great significance in shaping social housing policy for the future. Many were incorporated in the 1965 Housing Act that was enacted along with a sophisticated physical planning system, considered one of the most progressive to this day.

The first of the Committee's policy recommendations dealt with the characterization of the housing associations as 'private initiative', not simply a tool of government. The original 1901 concept was revived—that of associations as developers with the ability to construct new units through profits on the initial developments without further government aid. So long as rent controls persisted, however, subsidies would still be required.

Second, the Committee recommended that associations become the preferred mode, rather than municipalities, for the construction of social housing. This preference was enacted in 1962 legislation. Local government was to act only if associations were unable or unwilling to do so. Since about 80 percent of all cities had local housing associations, the need for municipal action was considered to be low. Nevertheless, a 1969 government circular had to be issued to remind municipalities of their limited role and the need to defer to associations.

Third, the Committee recommended that housing associations be permitted to build housing for sale supported by premiums. This would allow them a broader constituent base and would help increase their financial strength and independence. This provision was embodied in legislation in 1968 and was expanded to permit construction of free sector dwellings, too, in 1975.

Fourth, the Committee recommended that loan conditions and municipal control over associations should be standardized and limited to a nationally approved format. The objectives were greater flexibility and initiative for associations and their release from the 'web of regulations' that had developed. This provision was enacted in 1968.

Fifth, the need to pay back subsidies had long been a sore point with associations, and the Committee recommended that this requirement be deleted. Without it, associations could accumulate reserves for new development. This was authorized in 1965.

A sixth recommendation was that associations be permitted to accumulate reserves to enable them to finance additional construction and to maintain their existing stock. This, too, was enacted in 1965.

Thus all of the Committee's major proposals soon became national policy. As a result, housing associations activities increased (Fig. 10-2). Their expanded volume of production, however, caused the government to increase the cost to associations of the loan interest they had enjoyed on housing act loans from 4 percent to the prevailing market rate in 1968. The effect was to take away a significant subsidy they had enjoyed, since market interest levels were substantially higher by then.

Rent Controls

Attempts were also being made during this period to deal with the effects of rent controls. A policy of 'liberalization' was instituted in order to gradually free private rental units from controls in areas without shortages (with more than 1 percent vacancies). At the same time, 'rent harmonization' policies were applied to older units still under controls.[11] Harmonization was to enhance filtering and mobility by increasing rents on older units above their individual historic costs bringing them more in line with newly constructed units. This policy resulted in a financial windfall for associations with older units. As harmonization evolved, individual rent subsidies became available in the 1970s to reduce the impact of rent increases on those with lower incomes. By 1973 all but the Randstad has been liberalized. Controls remained, however, on Housing Act and premium rentals. The harmonization policy, however, increased rentals on many of these units too.

At the same time, to ensure maintenance and to relate unit rentals to housing quality, a point system was established which took into consideration such factors as state of repair, number of rooms, room size, availability of central heating and shower or bath, useful cellar or attic space, and presence of a garden in establishing rents. Procedures for handling complaints and for outside evaluation of established rents were also created. Rent advice committees were provided to mediate disputes.

1970 to present: Emphasis on Housing Production, Growth Centers, Finance, Subsidies, and Preservation

Progress in dealing with housing shortages was being achieved until about 1975; at that time, however, shortages again started to increase.[12] The government employed a number of tactics to deal with this problem and its related effects.

The cost of producing government assisted housing encouraged the development of ways to resolve shortages. The multi-faceted policies included:

—creating housing for a designated population;

—meeting housing pressures created by immigration;

—developing innovative housing finance mechanisms;

—creating individual rent allowances to help those with lower incomes afford housing costs;

—focusing housing development more specifically on population segments most in need of housing, such as one and two person households and the handicapped; and

—continual utilization of housing associations to develop and manage social housing.

Growth Area Strategies[13]

Growth centers were designed to meet the pressure for additional housing. Through them, new development was to be directed outwards into New Towns built upon polders created from the sea or to areas on the edges of existing cities which had, or

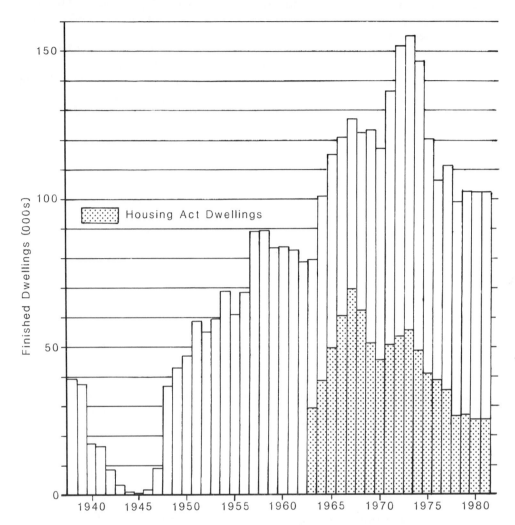

Fig. 10-2   Total Dwellings built and Share of Housing Act Dwellings since 1965
(Source: Annual Statistics of the Central Bureau of Statistics)

could develop, the necessary facilities to support new housing and meet the needs of
the resultant additional population.

Planning for this growth, with its concomitant requirements for the coordination of
transportation and employment policies for the new communities, required that decisions be taken at the national level subject to local consent. The latter, at times, has
been given reluctantly. Without such an approach, however, existing unprepared rural
provinces would have had to endure scattered urbanization with all the attended problems of sprawl.

Fourteen growth centers and six growth towns had been created by 1981. Growth
areas in the provinces of North Holland, South Holland, Utrecht, and the new polders
of Zuiderzee accounted for 27 percent of housing production in 1978, 26 percent in

1979, and 33 percent in 1980. Overall, the growth areas' share of total national production was 15 percent in 1978, 15 percent in 1979, and 19.6 percent in 1980; and in 1981, 20 percent was estimated.

Additional central government subsidies for infrastructure were provided for cities in growth areas. Major traffic arteries were needed and were fully funded by the central government. Additional welfare funds were allocated to these areas, as were funds set up to attract employment through industries. In addition, grants were given on the basis of the envisaged growth and planned housing production. Location subsidies to help meet the greater expenses in high cost areas were also provided.

Housing for Immigrants

While the pressures for new housing came from several sources,[14] expansion of immigration was a major factor. Immigration from former Dutch colonies and immigration of foreign workers rose substantially in this period. Foreign workers began to arrive in greater numbers. They then brought their families to join them, increasing the demand for housing even further. Pressure for housing in the Randstad, where the employment opportunities for these newcomers were greatest, created social disruption during this period.

Well-publicized disruptions occurred when 'krakers', or squatters, literally broke in and took over vacant dwellings.[15] Such actions by young adults resulted in open clashes with authorities over housing. They also focused attention on the shortage of housing, the need to make the cities more liveable in and to avoid population spillover in adjacent communities unable to handle pressures for housing.

The immigration of new ethnic groups into the Netherlands created social problems in a country renowned for its tolerance and acceptance of diversity. The integration of these new groups into Dutch society was probably most difficult with respect to housing and employment. However, the immigrants from Surinam and the foreign workers from Turkey, Morocco, Italy, Tunisia, Greece, Spain, Yugoslavia, and Portugal have tended to follow and group together with earlier arrivals in low quality housing areas. Overcrowding in these areas has further strained social relations with the existing residents. In contrast with the relative ease with which the immigration from Indonesia and, in general, that from Molucca was accepted during the 1950s, these recent immigrants (except from Surinam) know little of Dutch culture and have had, in the case of foreign workers, the additional problem of a language barrier.

In order to avoid further concentrations of immigrants in quarters with low quality housing, particularly in cities, and to encourage integration of these groups, two programs were instituted. A Preferential Scheme for foreign workers and Moluccans was announced in 1978. Under this program, 5 percent of the annual Housing Act Dwellings production was to be set aside for them, as was done in the 1950s with the earlier repatriates from Indonesia; this amounted to about 2,000 units annually, spread throughout the Netherlands. Local employment opportunities and educational facilities were to be considered in making placements, as was the need to allow clusters of immigrants so that they would not be isolated from others of their culture and life style.

Efforts to obtain voluntary cooperation with these integration programs, however, have not been fully successful. Recent attempts at the municipal level to prevent the concentration of immigrants in particular neighborhoods by means of allocation policies have been held legally impermissible. A voluntary acceptance by the affected groups seems, therefore, to be required before these government efforts can succeed.

Preserving the Existing Stock

Another significant policy initiated in this period was the effort to preserve the existing housing stock. New programs were developed to support conservation, rehabilitation, and improvement of existing dwellings. After 1960, greater attention was given to improving the quality of housing, primarily in respect of the technical standards for new construction. Government action regarding the deterioration of existing housing, however, was largely confined to demolition of inferior housing. It was not until the early 1970s—partly under pressure from residents who were opposed to demolition policies—that a change of policy took place.

The principal programs for the granting of government financial assistance for housing rehabilitation and improvement were introduced in 1970 and 1971. These issues have been primarily an urban concern for urban areas exhibited the most serious deterioration in housing.

Assistance has been given to individual units, to large social housing developments, and to neighborhoods. Initially, improvement of individual dwellings in different locations was stressed. Subsequently attempts were made to interest housing associations which owned whole blocks of houses to improve their properties. Municipalities offered to undertake the coordinated improvement of the immediate surroundings of the assisted housing at the same time. Finally, whole neighborhoods were selected in which assistance would be provided for improvements to privately-owned units.[16]

A good deal of progress has been made with the improvement of the social housing portion of the housing stock, since large numbers of dwellings are under the control of one entity, either city or housing association. For improvements by associations, the government contributes the entire cost for units built before World War II and half the cost of modernization for units built more recently. The government makes long-term loans to associations and provides the annual payments for its share. Associations must use their own financial reserves for their share. The government assumes that the 50 percent which the association must contribute constitutes deferred maintenance.

Rent increases also require tenants to contribute to the costs of the improvements they obtain, normally 2.5 percent of the cost of improvements (up to 4 percent for improvements to a 'high standard'). Individual rent allowances are available to mitigate the effects for those with lower incomes.

With respect to private owner-occupied dwellings, improvement activity has been modest. Despite some success, a number of difficulties have been encountered. First, municipalities have not always made clear their intentions or commitments towards implementing a policy of renovation and improvement. The resulting uncertainties have discouraged potential improvers from acting.

Second, municipalities have encountered management problems in connection with area improvements even where plans have been adjusted to the wishes of the residents by means of citizen participation and consultation. This has occurred when improvements have been undertaken on too large a scale and where temporary accommodation has had to be arranged for too many residents at one time. Third, the economic crisis has led to insufficient funds being available for these purposes from the central government. Finally, citizen consultation processes and the need for tenants' approval have in some instances prolonged the entire renovation process.

In the private rental sector, improvements have been curtailed even more because further investment is risky and yields are too low. Access to sources of finance is also lacking. Often the non-professional landlord is elderly and ignorant of the relevant government programs.

Before improvement can start, landlords must confer with tenants over the rents to be charged after improvements have been made. Thus, improvements in private rental housing are often possible only when fairly high subsidies are available; otherwise tenants will not concur.

Provisions under the Housing Act of 1965, giving municipalities substantial powers to require housing rehabilitation within a given period, have been put to work as part of the new emphasis on renovation. If necessary, the city can carry out the work itself, assessing the expenses to the owners. If the owner fails to comply with the order to effect repairs, dwellings may be condemned.

Under existing statutes, subsidies are provided by the central government to support the municipalities'renovation activities. Funding for improvements for individual houses are given to the owners from the central government. To ensure better planning, and to encourage municipal participation, multi-year funding commitments to municipalities for overall renewal activities have been made. In fourteen cities with particularly severe problems of housing deterioration, a deficit subsidy has been provided whereby the central government assumes any approved deficits caused by the need for the extensive rehabilitation activities.

A number of subsidies are made available to private individuals for improvement of individual dwellings. The major support is provided by a subsidy of an often changing but still substantial percentage of the improvement costs, within a ceiling adjusted for inflation. In 1981, 28,000 Housing Act Dwellings were improved along with 53,000 owner-occupied and other rented units. The subsidy can also be given in the form of annual grants over a period of 10 years in certain circumstances. Subsidies are shared by the central government and municipalities in a ratio of 4 to 1.

Where groups of dwellings are improved, as well as the immediate surroundings of the housing, more liberal subsidies are available. The intention here is to stimulate improvement of whole blocks of houses and even portions of neighborhoods. A subsidy may also be given for the rehabilitation of buildings other than housing, if necessary, to improve the surroundings in accordance with the residential improvements.

The central government, in addition to providing 80 percent of improvement grants, can also give the municipality a special surrounding subsidy grant of dfl. 2,500 for each dwelling in the improvement area for improvements to its immediate surroundings. In addition, a sum of dfl. 250 per dwelling is also available to the city to meet certain costs, such as those connected with citizen consultation. Subsidies from the central government are made available through the city for temporary housing accommodation for residents whose units are undergoing rehabilitation.

Special subsidies are made available to private individuals and cities for the restoration and improvement of historic dwellings. The central government can subsidize, depending on the circumstances, up to 60 percent of the total cost of restoration and improvement; municipal and provincial authorities can also make grants to bring the total subsidy up to 70 percent of the costs involved.

To alleviate basic defects in housing for which longer term rehabilitation is not feasible, special subsidies are made available to private individuals for the temporary improvement of housing of doubtful quality and questionable useful life. This may apply also when no final decision on the treatment for all areas has been taken. The assistance is provided where better housing is not available to residents in the short term. In such cases, the subsidy cannot exceed dfl. 10,000.

In order to encourage expensive development of new housing to fit sites within improvement sites, special subsidies from the central government are available to municipalities, housing associations, and private individuals for 'infill' housing in improvement neighborhoods to replace individual units that have had to be demolished. Amounts vary considerably, depending on the special circumstances and costs encountered in individual cases.

Rent Allowances

Individual 'subject' rent subsidies were introduced in 1970-1 and expanded in 1974. The subsidy is computed on the basis of the highest earning spouse, reduced 15 percent for each guilder earned by the other spouse in excess of dfl. 1,500. Computed quarterly, after verification of a tenant declaration, the amounts can be adjusted where income varies more than 25 percent from the previous year's level. Welfare recipients' payments are also taxable, if the individual's income is sufficient to be taxed. Rent is construed as the amount paid the landlord less amounts for utilities (heating, gas, electricity, water, and garaging costs), furnishings, meals, or nursing expenses. Amounts are apportioned where shared accommodation is involved. If the city decides that an appropriate, lower cost unit was available, the subsidy may be lost. Tenants may authorize payment direct to the landlord, who will deduct it from the rent; otherwise, as much as a two-month lag may occur before bank giro payments are received. Payments to landlords, however, involve providing landlords with the tenant's income data. Some 450,000 households and 1,000,000 recipients received benefits in 1980. This amounted to about 80 percent of those eligible.

Housing Financing Innovations

Dynamic Cost-Price Rents

A significant housing policy, dynamic cost-price rents, conceived of in 1970–1, emerged in the government's 1974 Rent and Subsidy Policy Memorandum. This document also expanded application of individual rent allowances, established annual rent increases, set 16 percent of an average worker's family income as the norm for housing costs, created support for home-ownership for moderate income families and announced that housing for those over 18 was a 'merit good' the state would assist them to achieve.

The dynamic cost-price rent concept anticipated that government-assisted developers would be attracted by a guaranteed, fixed rate of return even without the advantage of inflation in rents. Readjustments every ten years are used to achieve the promised yields. Rent controls with annual adjustments for inflation apply to assure rents are kept within the norm. Operating subsidies are provided to assure developers their promised returns. To stay within the 16 percent norm involves reducing initial rents set at 6.4 percent to 5 percent of construction costs by an initial government payment to the developer. Loan costs are calculated annually at the yearly adjusted market rates for government securities.

Savings in subsidies were envisioned since initial rents would be lower than the normal 10 percent of construction costs. These lower rents were also seen as enhancing the filtering process. As rents rose annually, moreover, it was anticipated that construction subsidies could be reduced.

The intended results did not occur. Private investors temporarily withdrew from housing financed with government assistance and associations had to be funded to fill the production gap. The effects of annual rent increases were overestimated; construction subsidies have not diminished as anticipated. Additionally, the cost of individual rent allowances was underestimated and these payments have become a major housing cost.

Financing Homeownership

In addition to creation of major new concepts of housing finance and subsidy, several revisions to existing approaches to housing finance took place during this period. Greater assistance was given to people wishing to own their own home. This even included a short-lived enthusiasm for selling Housing Act Dwellings. The relevant government circular was withdrawn, however, after parliamentary debate. Since sale required specific ministerial approval, only some 3,000 units were sold.

Premium subsidies for homeownership, on a ten-year decreasing basis, were split into an A and a B format, the former being substituted in 1979 for the support provided under the 'Owner-Occupied Housing in the Sheltered Sphere', a previously available subsidy for those with moderate incomes. The essential difference in the two 'premium' subsidies is based on the income level of eligible applicants, unit cost, and the extent of the premium provided. The fact that premiums are taxable income also makes the subsidy a graduated one, given the Dutch tax system.

Mortgage guarantees for private funding were provided by the municipalities under the premium schemes, supported up to 50 percent by the central government in the case of defaults. Defaults, initially minimal, increased somewhat during the economic recession in the earlier 1980s.

Limits on construction costs are also applied and reviewed annually; premiums are related to the capital costs of the individual unit. Premium units are on average about 22 percent higher in construction costs than Housing Act Dwellings. Provisions in the ground lease restrict resaleability in order to prevent speculation.

In a related action, location subsidies have been made available in high-cost, specially selected areas, specifically because of high land prices. These were instituted in 1978 to keep down rents or sales prices for subsidized housing.

Combined developments, including free sector, premium, and Housing Act Dwelling rental units, have been built to create income mix within the same project. In order to get rentals and purchase prices lower on the more heavily subsidized units, land costs were sometimes allocated more heavily to the free sector portions of the project.

CONCLUSION

The Dutch have committed themselves to increasing and improving the housing available to the country's inhabitants. They have provided substantial national financial support for these objectives. Since World War II, however, the increase in the number of people wanting housing has caused constant shortages which have frustrated these objectives. These demands, given the inflationary trends in land costs, building materials, and labor, have put a significant strain on budgetary commitments to housing.

Along with problems of housing shortage have also come the need to control rents and, at times, to restrict by means of allocation policies the areas in which individuals can reside. Government, indeed, has extensively regulated and intervened in housing markets and has controlled housing construction largely by means of fiscal policies and the use of housing subsidies.

While following policies of extensive government intervention, the Dutch have also encouraged an active role for private non-profit housing association as a means of providing social housing. The private sector, for example, has worked with local government to achieve housing objectives. The Dutch have also shown considerable ingenuity in expanding residential areas by means of new towns and growth areas (especially in areas reclaimed from the sea). They have substituted housing rehabilitation policies for policies of land clearance, thereby preserving older urban centers and their mixed residential and commercial uses.

At present there is a good deal of rethinking because of the strong impact of housing expenditures on the budget.[17] While the fiscal problems of housing shortages in the face of escalating costs for construction and management have not yet been mastered by Dutch governments, their problems are not unique to most 'free market' economies. Given the longstanding Dutch commitment to government support for housing costs and the variety of government interventions that have been employed, one would not be surprised to see a country that has demonstrated such foresight and ingenuity become one of the first to resolve these mutual problems.

NOTES

1. Ministry of Housing and Physical Planning, *Some Data On Housebuilding in the Netherlands*, The Hague, 1981, p. 2.
2. Netherlands Central Bureau of Statistics, *A Statistical View of the Netherlands*, The Hague, 1979, p. 2.
3. Ministry of Housing and Physical Planning, *Some Data on House building in the Netherlands*, The Hague, 1981, p. 4.
4. Ministry of Housing and Physical Planning, *Factsheet, Government Control Over Housing in the Netherlands*, The Hague, 1981.
5. For an interesting discussion of the dynamics between province and municipalities in this regard, see, Faludi and Hamnett, 'Leiden South-West: A Study of Plan-Making', *Lieden–Oxford Comparative Study*, Research Note 8, 1975.
6. See generally, Hugo Priemus, 'Rent and subsidy policy in the Netherlands during the seventies', 4 *Urban Law and Policy* 299, December 1981, (hereafter *Priemus*).

7. Joel F. Brenner and Herbert M. Franklin, *Rent Control in North America and Four European Countries*, The Potomac Institute and The Council For International Urban Liaison, Washington, DC, 1977, p. 38.

8. See Ministry of Housing and Physical Planning, *Factsheet, Non-Profit Housing Associations*, The Hague, 1981.

9. Donald I. Brinberg, *Housing In The Netherlands 1900-1940*, Delft University Press, Delft, 1977, p. 28.

10. Ibid., p. 38.

11. *Priemus, supra* n. 6, p. 307.

12. Contributing to this resurgence in demand were several factors. Government decisions to provide individuals over the age of 18 with the right to housing as a 'merit good' (in 1974), security of tenure laws making rentals less attractive to resident landlords who resist renting surplus space, and changing life patterns because of old age pensions, education scholarships for students, and increases in divorce rates, have all contributed to increased demands along with pressure from immigration and influxes of foreign workers.

13. See Ministry of Housing and Physical Planning, *Growth-centres and growth-cities*, The Hague, 1981.

14. See n. 12 *supra*.

15. One legislative response to this problem was the Empty Property Act, passed in 1981, to regulate such takeovers where units are vacant for over five months. Its provision had not come into effect, however, by the end of 1982. See Ministry of Housing and Physical Planning, *Factsheet, Empty Property Act*, 1981.

16. Ministry of Housing and Physical Planning, *The Neighborhood Approach*, The Hague, 1980.

17. *Priemus, supra*, n. 6, pp. 3 and 5.

11
Planning for Urban Renewal in The Hague

F. van der Sluys and G. van Evert

HISTORY AND TOPOGRAPHY

The Hague is the third largest city in the Netherlands. It is the only capital city in Western Europe that directly borders upon the North Sea.

The history of the Hague goes back to the mid-thirteenth century. Floris IV, count of Holland, had purchased a farmhouse around that time for use as a hunting lodge. For this purpose it was ideally situated: near a large forest, on a high ridge in the dune lands bordering the coast and adjacent to a small pond filled with clear water from a brook running through the dunes. Many types of game were to be found in the nearby forest and dunes. In addition, the surroundings provided wood and peat (in dune valleys) for heat in winter. The site was so desirable that soon the county administration was moved there and the lodge was enlarged into a castle, complete with inner and outer courts, a moat, and gates (Photo 11-1.).

This development in turn attracted commoners to serve the counts and their civil servants. A small hamlet came into existence west of the castle, housing pubs, art and craft workshops, etc. In the year 1370 the estimate of population was some 1,500 persons. By that time there were no more counts in Holland in the direct line. Not only did the county administration stay, but, by virtue of heritage and marriage, the area controlled from this village steadily grew larger and larger.

The Hague is referred to as a village because it never obtained the rights of a town or municipality. Those who ruled from the castle site did not like influential citizens on their doorstep.

The inhabitants could build a large church—St. James's and even, in 1565, a beautiful town hall (Photo 11-2) in the style of the Flemish Renaissance, but they never obtained the rights that many other towns were granted in the Low Lands.

After the revolution against the Spaniards, which began in 1568,[1] a federal republic was formed. There were seven 'provinces', of which Holland was by far the most powerful. Holland as well as the federation had its seat in the Hague. This did not change when the Netherlands became a kingdom in 1813. Thus for over seven centuries the Hague has been a center of government. Such a long tradition tends to put a stamp upon a community, for better or for worse.

Because the town was traditionally accustomed to administration, large private organizations are to be found in the Hague even today: oil and insurance companies, banks, etc. As in former times when administrators of county and republic hardly

Photo 11-1   (1) The Pond, (2) The Castle, (3) The Buildings surrounding the Inner
             Court, now housing Parliament, Office of the Prime Minister and the
             State Council, (4) Covered Shopping Mall built in 1885

Photo 11–2   The Town Hall built in 1565. To the Left of the Tower an Eighteenth-
Century Extension

recognized the citizens at their doorstep, it still seems, sometimes, as if the national government is not much inclined to consult the local authority (for example with respect to its policies concerning the housing of the national civil administration, or helping the city of the Hague financially in coping with its economic and social problems as the cities of Amsterdam and Rotterdam have been helped to enlarge their harbors and industrial sites). Tradition is one of the many aspects of society perhaps not recognized sufficiently in planning procedures.

Let us return to the Middle Ages for a moment. When the counts of Holland discovered the area to be a pleasant and healthy spot in which to live, fishermen had already lived on the coast for a long time. It took at least half an hour's walk from the village of the Hague to reach them, or rather, for them to reach the village to sell fish. Around 1650 a turnpike road, with four rows of trees on either side, was built through the dunes to connect the village of the Hague with the fishermen's hamlet, Scheveningen.

On clement summer days burghers went to Scheveningen on foot, or by coach, or on horseback to get fresh air from the sea and to watch the fishermen toiling, but not to bathe. People did not begin to bathe in sea water until the beginning of the nineteenth century, first in bathhouses, later from carts drawn into the sea, and finally by plunging into the water.

The Hague thus became not only the main administrative center in the Netherlands, but also a seaside resort, with the special attraction of being part of a larger city with its concert and Congress halls, its museums, theaters, and cinemas, and its pedestrianized shopping streets in the center of the city.

At the beginning of the seventeenth century a canal was dug around the Hague, not for protection in wartime, but to keep out brigands, mutinous soldiers, and the like at night.

The castle and its surrounding buildings are still there, serving as the seat of Parliament, the Office of the Prime Minister, and the State Council. The pond next to the castle is still there as well as a large part of the seventeenth-century city and the canals around it. A large part of the area inside the canals is now the Central Business District.

Essential Statistics

Until the middle of the nineteenth century most of the inhabitants of the Hague lived inside the line of encircling canals, separated from Scheveningen by dunes and park land (Fig. 11-1.). After this period the influence of the industrial revolution was felt in the Netherlands. It affected the Hague, not so much by industrial growth as by the growth of administration and, of course, population increase.

The war (1940–5) brought a decline, but soon the growth began again. In 1959 the number of inhabitants reached its pinnacle, 606,973. The number of dwellings was then 162,755 and the average number of persons per dwelling was 3.73. Today these figures are 456,725 inhabitants, 186,774 dwellings and an average number of persons per dwelling of 2.45.

This trend highlights a phenomenon with which Dutch physical planning has been confronted for the last twenty-five years. The number of persons per dwelling is decreasing steadily and the termination of this trend is certainly not evident yet. This means that, given a finite quantity of population, there exists a continually increasing

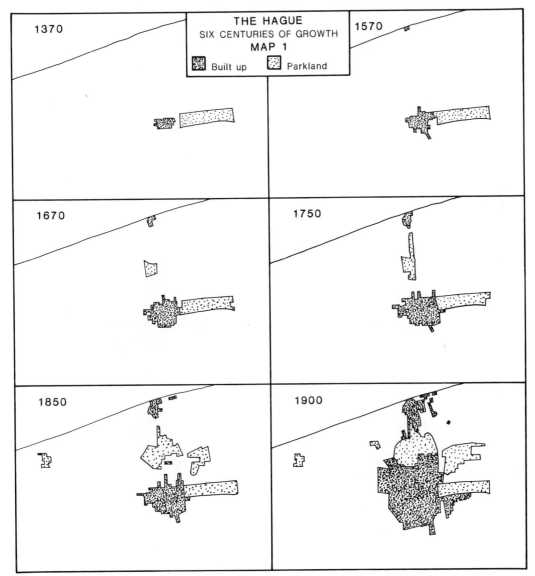

Fig. 11-1   (Map 1) Successive Stages of Growth: The Hague, 1370–1900

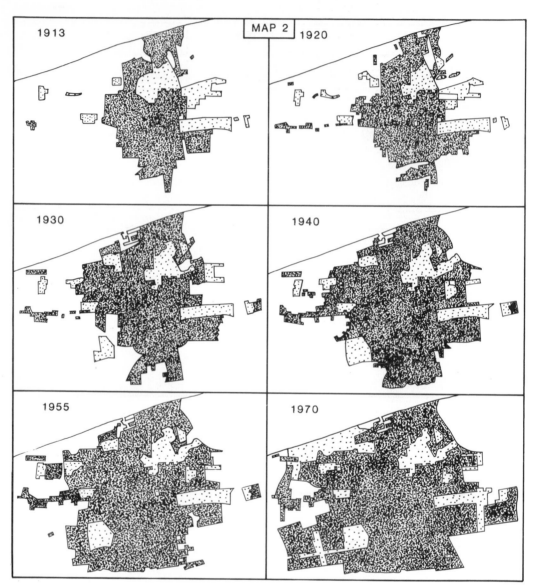

Fig. 11-1   (Map 2) The Hague, 1913-1970

demand for housing units. The Hague cannot provide these and, as a consequence, people leave the municipality to find housing eleswhere. Later we will return to this phenomenon, especially its consequences.

Employment in the Hague is about 210,000, far more than the city's work force of 180,000. This means that traffic facilities have to deal with a heavy stream of commuters twice a day.

As has already been mentioned, the Hague is the seat of the Netherlands government. Together with the provincial and local authorites, 30 percent of the employment is in the civil service. In private enterprise, employment is mainly administrative. Just over 80 percent of the total employment is in the tertiary sector and almost 20 percent in the secondary (industry and small technical trades).

The municipality covers an area of about 67.5 square kilometers. This area is highly built-up (98 percent). The total urbanized area, however, is much more extensive and is under the jurisdiction of several local authorities (Fig. 11-2).

The authorities of the municipalities named on the map have voluntarily formed an organization to deal with common problems such as physical planning and housing. It has not been a great success up to now since the interests of each individual municipality invariably turn out to be very different from those of the others. Moreover, the smaller communities are generally not inclined to make the problems of the large central city, the Hague, their own (for example housing low income groups, taking care of ethnic minorities, paying part of the losses on public transportation and cultural facilities, etc.).

Table 11-1   Population growth of the Hague (1870–1940)

Year	Population
1870	90,497
1880	113,460
1890	156,809
1900	206,022
1910	271,280
1920	354,987
1930	437,675
1940	495,518

TOPICS IN PLANNING FOR THE HAGUE

The loss of population, from nearly 607,000 in 1959 to just over 450,000 today, has already been mentioned. This has to do with the tremendous rise in Dutch prosperity over the past twenty years. As a result people can afford much more space per person than ever before. Families as well as other households that are decreasing in size demand more and larger dwellings. Further, many older people still occupy houses in which they once raised a family of two or three children. Young people of eighteen years and older tend to want their own housing. Thus, there is a constantly increasing demand for housing which cannot be met.

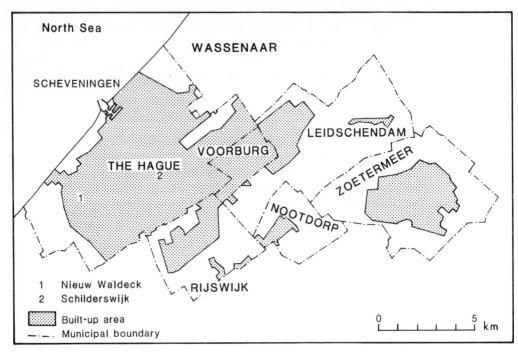

Fig. 11-2   The Hague and Adjacent Municipalities

Why is the Dutch community unable to build enough housing? It is not a problem of physical planning but a socio-economic one. When World War II ended, the Netherlands not only had to cope with a tremendous amount of war damage but they also lost their colonies, the Dutch East Indies. To survive, the country had to change from a mainly agricultural society to an industrial one, and, what is more, an industrial society that had to export!

This could only be achieved if wages were kept low; rents of dwellings were therefore put under government control. Rents were fixed at the May 1940 level and could only be raised by law. The percentage increase in rent, however, lagged behind the percentage increase in building costs, if the worldwide inflationary situation is taken into account.

This indicates a growing gap between the economic rent of newly built houses and that of the older ones. Therefore the difference in rents of new dwellings resulting from real building costs, as opposed to the rents of older ones, is subsidized by the national government. Since the national budget has its limits too, the yearly building program is limited. To build for the free market is not forbidden, but the prices (whether for rental or for ownership) are so high that only a few people can afford them.

In the Netherlands there still are dwellings available at a monthly rent of under six hundred guilders. To occupy a dwelling in that rent class one needs a license from the local authority.

In the Hague the situation is worse than elsewhere for several reasons. First, there is not enough space within the boundaries of the municipality to build a sufficient number of new dwellings. As already mentioned, almost the entire municipal area is used for urban purposes. In fact two new neighborhoods are under construction: New Waldeck with approximately 2,750 dwellings (nearly finished); and Houtwijk with some 4,250 units (of which just over 1,500 are ready). Both these quarters are built on land that was used for horticulture (Photo 11-3), a very productive form of land use and therefore very expensive to replace. Nevertheless, it has been done (although at high cost) and replacement horticultural land has had to be developed for the horticulturalists to begin a new, ultra modern and costly 'bio-industry'. The best horticultural land is sandy soil. The area into which they were moved consisted of heavy clay with good sand approximately 4 m. deep. The land, therefore, was turned over a depth of 4 m. and thus exceptionally good horticultural land was created for producing abundant and early crops in computer-controlled hot (or green) houses. All in all this was a very expensive operation and one which could not be paid for out of the profits on the building lots obtained; subsidies from national and local funds were therefore necessary.

A second reason for the difficult housing situation in the Hague is connected with the quality of part of the stock. One-third of all dwellings are over seventy-five years old and about half of these are in disrepair. When the Hague began to grow, around 1870, new residential areas were developed in two directions: towards the sea, on good, dry, sandy soil for the higher income groups; and landward on wet, peaty soil for the lower income groups. The soil required a foundation of wood piles, which were not too carefully laid; and the rest of the construction was also thrown together hastily. No space was wasted on greenery or even on a few trees: block after block was built along long and rather monotonous streets.

When a loophole in the building regulations was discovered, additional houses were built inside the blocks which could only be reached through small gates in dwellings located along the streets. These extra houses were on the areas intended for gardens and very often consisted of no more than one or two rooms. One common watertap and lavatory served for as many as twenty of these houses. Nevertheless they were occupied by families consisting of five, six, or more persons.

Although the worst examples of nineteenth-century building construction have been cleared away during the last twenty-five years, the quarters which were intended from the very beginning for the lower income groups remain in the city. Today they house the lowest income groups, those who earn a living by unskilled labor.

In the Hague this group includes not only those Dutch who did not have the opportunity for higher education but also people from Mediterranean countries such as Turkey, Morocco, Spain, and Greece, who are willing to perform unattractive work. There are also people from former Dutch colonies in South America and the West Indies (particularly from Surinam) all bringing their own religion and their own customs. Together these groups make up 10 percent of the city's population.

This ten percent lives in qualitatively poor and cheap dwellings. Since the law that controls the level of housing rents also connects quality to rent level, every action to renovate these dilapidated dwellings, means a considerable rise in housing costs for the people living in these quarters; and it makes no difference whether they are Dutchmen by birth or people from abroad.

Before discussing ways and means of urban renewal in the Hague, let us give some attention to other general planning aspects. The considerable loss of population since

Photo 11-3   Horticultural Area as removed to develop New Residential Areas

1959 has already been mentioned. Planners ask themselves: where did these people go, since most of them had (and still have) their jobs in the Hague?

First of all, as is the case in all major developed cities throughout the world, the localities directly neighboring the Hague started to grow. They are now in the same position as the central city, insofar as they have hardly any space left to build new houses. In the 1950s it was already recognized that this was going to happen and that these suburbs, along with the Hague itself, could not house everybody. Thus the municipality of Zoetermeer, 15 km. from the Hague, was given the status of 'expanding town', which means that it receives financial as well as other help from the government to build houses, schools, community centers, and so on to house the 'overspill' population from the city of the Hague. In the case of Zoetermeer it meant an expansion of the community from 8,000 to 100,000 within twenty years.

We will not go into the difficulties that such developments entail in a country organized politically like the Netherlands. We must take note of two effects only, insofar as they influence the situation in the Hague itself.

The first has to do with the question of *who* left the town. They are people from the middle and higher income groups in the 25–45 age group, i.e. mainly the younger families with children. A group that hardly moved were the older people. While the percentage of people above 65 for the Netherlands as a whole is 11.7, for the Hague the figure is 18.6. Others that stayed in the city were the lower income groups. This lopsided development was strenghtened by the immigration of Surinamese and guest workers from the Mediterranean.

The second effect has to do with the way local authorities in the Netherlands are financed. They themselves have only limited tax authority; the main part of their income is derived from a fund provided by the national government from national taxes. The basis for distributing the money among Dutch municipalities is the number of their inhabitants. Since many local authorities face problems of one kind or another, a large number of adjustments to the basic system have been made. In the case of the Hague the result is that, whereas the problems grow in number and in scope, the money needed to tackle them diminishes.

Another more general item that should be mentioned when discussing physical planning for the Hague is the significance of the city as a center of national importance for activities which fall under the heading of the tertiary and quaternary sectors. Examples are civil administration as well as the administration of large private companies (many of them also with international range and influence), engineering firms, lawyers' and notaries' offices to serve the administrative sector, a diversity of educational facilities, a main shopping center serving a wide region, and, last but not least, cultural and recreational facilities, again serving a much wider circle of people than just the inhabitants of the city. Among these facilities is the seaside resort, subject to a large-scale renovation, which attracts tourists from many West European countries.

This background affords tremendous possibilities for those who want to find employment and, at the same time, provides a dangerous situation, mainly because of its onesidedness. As mentioned earlier, more than 80 percent of the jobs are in the fields described above. Thus, changes in the need for administrative employment may pose future problems of labor absorption or unemployment.

The labor force required to keep this whole complex going, with its many interrelations, is larger than the city of the Hague is capable of providing. The Hague provides work for many persons in the surrounding localities. Each morning about 68,000 persons[2] come into the city to their work and leave again in the evening. The traffic problems generated by these commuter movements raise the question whether deconcentration of offices is not advisable.

There can hardly be any objection to a certain amount of deconcentration inside the area as marked in Fig. 11-2, i.e. the Hague with its surrounding municipalities, Zoetermeer included. The danger of a more widespread deconcentration, however, might be the loss of the Hague as an administrative center of national importance. That would be a severe loss for the Hague, but much worse for the people now working there and for the earning power of the whole complex, because deconcentration would not mean 'going on in the same way elsewhere', but the disruption of an intricate system of interrelated activities developed over a long period of time.

While interrelations are known to exist, there has not as yet been sufficient research to quantify them. Nevertheless, in some case studies it has been shown that there certainly is a 'multiplier effect'. Certain types of activities attract others, or, indeed, cannot exist without them. If the basic activity decreases, or even disappears, several others are affected and have to shrink or be liquidated. In some case studies multiplier factors of more than two have been found. As a consequence, the local council wants the position of the Hague as an administrative center respected, in quality as well as in quantity. This fact is recognized in national reports on physical planning for the country as a whole. Nevertheless, there are marked differences in practical policy.

The last item to be mentioned is the traffic problem, which has been exacerbated in recent years by the energy crisis. Like many older European cities with historically and architecturally valuable city centers, which also serve as the Central Business Districts, the main question is whether or not private vehicular traffic should be allowed to flow freely into this center. If permitted, it may easily destroy characteristic parts of the center; if not permitted it may affect the Central Business Districts. In the 1960s roads were widened to accommodate traffic (especially the private motor car). More recently the local council decided that no more new roads were to be built, nor existing roads widened. In order to regulate private traffic, the number of parking places for all-day parking were limited and facilities for public transport and the use of bicycles were promoted.

PLANNING ACTIVITIES

These questions and problems are all dependent on physical planning measures for their solution. They raise a constant plea for help from the Hague officials to their neighbors, the provincial and national governments, to provide space for new residential quarters, industrial estates, public transport and roads, and recreational areas of regional or even national importance. They also require constant and intensive attention from the local authority for the area under its own direct planning control.

Practically every square meter of land is examined to see whether or not it is being used to the utmost. There is constant discussion within the municipal council as well as without as to whether a change in land use for certain plots or even whole blocks and quarters should or should not be promoted.

The National Planning Law gives the Dutch municipalities the planning authority to further as well prohibit changes in land use for their entire territory. Prohibition of change may be necessary, when, for example, a residential area comes under strong pressure for redevelopment for offices, while the local council wants to preserve the residential area. Discussion about future land use are most intensive in the case of urban renewal.

The total area around the city center is divided into eleven districts, in each of which a specific project organization has been set up. In each district a project leader and his assistants are responsible for the coordination and implementation of all activities that have been found necessary. These activities are planned by a group consisting of local civil servants as well as citizens living or working in the district; the project leader is chairman of the group. Each of the civil servants represents a certain department such as the Town Planning Department, the Housing Department, Public Works, Welfare Work, etc. He or she is responsible for seeing that the work to be carried out by his or her department can and will be done on time. All actions planned have to be approved by the municipal council.

Of the eleven districts one stands out as having the worst conditions. It is called the 'Schilderswijk', i.e. the 'Painters' Quarter', since most of its streets bear names of famous seventeenth-century painters. This quarter was the first to be worked on comprehensively and served as an example for other urban renewal projects. These are salient reasons to look more closely at 'Schilderswijk'.

The Painters' Quarter

The Painters' Quarter (Photo 11-4) is sometimes called the largest town renovation activity in Holland. The area is about 170 hectares (425 acres) of land on which there are about 16,500 dwellings which house 43,500 people and which for the most part were built between the years 1870 and 1900. From the very beginning these dwellings were never among the best. When they were built there was no Housing Act to provide rules and regulations for the construction of dwellings by housing associations for the lowest income groups.

The dwellings were built by private developers, few of whom lived in the Quarter themselves. The houses were built as investment, profit, or speculation projects and little consideration was given to the quality of their construction. But as this quarter was built on peat soil, every faultily constructed foundation soon showed cracks and sags.

In the post-World War II years the rent control administration was such that rentals were too low to permit the necessary maintenance work to be carried out. In other cases, despite reasonable rentals, the owners were not aware of the necessity for exhaustive repairs.

Public demand for the necessary replacement of the dwellings was first heard after the war. The publication of various schemes to achieve this end had the side effect of encouraging owners to refrain from maintenance, thus accelerating decay.

Between 1950 and 1970 various ambitious plans were presented for the demolition of extensive parts of the quarter. These plans were typical of the time: none of them had been drawn up in consultation with the inhabitants of the quarter concerned. In addition the question whether or not funds required for carrying out the plans were available had not been considered adequately. On analyzing these plans by hindsight, the above seem to be the central planning themes at issue in town renovation.

Photo 11–4   Typical lay-out of the Schilderswijk

1970: Start of Renovation

Between 1970 and 1980 the renovation of the Painters' Quarter was begun, and by a method of trial and error a successful approach was found. In the early 70s an attempt was made, this time in consultation with the tenants, to stimulate private owners to improve their houses. However, the owners did not have the means at their disposal, nor were they prepared to go to great expense for the improvement of these dilapidated premises. Purchase for demolition and new building by the city appeared to be the only possible solution.

In a section near Koningstraat in this period a fierce struggle took place between the city and the inhabitants when the rents, calculated on the basis of a realistic new building scheme, were made known. They were approximately Dfl. 250 a month for 1972. Not high for a new apartment house, but nevertheless nearly triple the rent people were accustomed to pay for their old dwellings. In the opinion of the people these rents were in fact far too high. Together with experts whom they themselves had hired, an alternative plan was drawn up with rents about Dfl. 50 lower. The Minister of Housing and Planning made a site visitation to the area, which at the time displayed its opposition to the official plan by raising black flags. Negotiations were then started between the city and the tenants and the ensuing compromise was close to the tenants' proposal. The compromise monthly rental was Dfl. 210 in 1973. Since then every project for new building, from its initiation to its completion, has been developed in close consultation with inhabitants, city, and housing associations. The inhabitants' action group became a permanent factor of importance and developed into a tenants' organization with regular staff members.

Apart from these building activities, which were of an incidental nature, there was a need for a structural approach to land use planning in urban renewal areas. A realistic structural scheme was developed within the municipal organization in 1974. Close attention was paid to the means necessary for the realization of this scheme, but as a result it was not possible to consult the inhabitants of the neighborhood while the discussion paper was being drawn up. First, many internally divergent views within the municipal organization had to be brought into a common view. When, in 1975, the document was presented as a discussion paper to the people, the latter were most dissatisfied. The forty-four cooperating action groups made the following demands:

(1) inquiries should be made by authorities among the inhabitants concerning their wishes for redevelopment;
(2) consultations should be organized in each section of the district;
(3) a clear pronouncement should be made that the present tenants could continue to live in the quarter, thus ensuring rents the present tenants could afford; and
(4) the discussion paper was to be discarded.

In order to break the deadlock, a delegation of the cooperating action groups sat down with representatives of the city and came to an agreement regarding the procedure to be followed in drawing up a structural scheme. The results were that the demands mentioned under (1), (2), and (4) were met through the following method of planning.

Planning in Accordance with Means

In drawing up the new structural scheme a critical factor was the time-limited character of the plan. One cannot set goals for an indefinite period of time, but must indicate which short-range and medium-range plans can be realized, while taking into account the means that will actually be available.

Another factor of paramount importance in this method is the need for agreement among the various participants concerned. Particularly in the Painters' Quarter, where the lowest-income group of the Hague lives, after years of making plans 'in the interest of housing the people' (attention focussed upon the houses) and after years of talking *about* the tenants, it was necessary to make the plans together *with* the tenants and to reach an agreement (attention focussed upon the tenants rather than the houses). Of course total agreement is an illusion, but this was something also notably appreciated by the tenants themselves. It was, therefore, agreed that the plan be drawn up in five stages:

(1) obtaining information and initiating a consultation process with the inhabitants;
(2) identification of problems;
(3) providing suggestions for solutions to housing problems and other aspects (green areas, traffic, etc.) and a choice of alternatives;
(4) integrating the alternatives into a structural scheme; and
(5) presenting the structural scheme to the City Council for its reactions and approval.

In the first stage the consultation structure was formed. In this a role of predominant importance was played by ten consultative groups, each one representing a particular segment of the quarter. In these groups from ten to sixty tenants participated. At each stage they reviewed with the officials the discussion papers, drawn up by specific aspect working groups, in which officials and tenants were working together. Each of the aspect working groups made proposals on themes such as housing, traffic, and education. Throughout the process, which took one and a half years, each of the consultative groups held about eight meetings. In the same period the other basic condition, i.e. adequate resources to achieve the objectives, was met to a certain extent.

The Minister extended state aid for the cost of town renovation by introducing the so-called interim balance regulation. He was prepared in principle to make good any deficits in designated areas.

Many towns had raised the question whether future tenants would actually be able to pay the rents, which were to be fixed annually. In his reply the Minister announced that he had introduced a new system of guaranteed rents, which meant that rents would be payable dependent on the dwelling's size and quality, without regard to the year of construction.

In 1978 the structural scheme was backed by a large majority of the inhabitants of the quarter and in 1979 the scheme was adopted by the City Council. Although urban renewal in fact is a never-ending activity, the most important features of the scheme had to be implemented within ten years. This was illustrated in simple drawings (Fig. 11-3 to 11-6.). The main theme of the scheme was that the quarter was to be renewed for the benefit of the present tenants. The following were its prominent characteristics:

—the wishes of the tenants for a strongly decisive role in weighing the pros and cons of demolition and new building were recognized;

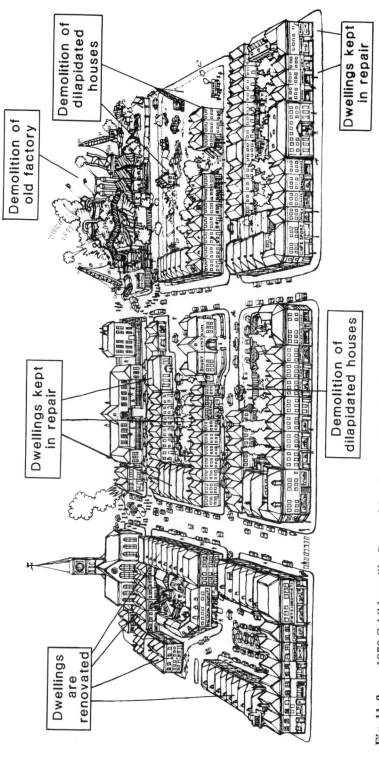

Fig. 11-3 1979 Schilderswijk: Start of Implementation. The Structural Scheme is accepted by the Municipal Council. Demolition, Repair, Renovation, New Housing Projects, all these Activities can take place according to the Scheme

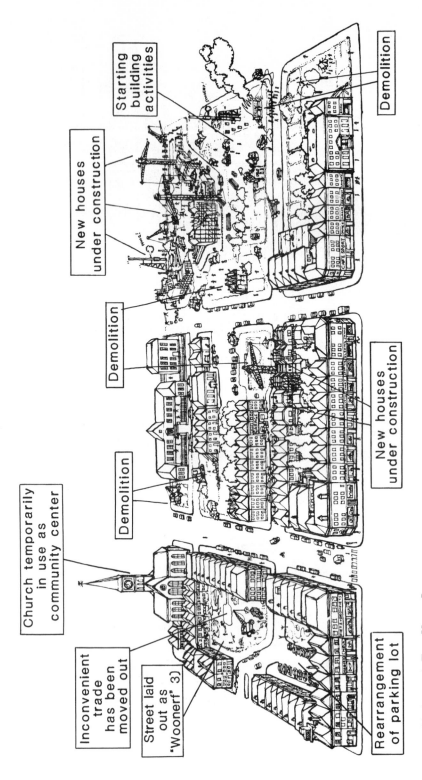

Starting building activities

Demolition

New houses under construction

Demolition

Demolition

New houses under construction

Church temporarily in use as community center

Inconvenient trade has been moved out

Street laid out as "Woonerf" 3)

Rearrangement of parking lot

Fig. 11-4   A Few Years Later

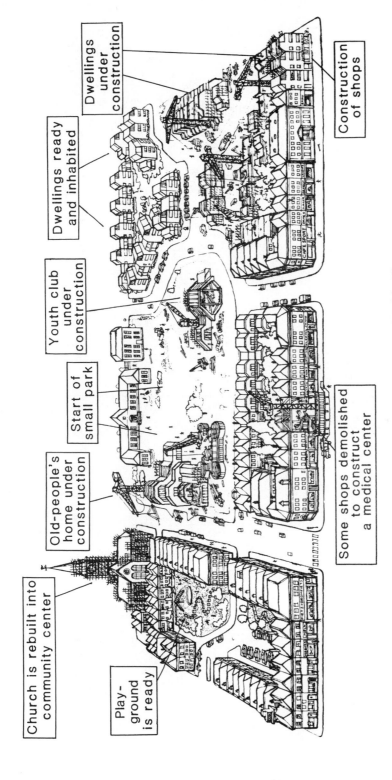

Fig. 11-5   Five to Ten Years after the Start. The New Lay-out becomes Visible. The New Housing Projects create a Pleasant Environment. Also Community Facilities are being realized. But still Demolition of Old Buildings is not finished

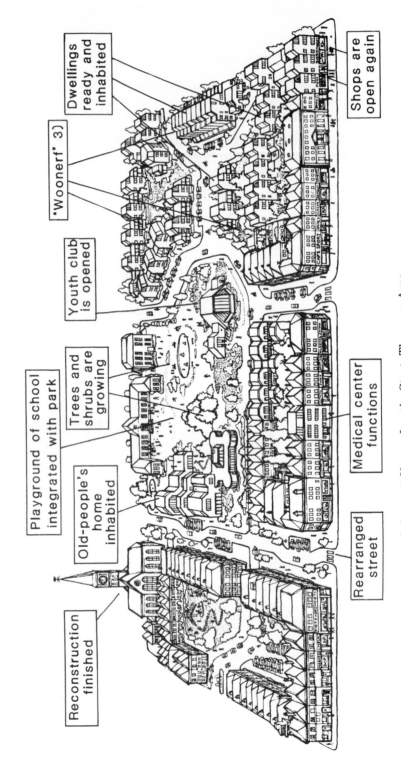

Fig. 11-6   The Operation is finished, Some 10 Years after the Start. The same Area as shown in Fig. 11–3, but radically changed

—new building was to be built for and with the tenants at rents the latter could afford;
—in order to house the largest possible number of tenants, as many dwellings as possible would be rebuilt, at fairly high densities;
—the planning period was to cover about ten years.

Structural Scheme—Implementation through Action Programs

In 1979 an action program for the next four years was added to the structural scheme. In this program all activities of the various municipal sectors (such as the purchase of private land, the demolition of dwellings, the development of building plans, and the laying-out of public gardens and green belts) were included in terms of time and manpower. On the basis of this action program, its implementation is now being energetically carried out. In each section of the neighborhood, the inhabitants of the section concerned are directly consulted.

Between 1972 and 1980 roughly 800 new dwellings were constructed. That the action program, together with the structural scheme, can have accelerating effects became quite clear in 1981. In that year the construction of about 700 dwellings, a shopping center, a sports hall, and two schools started, and a beginning was made in laying out two local parks as well as the improvement of various streets in a part of the quarter that was to be maintained. Renovation activities are well underway (Photo 11-5).

Town Renovation Demands Political Choices, Both Locally and Nationally

From the preceding it would seem that town renovation can be solved quarter by quarter, and this is largely the case as far as the formulation of problems, suggestions for solutions, and working methods are concerned. On municipal, and occasionally on national political levels, however, the means have to be made available. It is then a matter of priorities in the municipal budget, organization of the municipal machinery, and the application of national policy concerning the cost of housing.

The feasibility of carrying out town renovation very much depends on the priorities in the town's housing market. For every six new dwellings built, ten old dwellings have to be purchased and pulled down by the municipality, after the tenants have been given other dwellings. For six out of these ten therefore, a new dwelling is available in the Painters' Quarter, while the remaining four must be offered dwellings in some other part of the Hague.

If the process of town renovation is to proceed smoothly, 'normal' househunters will sometimes have to wait a little longer. The inhabitants of town renovation areas have been given the option of newly built dwellings on the outskirts of the town, in New Waldeck and Houtwijk. In these times of economic recession the municipal budget is showing increasingly that not every citizen or action group can have its own way. The need to make choices is growing stronger. It is not possible to erect a new school everywhere. The worst has to be replaced and more often than not the worst happens to be in a town renovation area.

The need to make choices also implies a change in attitude of the officials concerned. The work may become less spectacular, even contradictory to planning theories learnt and practiced before.

Cooperation in the project groups referred to is necessary for the coordination of work in all municipal sectors. In general, it is more necessary that ever to listen to the

Photo 11-5   The First Blocks are ready, the Second Phase has started

inhabitants and to see what can be done to meet their expectations. To the citizen the municipality is still too often a many-headed, multifaced monster working too frequently at cross purposes. Yet there is an inseparable connection between education, sports, housing, etc. An overall policy is required. The cost of housing is determined by the Minister in close correlation with fiscal policy. When, owing to the economic recession, increases in income fail to materialize while building costs and rents rise continually along with energy costs, it naturally follows that tensions increase. Is the citizen still in position to pay, or are the authorities still in position to subsidize on an even larger scale?

PLANNING: TIME-LIMITED AND DEPENDENT ON MEANS

It is now apparent that in a number of fields there are new influences on the process of town renovation which will lead to readjustments, a matter of logic in a cyclical process.

In the first place the approach to the main problems connected with the dwellings that are to be maintained appears to be ineffective. It would seem that demolition and new building, being more spectacular and impressive that the improvement of dwellings, have a more stimulating effect on the executives and officials concerned.

An opposite tendency becomes manifest among the tenants who, owing to the continual increase in the cost of energy, have to spend more and more on heating, in addition to already high rents, so that for them the problem which arises is whether or not they can still afford the cost of housing (rent + heating). In many cases, after weighing the pros and cons, those who at first opted for demolition and removal to a newly built dwelling now wish to continue to live in their old dwellings, which must then be improved.

The cost of new housing on outskirts such as New Waldeck is now so high that many who have to move from town renovation areas prefer an older post-war flat at a lower rent. Yet New Waldeck has certainly performed a useful function in accommodating tenants from the town renovation areas who had to be rehoused. The tenants of these areas are diverse and so are their tastes.

In view of these aspects, the process is one in which no timeless recommendations can be given. The only conclusion is that in a certain period of time the available financial means, manpower, and organizational expertise determine the result of the planning process.

NOTES

1. In those times Philip II, King of Spain, reigned over the Low Lands as he was by rights also Count of Holland. Although the revolt started earlier, officially the war of independence began in 1568. It ended in 1648 and is therefore called the Eighty Years War. In fact there were no more Spanish troops north of the Rhine after about 1575.
2. In 1975 an enumeration revealed 54,700 incoming commuters during the morning rush. At the same time 31,800 persons left the municipal territory to work elsewhere. For the traffic system the figure for incoming commuters of course is decisive. Although no new census has been taken, the figure for incoming commuters in 1982 is known to be about 68,000.

12
The Delta Works: A Dutch Experience in Project Planning

Ashok K. Dutt and Steven Heal

Water management has always been of the utmost importance in the Netherlands. Were it not for certain safeguards, a full 50 percent of the land area—home to 60 percent of the population of the Netherlands—would be flooded periodically[1] (Fig. 12-1). The most recent safeguards are incorporated in the Delta Project, a fascinating example of comprehensive project planning and regional development.

The project is a masterpiece of Dutch hydraulic engineering. Because of the length of time involved in its creation, changing planning values have prevailed in different stages of its implementation. The main objective of the Project is to protect the people, land, and property in the Delta Region from abnormally high floods. Throughout the Project implementation period, no compromise was made in this objective. In the seventies, when environmental conservation values took strong root in Dutch society, the Delta Project planners responded with an accommodating solution.

This chapter, while presenting the details of the above objectives and changes, describes how the Project originated out of a catastrophic crisis and finally evolved into a well conceived, exemplary effort of physical planning carried out on an incremental basis of various stages. In addition an examination of the technological, economic, developmental, and environmental benefits accruing to the Dutch people as a result of the Delta Project are also described in this chapter.

BACKGROUND OF THE PROJECT

Traversing the Netherlands are several large rivers, including the Rhine, the Meuse (Maas), and the Schelde, all of which enter the North Sea in the Provinces of Zeeland and South Holland in the south-western part of the country. This area is known as the Delta Region or the Delta Project Area.

Prior Land Reclamation and Flood Control Projects[2]

Initially, simple safeguards made against the onslaughts of the sea were adequate. For the last several centuries, however, the sea level has risen an average of ten centimeters per century.[3] The situation deteriorated until at high tide the sea penetrated from the north as far as Utrecht and through the Delta Region as far west as Dordrecht.

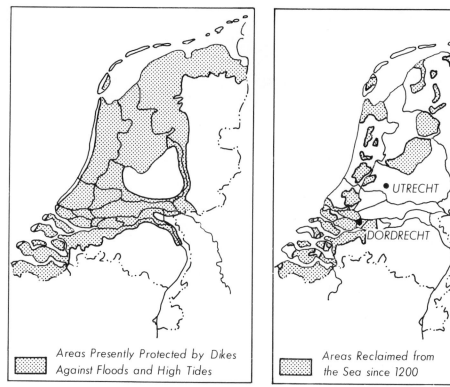

Fig.12–1   Areas of The Netherlands reclaimed from the Sea and protected against
              Floods

The earliest attempts to drain the land date back to ancient times. Early residents built mounds, called *terps*, on which to safeguard their property during periods of high water. When three or more terps were linked together, the interior could be drained by allowing the water during periods of low water to flow out through an opening that could later be closed during periods of high water. During the Roman period, elevated roads that acted as dikes were constructed parallel to the rivers.[4] The introduction of the windmill with rotatable heads in the sixteenth century and steam-driven pumps in the nineteenth century served to increase the efficiency of land drainage efforts, and both innovations have been instrumental in reclaiming much of the land. The Delta area islands have gained significant amounts of land in the last few centuries because of these measures (Fig. 12-2).

Perhaps the most extensive effort to reclaim land from the sea has been the Zuiderzee Project[5] which is discussed in the next chapter. With the north of the country in the Zuiderzee area sufficiently safeguarded, attention turned to the south where the rise in sea level presented an increasing hazard. Efforts to heighten sea defenses in the southern part of the country were hampered because many buildings stood on or near the hundreds of miles of dikes, and raising the dikes involved displacement of these structures. Before the present Delta Project, however, some work was accomplished in the Delta Region.

A project to close breaches in the dikes surrounding the island of Walcheren that resulted from Allied bombings in 1944 was carried out after the German surrender.

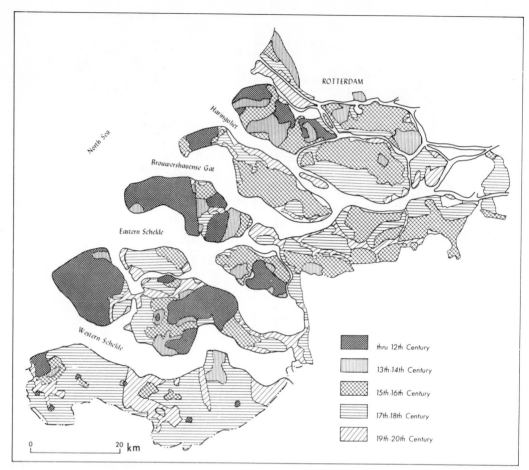

Fig. 12-2   Areas reclaimed in Southwestern Netherlands through the Centuries
(Source: John van Veen, *Dredge, Drain, Reclaim*, The Hague, Martinus,
Nijhoff, 1962)

The island had been exposed to the tides for nearly a year when the breaches were seal-
ed by means of concrete caissons sunk in the gaps.[6] This method, later perfected for
use on a large scale, has been employed repeatedly since. In 1950 the Brielse Maas
near Rotterdam was dammed by sinking reinforced concrete caissons, especially
designed for the project, into a previously prepared bed of sand. The caissons were
then filled with sand or loam, and a freshwater lake was created behind the dam. A
new highway between the islands of Rozenburg and Voorne was built, and the
coastline shortened by 38.4 km. Braakman, an inlet on the West Schelde was dammed
by a similar method in 1952; the main difference here being that the tide was allowed
to flow freely through gates in the caissons (called culvert caissons)[7] while construction was under way. Land for thirty new farms was reclaimed, road connections were
improved between east and west Zeeuws Vlaanderen, and the coastline was again
shortened. Perhaps most importantly, these three projects in the southern
Netherlands set the stage for a fully planned Delta Project, which unfortunately, required a catastrophic flood for its initiation.

The Flood of 1953: Genesis of Crisis Planning

On the night of 31 January 1953, gale-force winds blowing from the west and associated with a deep cyclone over the eastern part of the North Sea, prevented the tide from ebbing. When the next tide came in, water levels rose as high as 3.6 m. above the danger level. Sixty-seven major and 495 minor breaches were made in the dikes, inundating over 160,000 ha. of land (Fig. 12-3). In addition there were 1,835 fatalities, and 72,000 people were left homeless.[8] The loss of domestic animals was extremely high: 2,700 sheep, 12,000 pigs, 20,000 cows, and 165,000 poultry.[9] The central Netherlands, including the densely populated cities of Rotterdam, the Hague, Leiden, and Delft, were at one stroke seriously endangered. Extensive flooding had occurred on previous occasions, notably in 1894 and 1916, but a disaster of this magnitude had occurred only once: in 1421 when the St. Elizabeth Flood had drowned an estimated 10,000 people. The entire country was shocked.

In addition to the destruction of human and animal life, a variety of other problems are associated with such floods. Once areas below sea level are flooded, they remain inundated even after the termination of conditions responsible for the flood. As the tide flows in and out through breaches in the dikes, it widens them further. Marine sands cover fertile farmlands and fill in ditches, and eventually any sign of human habitation is erased. It was, therefore, imperative that repairs be made as soon as possible following the 1953 floods. Work on the Zuiderzee polders ceased as all available men and equipment were mobilized and rushed to the stricken area. Within a period of one year,

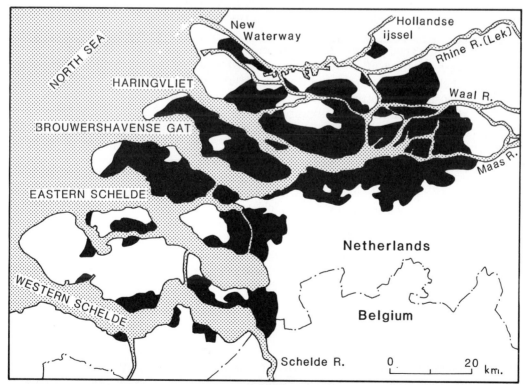

Fig. 12-3   Areas submerged in 1953 as a Result of the Storm originating in the North Sea

all the breaches in the dikes of the Delta Region had been closed and the flooded lands reclaimed with the help of methods used previously in other projects. The 1953 flood crisis became the main impetus in initiating a comprehensive flood control project for the Delta Region.

THE DELTA PROJECT DESCRIBED

On February 21, 1953 the Delta Commission was created as a special branch of the Government Water Control Department. Its task was to determine the best means of preventing a recurrence of the flooding of the previous month. The physical bias of the commission membership was reflected by the fact that except for the well-known economic planner, Jan Tinbergen, all others were engineers. It was, however, the world-famous hydraulic engineer T. Thysse, who supervised the planning details of the project. Two proposals were under consideration: (1) raising the height of existing dikes and (2) damming the sea arms of the delta altogether. The estimated expense for both solutions was approximately the same. The Delta Commission recommended the latter of the two proposals, and in 1958 the Dutch Parliament passed the Delta Act approving the Project.

The 1958 Delta Project Plan included (1) closing four broad, deep sea inlets at Haringvliet, Brouwershavense Gat, Veerse Gat, and the Eastern Schelde, (2) erecting a storm-surge barrier across the Hollandse IJssel, and (3) building secondary dams on the Zandkreek, the Grevelingen, and the Volkerak. In addition, the New Rotterdam Waterway, providing access to the port of Rotterdam, and the Western Schelde, providing access to Antwerp in Belgium, are to be left open and the dikes paralleling these waterways heightened and reinforced to provide maximum protection.[10] The project envisioned the creation of a vast reserve of freshwater in the outlets of Veerse Gat, Eastern Schelde, Brouwershavense Gat, and Haringvliet (Fig. 12-4). Before selecting the height, position and strength of the dikes two models wre prepared for experimentation at the Waterloopkundig Laboratory of the Delft Technical Institute. One was a miniature model of the area with a vertical dimension with water running through all rivers and sea arms, and changing positions of the dikes, followed by measurement of water velocities everywhere. The other model was one of electric wires whose resistence was proportional to the resistence water experiences in the real sea arms (about inversely proportional to the width of the arms). Based on the results of the above models, the location and strength of dikes was chosen.

With the eventual completion of the Delta Project, the coastline will be further shortened by 700 kilometers. Most existing dikes will be reduced to secondary defenses and will lie along nontidal or controlled tidal waters. Even if one of the large dams is breached, the residents of the area will not be exposed to the direct onslaught of floodwaters along the open sea arms.

The 1958 Project Plan

At the beginning scheduled parts of the 1958 Project were started immediately after the Parliamentary enactment. The parts of the overall Project included Hollandse IJssel and Zandkreek, Grevelingen, Volkerak, Haringvliet and sections of Eastern Schelde Dams (Fig. 12-4). Until the middle of the seventies no change was sought in the initial plan.

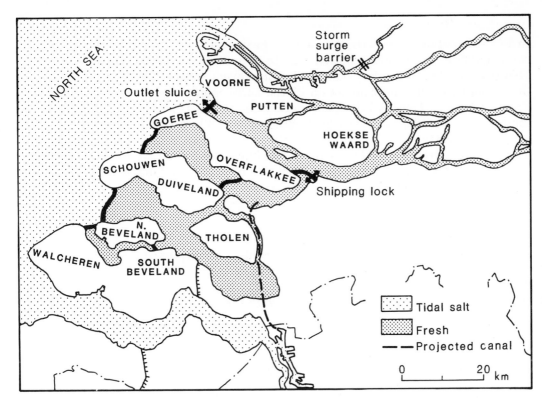

Fig. 12–4   The Delta Project, 1958

Hollandse IJssel

A storm-surge barrier, 72m. long and 9.9m. high, was constructed across the Holland-se IJssel in 1958. This barrier remains raised under normal circumstances and lowered into place during periods of high water to prevent the dikes paralleling the Hollandse IJssel from being breached. The barrier has been closed several times since 1958 to hold back the water. An additional but much stronger gate was added in 1976. A lock adjacent to storm barriers, allows for the passage of ships.

Zandkreek Dam

The first dam to be completed was across the Zandkreek in 1960. Standard caissons were floated into place and sunk. The Zandkreek was one of three secondary dams built to prevent troublesome currents from flowing through certain stretches while the Project was under way. The Zandkreek is part of what is known as the Three-Island Project; with completion of the Veerse Gat in 1961, the three islands of North Beveland, South Beveland, and Walcheren were linked. A lock on the Zandkreek dam serves to connect the south basin.

In constructing the dam across the Veerse Gat, sluice caissons were used for the first time on the Project. As with standard or culvert caissons, sluice caissons have passageways that remain open until all are in place and then are closed simultaneous-ly.

Grevelingen Dam

In l962 the southern gap of the dam across the Grevelingen was completed. An island in the middle of this estuary allowed work to be undertaken on the dam in two stages. This, and the other secondary dams, will help prevent strong currents from arising in the estuaries before the completion of the three major dams on the Haringvliet, Brouwershavense Gat, and the Eastern Schelde. In constructing the dam across the southern gap, standard caissons were employed, and a lock was incorporated into the design. In constructing the dam across the northern gap, a different technique was used; boulders, transported by gondolas running along a cable, were dumped into the estuary. The dam across the northern gap was completed in l965, and the islands of Overflakkee and Duiveland were linked by road.

Volkerak Dam

Constructed with sluice caissons, the Volkerak Dam was completed in 1970, although the locks have been in use since 1967. Thousands of ships passed through these locks annually, even before the new inland waterways between Rotterdam and Antwerp (Rhine-Schelde Canal) was completed in 1975. The Volkerak dam also serves to link the islands of Overflakkee and Hoekse Waard with the province of North Brabant.

Haringvliet Dam

Because over half of the Rhine's flow and almost all of the Meuse's flow once entered the North Sea through the Haringvliet, the closure of Haringvliet was considered particularly vital. Not only would a considerable land area be protected, but great quantities of fresh water would be diverted to the New Rotterdam Waterway.

A new technique was used in constructing the sluices and the locks across the southwest gap of the Haringvliet. A ring dike was built, and the area within it pumped dry. Construction of the sluices and locks commenced and on completion the ring dike was removed, leaving behing the completed works. The northern gap was dammed by means of a gondola cableway similar to that used to close the northern gap across the Grevelingen. Instead of boulders, however, locally produced concrete blocks were used. This proved economical because boulders would have had to be imported, a costly measure in terms of both time and money. Furthermore, Zeeland has an abundance of the materials needed to make concrete. The entire length of Haringvliet dam was completed in 1971, and the dam across the Brouwershavense Gat, which was started in 1962, has since been completed as well. Sluice caissons were used for the northern gap, and the cableway for the southern gap.

Eastern Schelde Dam

This part of the Delta Project was left until last because of the magnitude of the task. Because the Eastern Schelde is very deep its closure required the same volume of materials as was needed for the construction of the Zuiderzee enclosure dam, which is three times as long. The actual construction of the dam on a 9.6 km. stretch of Eastern Schelde started in 1968 in accordance with the 1958 Project Plan. Three construction islands: Roggenplaat, Neeltje, and Jans were artificially created in 1969, 1970, and 1971 respectively.

The Geul dam section was built in 1972, whereas the pier and mattress building sites were completed in shallow water parts of North Beveland and Schouwen in 1972 and 1973 respectively. A dike 4.8 km. long was completed in 1973.

According to the plans, the remaining three channels, Hammen, Schar and Roompot should have been plugged with quarrystone and slag, followed by concrete blocks, gravel and sand between 1974 and 1980. The intention was to dump the slag and the stone from barges, the concrete blocks from cableways, the gravel by means of trailer dredgers and the sand by means of suction and trailer dredgers . . . In 1973 when the idea was still to close off the Eastern Scheldt completely, a start was made with laying the protective mats in the three remaining channels. The mats were needed during the construction of the dam to prevent scouring of the seabed and to keep the erosion expected on each side of the concrete block dam far enough away from the dam itself.

   At first the protective matting consisted of filtercloth and wood, with rubble as ballast. Later mattresses with fixed ballast were used: in the Hammen and the Schaar van Roggenplaat mattresses of stone asphalt made on floating asphalt ship, the 'Jan Heymans', and in the Roompot concrete block mattresses made in the factory at the Sophia work harbour. The 13 towers for the cableways which were to be used for dumping the concrete blocks were installed in the three channels in 1973 and 1974 by means of a lifting platform.[11]

The 1976 Revised Plan

While these activities were in full swing, a heated controversy surfaced between environmental groups, who vehemently opposed the closure of the Eastern Schelde, and the government planners. Planners upheld the need to provide security for human lives, habitats, and land on the one hand, while environmentalists called for the protection of the natural ecology of the area and of the environment on the other. Supporters of the plan argued that only closure could guarantee complete safety, while the opponents declared that the strengthening of existing dikes around the Eastern Schelde would provide adequate protection. In the midst of the controversy, the Transport and Public Works Minister appointed an advisory committee which in 1974 proposed the erection of a storm-surge barrier across the Eastern Schelde which could be closed whenever necessary, thus satisfying both environmental and safety needs. The selected design of the storm-surge barrier (Fig. 12-5), approved by the Dutch Parliament in 1976, has the following characteristics:

A. The length of the storm-surge barrier is 2,800 meters long with 63 closable openings;

B.   Hammen, Roggenplaat, and Roompot channels where the openings are, are to have 16, 17, and 33 pre-fabricated, reinforced concrete, monolithic piers;

C. The seabed between the piers is to be raised by a sill construction and threshold beams;

D. The piers, the sill, and the beams together form the frame within which the 63 sliding gates, made of steel, can be raised in normal circumstances (thus allowing the tidal water to pass freely and preserving the saline environment) and lowered during gales for safety;

E. The piers, with baseplates of 25 x 50 meters, heights between 35 and 45 meters and with a maximum weight of 18,000 tons, are to be constructed in the artificially created construction dock at Schaar [pier building started in 1979] and transported and sunk in exact position by a specially designed lifting barge [the first pier was placed in August, 1983]; and

F. With the completion of three storm-surge barriers a roadway is to be built across

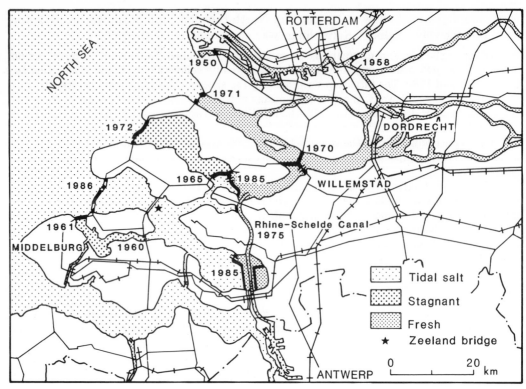

Fig. 12-5   Revised Delta Project, 1976

the Eastern Schelde using the top surface of the barriers and dike on the Geul (Fig. 12-6.)[12]

This revised plan was a great victory for environmentalist groups, because it preserves the saline ecology by keeping the sluice gates open in normal circumstances. The sluices may, however, be closed, if there is any possibility of coastal flooding. Before any construction was undertaken, careful study of the Project was completed at the national hydraulics laboratory. A scale model of the complicated systems of dams, sluices, and dikes was first tested here. Engineers also benefited from experience gained in previous projects, although none of the earlier endeavors came close to matching the magnitude of the Delta Project. The revised plan has put back the completion date of the project from 1978 to 1986. This revision also substantially raised the cost of the project.

Philips Dam

After the completion of the storm-surge barrier in 1986 only 75 percent of the tidal water will enter the Eastern Schelde and, to compensate for the loss, the 1976 Revised Plan called for the construction of Philips and Oester Dams. These dams are intended to reduce the tidal area of the Eastern Schelde and prevent any level changes by tidal movements in the Rhine-Schelde canal. As the Dutch government has already guaranteed the Belgian government by means of a treaty that it will maintain a fixed

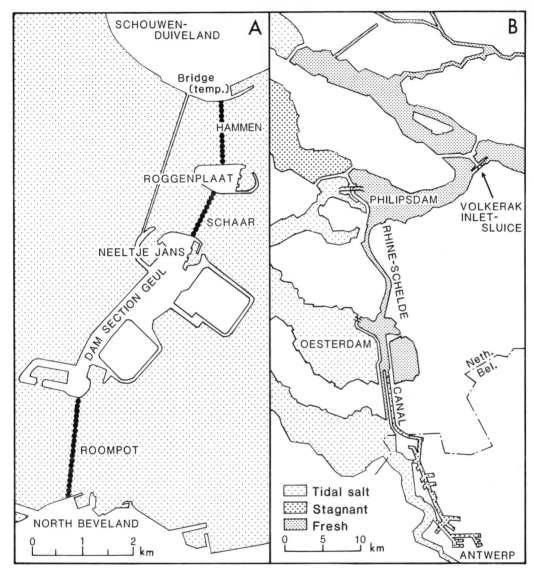

Fig. 12-6 (A) Storm-surge Barrier at the Eastern Schelde. The Temporary Bridge
will be removed on Completion of the Project. (B) Rhine-Schelde Canal
linking Antwerp with Rotterdam

level in the canal, the canal has to be tide free.

The Philips Dam is especially noteworthy because it incorporates a novel
freshwater/saltwater separation system which does not allow the transfer of the salt
water of the Eastern Schelde to Krammer or any fresh water from the latter to the
former, through its shipping locks. Two large locks are big enough for four barge push-
tows. The system, which makes use of the simple fact that freshwater is lighter than
salt water, runs in the following manner:

While the ship is in the lock and the gates are closed, the salt water in the chamber is drained
away through culverts in the floor to one of the two storage reservoirs of 101 and 111 acres
which lie along the Slaak.

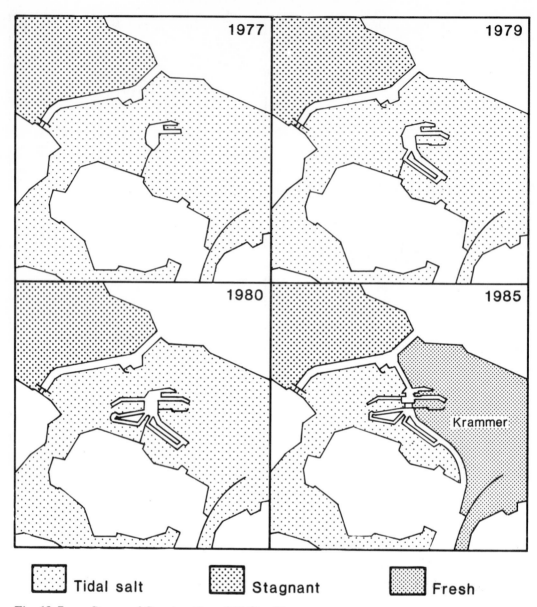

Fig. 12-7   Stages of Construction of Philips Dam

As the salt water leaves the chambers, fresh water is allowed to enter from the sides, flowing over the top of the salt water and maintaining a constant depth of water in the chamber. When the salt water has been completely replaced by fresh water, the gates of the chamber can be opened to allow the ship to leave. The storage reservoirs are equipped with a large pump with a capacity of 40 m^3/s, by means of which the salt water can be pumped from the lower reservoir to the higher one; it is then ready to be readmitted to the lock chamber when needed. The pleasure boat lock will not have storage reservoirs but only a small pump (capacity approx. 4 m^3/s). The fresh water will be expelled and readmitted through apertures in the chamber walls which can be closed by means of steel gates.[13]

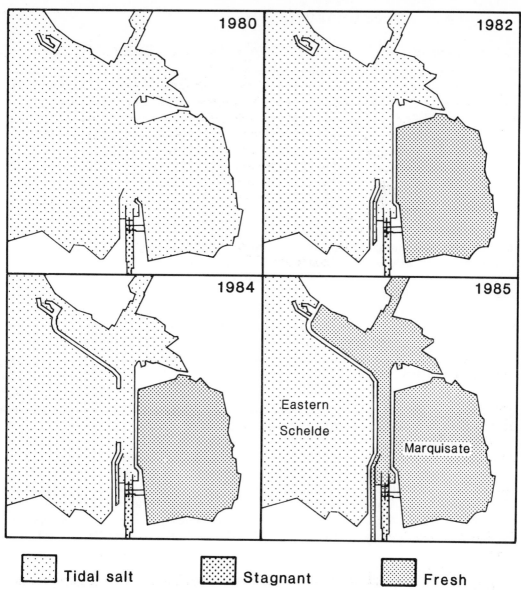

Fig. 12-8   Stages of Construction of Oester Dam

Oester Dam

This dam not only shortens the tidal basin of the Eastern Schelde but it also ensures a
tide-free Rhine- Schelde canal along with the creation of a freshwater lake, Marquisate
(Fig. 12-8). A lock south of Tholen will allow shipping, and Bergen op Zoom will continue to maintain its minor port function. Moreover, this lock, like Philips Dam, also
has a freshwater/saltwater separation system.

TANGIBLE BENEFITS ACHIEVED

Control of Salt Water

Since World War II the penetration of saline water from the North Sea has reached as far as 15 miles (24 km.) up the River Rhine. This incursion of salt water was aided by the diversion of the freshwater of the Rhine and by harbor improvements and the dredging of shipping channels for Rotterdam, now the largest port in the world. As a consequence of the increased salt water penetration, agricultural activities in the area were adversely affected, and Rotterdam's domestic water supply also suffered.

The Delta Project has halted the incursion of massive amounts of salt water through the Haringvliet and the Volkerak as a result of the construction of dams. Raising the bottoms of the shipping channels has further inhibited the inland incursion of salt water. Withdrawal of the Rhine's freshwater from Haringvliet and channeling it through the New Rotterdam Waterway has also pushed the salt water back toward the sea. All these changes will gradually produce an increasingly less brackish north basin of the Delta area as time passes, alleviating agricultural irrigation problems and providing the southwestern part of the country with a freshwater supply similar to that of Lake IJssel in the north.

Sluices can be opened on the Haringvliet dam to allow freshwater to flow into the North Sea when the rivers are high. These same sluices can be opened at high tide to admit salt water, thereby preventing formation of ice during severe winters. Sluices on the Volkerak dam can be opened to permit the flow of a desirable amount of freshwater into the south basin.

Increased Communication

As part of the Project, roads are being built over every dam, and a highway system is being established to link the islands with one another and with the mainland. Before these transportation improvements had been made, the Delta islands were dependent on a limited ferry system. The Zeeland bridge, although not directly part of the Delta Project, has been built across the Eastern Schelde connecting the islands of Duiveland and North Beveland. This 4.96 km. bridge was constructed of prestressed concrete and completed in 1965. With the completion of the storm-surge barrier on the Eastern Schelde, a 55 km. highway paralleling the North Sea, will run from Brielle to Vlissingen.

The transportation improvements have significantly aided Zeelands's potential growth. Port connections also are available. The new network of roads and bridges. Rotterdam lies just to the north and is reached by the new inland waterway (Rhine-Schelde Canal) connects Antwerp and Rotterdam, the largest ports of Belgium, and the Netherlands, respectively.

Increased Recreational Use

The Delta Project has increased economic activity in the South-West particularly, because of newly created opportunities for tourism and recreation. The Netherlands is a crowded country with 881 people per square mile or 339 per square kilometer (1977). It is, therefore, vital that areas such as the Delta Region, situated adjacent to the densely populated Randstad, be made accessible for recreational purposes. The most important recreational activities in the region center on the beautiful beaches and clean riverine water courses. Fishing villages such as Veere and medieval towns such as Middelburg, Goes, and Zierikzee are especially attractive. Moreover, a visit to various Delta Project sites is in itself an attraction for tourists.

Urban Development Potential

To the north-east of the Delta Region lies the Randstad, home for 46 percent of the population of the Netherlands, but comprising only 21 percent of the country's land area. It has already been noted that the government is trying to discourage further urban growth in the heart of the Randstad, although population projections indicate that the core of the Randstad (southwest flank) will still be the most densely populated area of the Netherlands in the year 2000. In the midst of the Randstad is the 'Green Heart' or central green belt, an area that would appear to be a natural outlet for the Randstad's urban overspill. Because of the Green Heart's suitability for high-intensity agricultural uses such as horticulture and the need for open space in the midst of the Randstad, however, the government is discouraging urban development in the area.[14] Instead, urban growth is being encouraged in other areas, including the three northernmost provinces of the Netherlands, Limburg in the extreme south, Brabant, part of Zeeland and in the growth towns near Randstad. The northern segment of the Delta Region, adjacent to Rotterdam, is already becoming urbanized and is expected to be a part of the very high-density area of the south-west flank.[15] The safety guarantee and increased accessibility resulting from the Delta Project have thus augmented the region's capacity to accommodate the Randstad's population overspill.

EVALUATION OF ISSUES

Owing to revisions to the way in which the final gap in the Eastern Schelde will be closed, the Delta Project completion date has been set back to 1986. Moreover, the impact of the Delta Project on the region and the nation will not be fully appreciated for years to come. Nevertheless, a number of questions and issues concerning the Delta Project may be raised, and a few conclusions may be reached.

Safety

The Delta Region will become safe after the completion of the Project. The dikes, the natural dunes, dams, and the storm-surge barrier have not only shortened the coastline, making it easier to maintain, but are expected to withstand the *violence* of a storm that is likely to occur only once in 10,000 years.

Technological Considerations

The Delta Project has been a massive undertaking. It was well planned, and few problems were subsequently encountered. More importantly, however, new construction techniques were employed that will be beneficial in future flood control and land reclamation projects, not only in the Netherlands but all over the world. The Dutch have long shared their technological superiority in the field of hydraulics. The successful accomplishment of the Project establishes that, if modern technology and the will of a nation are combined with a scientifically based long-term planning process, many natural calamities can be averted permanently, and a hazard-free, peaceful environment can be created.

After a rather modest beginning in the late fifties and early sixties, the Dutch hydraulic engineers had created some technological marvels by the seventies. Their perfecting of caisson building, the storm-surge barrier across the Eastern Schelde—particularly the skill in constructing massive piers, their transport by water, and their accurate positioning, and the freshwater/salt water separation system at the Philips and Oester Dams—are not only highly innovative feats but also significant contributions to hydraulic engineering. These only became possible because of research that matured in the process of finding answers to the problems encountered in the Delta Project.

Cost Considerations

The original cost of the Delta Project, estimated at 3 billion guilders (at the 1978 rate, 1 guilder = US $.50), was to be spread over a period of twenty years. This is equivalent to 150 million guilders or 2 percent of the national budget every year. Increased costs, particularly those resulting from the construction of sluices on the Eastern Schelde, however, will add another 3.7 billion guilders at 1976 prices to the expense of the Project. [16] Direct benefits from the Project will account for only half the original expense of 3 billion guilders. Thus, 5.2 billion guilders will have been spent on safeguarding the region against a flood of a magnitude that might occur only once every 10,000 years. Because it is impossible to place a value on human life, the cost of such indirect benefits cannot be reasonably evaluated.

Developmental Considerations

The social and economic effects of development on the people of Zeeland are difficult to predict. The Project has brought machinery, building materials, people, and money into what was essentially a backwater area. Zeeland has been freed from centuries of isolation as a result of the roads and bridges thus far constructed. Distances have been shortened. The new roads provide a direct link with the densely populated Randstad and economic growth has ensued. Industry is being attracted because of local manpower. [17]

On the other hand, residents of small communities, such as Veere, can no longer rely on earning their living by fishing because they have been shut off from the sea. Many of the fishermen's cottages have been transformed into vacation homes and tourists by the thousand are being attracted to these 'quaint medieval villages' and the area's beaches. One might question whether or not such developments are desirable. Meanwhile, Zeeland is changing from a traditional isolated corner of the Netherlands into a fully integrated part of the nation.

Environmental Considerations

The decision to leave the Eastern Schelde open to tide water was made after research into the ecological consequences of three alternatives: (1) Closing the estuary, (2) Erecting a storm-surge barrier with an aperture between 6,500-20,000 square meters, and (3) Maintaining an open estuary. Closing the estuary was considered to be ecologically disastrous because it would not only greatly reduce the density and amount of biomass but would also eliminate commercial shellfish (mussel) cultivation. In the case of the second alternative (erecting a storm-surge barrier), the size of the barrier would determine the character of the ecological changes. Apertures of at least 20,000 square meters would retain original ecology, and apertures smaller than 6,5000 square meters would cause much smaller total amounts of biomass.[18] The third alternative, maintaining an open estuary, would entail much stronger and higher dikes along the shoreline of the estuary; these dikes are not only more costly to build and maintain but are a risky protection against severe storms. The Dutch Delta Project planners and the Parliament selected the second alternative. This meant that valuable sea fisheries and mussel and oyster beds would not be destroyed. Also, the south basin of the Delta area would not become a freshwater lake, obliterating the saltwater-based ecology that has been in existence for centuries.

The revision of the Delta Plan in the mid-seventies took place in large part because of the heightened environmental consciousness of the Dutch people. National surveys conducted by the Social and Cultural Agency indicated that (a) 9 out of 10 people in the country agreed that the government ought to take radical steps to combat environmental pollution and (b) between 1970 and 1975 there was actually an increase in the number of people who were willing to pay for the improvement of the environment.[19] But for the consciousness and will of the people to pay for environmental conservation, the revision of the Delta Plan in 1976 would not have been possible.

REGIONAL PLANNING FRAMEWORK[20]

Four regional planning approaches, including regional safety and protection, maximization of regional specialty, balanced development of regions, and conservation and ecological balance, have played significant roles in shaping the strategy and objectives of the Delta Project at different stages.

For simplification, let us give an analogy of a tetrahedron (equilateral prism) and regard its four corners as the four different approaches. At any given time, four approaches exert requisite force. The ideal point resulting from such force must be well balanced and result from the absorption of force generated by all four corners of the equilateral prism simultaneously in accordance with the need of the situation. In such case the point may or may not stay equidistant from all the corners at the center of the prism. The achievement of balance that allows formulation of an ideal solution for any given situation is highly unlikely in any practical context, yet consideration of each of the various approaches is paramount in evaluating the regional planning approaches in the Delta Project (Fig 12-9).

It has already been mentioned that the primary objective in Delta Project planning was protection of the region from unusual floods associated with sea storms. The objective is in the final process of realization with the completion of the Project in 1986. However, at the end of the fifties, when the Project plan was first prepared, the pull of the safety factor was paramount and the other planning approaches were given only minor consideration.

As the exchange economy advances and the transportation system matures, the idea of regions specializing in the production of certain commodities and rendering certain services that are intrinsically suitable to particular regions becomes a feasible approach in regional planning. In the case of the Delta region, the planners, by constructing inland roads, bridges, and roads over dams and dikes, have opened up the regional potential for an advanced exchange economy. This has resulted in an accentuated

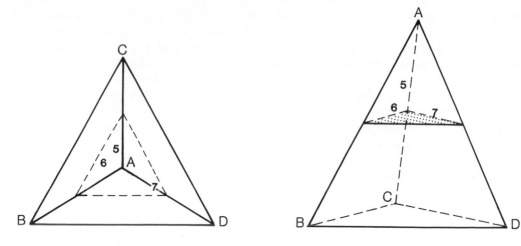

A Safety
B Regional Specialization
C Balanced Regional Development
D Ecological Conservation

Position of the approaches resulting from the pull:
5 at the end of the 50s
6 at the end of the 60s
7 at the end of the 70s

 Limit to safety of the region

Fig. 12-9   A Diagramatic Representation of Regional Planning Approaches to the
Delta Project in the Fifties, Sixties, and Seventies

development of the Delta area not only as a focus of international tourism and recreation but also for agricultural development. In addition, the regional potential for commercial fishing has increased. A selected number of municipalities have also attracted industries. Thus, the Delta area's agricultural and recreation based regional specialty has been given remarkable stimulus by the Project.

The balanced development approach implies that the regional development of a country should occur in a way that allows each region to be at an approximately equal level of development. The policies, therefore should be aimed at minimizing the development of the already developed and maximizing the development of the less developed regions. The Dutch government identified the Delta region as a 'stimulus area' in the fifties because it was considered to be economically depressed. The main purpose of this was to promote economic growth. At the end of the sixties and the beginning of the seventies the Delta Project stimulated the growth of the transport network and decreased the region's isolation from the rest of the country. Then its depressed status was lifted because the region no longer needed economic assistance from the government. The Delta area was not only open to the tourists, recreators, and industrial entrepreneurs but its agriculture was placed on a sound footing. The Delta region is no longer considered a backward or a depressed region and its economic potential compares well with the rest of the country. Thus, by the end of the sixties, there was a relative balance between the three approaches: safety, regional specialization, and balanced development of regions (Fig. 12-9).

Ecological conservation, not a part of the original Delta Project Plan, became an accepted objective by the middle of the seventies. As by then the goal of balanced development of regions was nearly achieved, balance among safety, regional specialization and environmental conservation approaches became the matter of greater concern. The Eastern Schelde's ecology has been preserved and conservation of esturine ecology has become one of the project's main aims.

CONCLUSIONS

In undertaking the Delta Project the Dutch set down very definite objectives, foremost of which was flood control. When the storm-surge barrier across the Eastern Schelde is completed in 1986, the people of the Delta Region will no longer need to live in fear of another flood. Other objectives were (1) desalinization of the country's rivers and channels; (2) increased communication; (3) new opportunities for industry, tourism, and recreation; and (4) the establishment of an inland waterway between Antwerp and Rotterdam. All these objectives have been, or are, in the process of being met. If achievement is measured in terms of meeting objectives, the Delta Project has been an unqualified success.

The Delta Project has also demonstrated how regional planning approaches can be implemented with varying degrees of emphasis at different stages. Though the predominant consideration in the initial phases of implementation of the Project was regional safety, other objectives, such as balancing the Delta region's development with other regions, accentuating its potential for tourism and recreation, and creating a strong agricultural base, became important at a later stage. At no time was the regional safety element compromised to accommodate newly emphasized approaches. The aspect of regional safety was given paramount consideration even though it entailed significantly augmenting the Project cost, when through pressure from conservation groups, the Eastern Schelde was saved from being closed entirely to sea water. Thus, the Delta Project experience teaches us how different regional planning approaches can be appropriately blended without ignoring the main objective.

Many people in the sixties expected that, with the completion of the Delta Project, attention would then be turned to the possibility of another ambitious and expensive project, the closure of the Wadden Sea in the North in a manner similar to that of the Zuiderzee. However, as the Netherlands' recent drastic reduction in its birthrate (13 per 1,000 in 1977) has slowed the build-up of population pressure and diminished the need for expanding farmlands, there is no incentive to reclaim more land from the sea. Moreover, pressure exerted by the environmentalists to preserve the natural features of the relatively unspoilt Wadden Sea region is very difficult to ignore. Finally, the main commitment for the expensive Delta Project was made when the Dutch economy was growing rapidly. Any new large-scale project will be almost impossible to initiate in the depressed economic situation of the eighties.[21]

NOTES

1. M. Snikdelaar, 'The Water Management of the Netherlands', *Planning and Development in the Netherland,* vol. 4, no. 2, 1970, p. 171.
2. For more details, see Johan Van Veen, *Dredge, Drain, Reclaim,* The Hague, Martinus Nijhoff, 1962.
3. Ir. F. Van Schagen, 'The Dutch Deltaplan', *The Snowball,* Institute of Social Studies, The Hague, October 1966, p. 31.
4. Audrey M. Lambert, *The Making of the Dutch Landscape,* London, Seminar Press, 1971, pp. 39-41.
5. Ashok K. Dutt and Robert B. Monier, 'Zuyder Zee Project', *Journal of Geography,* vol. 67, no. 6, 1968, pp. 374-7; A. K. Constandse, *Planning and creation of an Environment: Experiences in the Ysselmeerpolders,* Lelystad, Rijksdienst voor de IJsselmeerpolders, 1976.
6. A Caisson has been defined as a 'huge reinforced concrete box subdivided internally by longitudinal and transverse partitions or bulkheads. A caissson usually has a fixed bottom... It can be floated (towed by tugboats) into position and sunk by admitting water to its compartments through valves. In this way, it will settle down on a prepared base'.... J. S. Lingsma, *Holland and the Deltaplan,* The Hague, N. V. Nijgh and Van Ditmar, 1966, p. 31.
7. The culvert caissons, originally designed in 1922, were not actually used before 1952. They have 'long sides' comprising 'large openings, which can be closed by vertically movable steel sliding gates...'. Van Schagen, op. cit., p. 35.
8. Lambert, op. cit., p. 316.
9. Van Schagen, op. cit., diagram opposite p. 37.
10. For more detailed English-language treatment of the Delta Project see Lingsma, *Holland and the Deltaplan; Report of the Delta Committee: Final Report,* The Hague, State Printing and Publishing Office, 1962; A. Spits, *The Delta Works, Holland's Struggle against the Water,* Amsterdam, Society for Making Holland Better Known Abroad, 1966.
11. *Verkeer en Waterstaat Informatieblad,* no. 22E, The Hague: Information Department, Ministry of Transport and Public Works, 1980, p. 1-2.
12. Ibid., pp. 3-7.
13. *Verkeer en Waterstaat Informatieblad,* no. 22E, The Hague: Information Department, Ministry of Transport and Public Works, 1980, p. 3.
14. See, for more details, Ashok K. Dutt, 'A Comparative Study of Regional Planning in Britain and the Netherlands', *The Ohio Journal of Science,* vol. 70, no. 6, 1970, pp. 32-5; and Ashok K. Dutt, 'Levels of Planning in the Netherlands, with Particular Reference to Regional Planning', *Annals of Association of American Geographers,* vol. 58, no. 4, 1968, pp. 670-85.
15. Based on discussions with Jan kits Nieuwenkamp, Member of the Secretariat, National Physical Planning Agency, the Netherlands.
16. *The Delta Project,* The Hague, Ministry of Transport and Waterworks, 1977, p. 7.
17. Anthony Bailey, 'Profiles: The Little Room', *New Yorker,* 15 August 1970, p. 7.
18. B. F. Goeller *et. al., Protecting an Estuary from Floods—A Policy Analysis of the Oosterschelde,* vol. 1, Santa Monica, Rand Corporation, 1978, pp. 60-90.
19. J. W. Becker, 'Public Opinion and Environment 1970-75', *Planning and Development in the Netherlands,* vol. 11, no. 2, 1979, pp. 179-85.
20. This section is derived from a paper written by the Senior author entitled, 'Approaches to Regional Planning', presented at the Association of American Geographers Annual Meeting in 1981.
21. This chapter is mainly based on an article by the present authors published in the *Journal of Geography,* vol. 78, no. 4, 1979, pp. 131-41, and is printed here with modifications by the senior author by permission of the *Journal* editor.

13
Evolution of Land Uses and Settlement Policies in Zuiderzee Project Planning

Ashok K. Dutt, Frank J. Costa, Coenraad van der Wal, and William Lutz

The Zuiderzee, a bay of the North Sea, was considered for draining in order to extend farmlands and human settlements as early as the seventeenth century. The proposal was given final form in 1918 when the Dutch Parliament approved the Act of Enclosure, an ambitious plan for reclamation of the Zuiderzee. Thus an old idea gradually became a reality through the incremental implementation of a master plan. Rigid adherence to original goals was maintained until the end of the fifties when demands for urban and recreational land use made significant impacts on national policy formulation. By the end of the sixties Dutch environmental groups had become so powerful in molding national policies that they succeeded, not only in shifting emphasis toward preservation or creation of natural surroundings in the newly reclaimed lands of the Zuiderzee but also in calling into question the very completion of the basic master plan. Thus, a rigid master plan process tied to the original objectives gave way to a more flexible approach capable of absorbing different sets of objectives. This new planning process can be called dynamic incrementalism. Table 1 illustrates this concept. The development of the process is the focus of the discussion in this chapter.

In addition to published materials, this study uses unpublished documents and statistics of the IJsselmeer Authority. Farmers were interviewed and several field trips were made in the polders. Though earlier publications on the Zuiderzee Works came primarily from the government or its agencies,[1] by the late 1960s several geography journals published studies on the Zuiderzee Project.[2] Thereafter, planning journals published a number of analytical papers on the planning implications of the Project.[3] In addition, several documents and information materials were published by the IJsselmeer Polder Development Authority.[4] Publications concerning the Project are found in other popular and technical journals.[5] In 1970, *Planning and Development in the Netherlands* published a special issue on the Zuiderzee Project with contributions from seven specialists.[6]

INITIAL FORMULATION OF THE PLAN

Records show that almost all of the Zuiderzee and most of the Wadden Sea were land areas that lay above sea level during the pre-Roman period (Fig. 13-1). During the Roman era inlets from the North Sea began encroaching the Zuiderzee. This encroachment continued throughout the thirteenth century, greatly accentuated by storms and

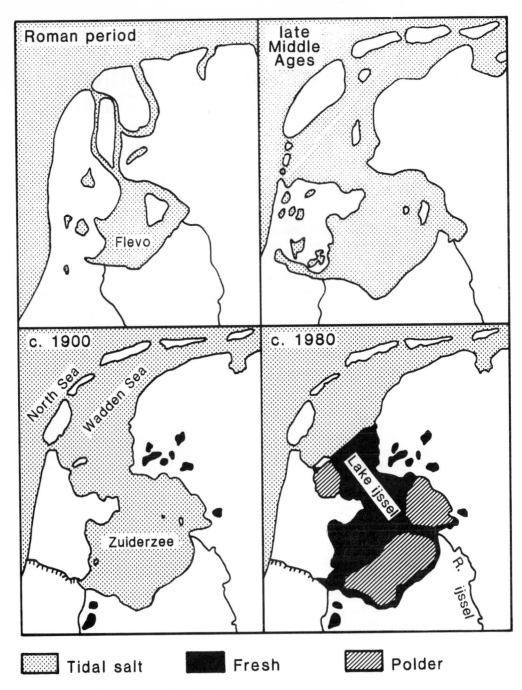

Fig. 13–1   Evolution of the Zuiderzee

floods which created unprecendented havoc in the coastal region of the Zuiderzee. Sizeable coastal areas were reclaimed between 1400 and 1900 through increasingly more advanced forms of technology for impoldering: windmills from the sixteenth century and steam-driven pumps from the nineteenth century. Nonetheless, by 1900 the island of Texel had been reduced to less than half the size it had during the late middle ages. It was against such a background of battle that the plans for the Zuiderzee Project was devised.

As early as 1667, Hendrik Stevin prepared a plan in which he proposed that a series of dams be built to join the mainland with the islands of Texel, Vlieland, Terschelling, and Ameland, that the Wadden and Zuiderzee be reclaimed by draining, and that a new shipping route be constructed along the route of the modern North Sea canal to join the port of Amsterdam with the North Sea.[7] This ambitious plan could not be carried out with the means available in the seventeenth century. Even by modern standards, enclosure of the Wadden Sea, which could entail the damming of deep inlets and draining the deep beds of the Wadden Sea, may be technologically possible, but would be an extremely costly and risky venture. Similarly ambitious but technologically impossible plans were proposed in later times by Van Diggelen (1849) and Wenmaekers (1863–83) (Figs. 13-2B, C). Buma, in 1882, proposed yet another design for the Zuiderzee Project.

In 1848, for the first time Kloppenburg and Faddegon came up with a more practical idea of enclosing the Zuiderzee while retaining the Wadden as saline sea water (Fig. 13-2A). Leemans, in 1875–7, proposed reclamation of only the shallower parts less than 5 meters deep of the Zuiderzee (Fig. 13-2D). All these early plans remained unimplemented, however, until Cornelis Lely (1854–1929) proposed a pragmatic and innovative plan in 1891, which contained the following elements:

1. Enclosure of the Zuiderzee by a dam (later called the Barrier Dam or Afsluitdijk);
2. Retention of the deeper parts of the Bay (more than 5 meters deep) as a freshwater lake, call Lake IJssel;
3. Reclamation of sand and sandy clay parts of the Bay which were better for agriculture than clay soils[8] (Fig. 13-5);
4. Connection of Wieringen island with the mainland of North Holland by a dam;
5. Creation of five polders (Wieringmeer, Northeast, East Flevoland, South Flevoland, and Markerwaard) one after the other; when completed each polder to be used as farmland to augment agricultural production.

Open water areas were to be left between the Northeast and East Flevoland Polders, so that the river IJssel, which carries 10 percent of the Rhine water to the sea, might continue to discharge its water uninterruptedly. The area between the Markerwaard and Flevoland Polders was also to remain open to maintain inland shipping connections between Amsterdam and north-eastern parts of the country. Deeper parts of the lake were avoided from being reclaimed (Fig. 13-5). It was estimated that the plan would require a completion time of thirty-two years with a total estimated cost of 190 million guilders.

Adoption of Lely Plan by the Government

The question of government involvement in a reclamation project involving the creation of polders was resolved by the middle of the nineteenth century, when safety, not the gain of private farmland, became the main objective of large-scale reclamation.

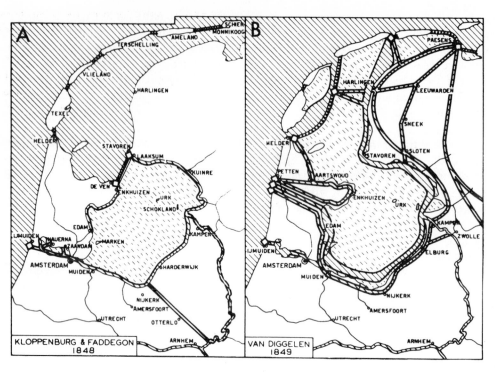

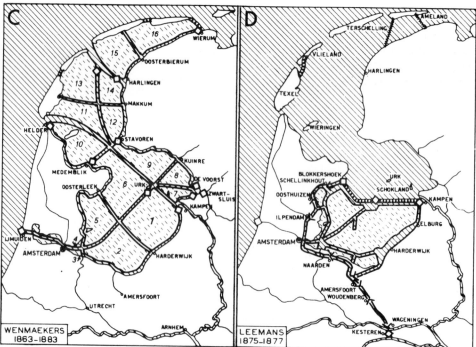

Fig. 13-2 Early Plans prepared for the complete or partial Reclamation of the Zuiderzee (Reproduced from *I.D.G. Bulletin*; permission given by the Netherlands Geography Institute)

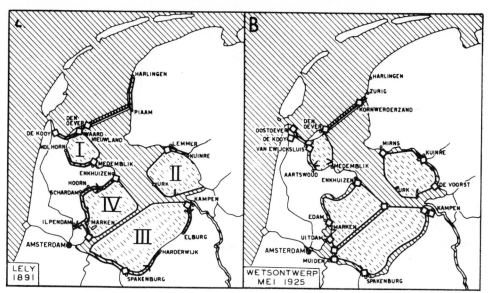

Fig. 13-3   Lely Plan and the Bill (*Wetsontwerp*) of 1925 basically followed in
Reclaiming the Zuiderzee (Reproduced from *I.D.G. Bulletin*; permission
given by the Netherlands Geography Institute)

The Haarlemmer Lake south of Amsterdam, covering an area of 18,000 ha., came to be
regarded as a great danger to the people living nearby as it was likely to overflow during storms and cause floods. Before the advent of the steam pump it was technically
impossible to drain this huge lake, but by the time the new pumping technology had
been acquired, private investment proved shy because any large-scale reclamation
would not bring forth profitable returns. Therefore, the Dutch government assumed
responsibility for draining the Haarlemmer Lake and by 1852 the lake was drained.[9]

Lobbying the government to embark on a Zuiderzee Project for safety and reclamation of land for farmlands took definitive shape in 1886 when a Zuiderzee Association
was formed by private initiative. Lely played a leading role in this association. The
cause received further impetus when Lely became the Minister of Water Affairs in the
1890s and a bill was presented in the Dutch Parliament in 1894 calling for adoption of
Lely's basic plan. Similar bills were reintroduced in 1901 and 1908 but were not approved. Eventually a catastrophe in the form of a flood disaster in 1916 which affected
the low-lying areas of the Zuiderzee coast caused Parliament to embark on the project
by adopting the Act of Enclosing (Official Gazette, No. 354, 1918). After the enactment, the Lely Plan went through some minor changes as described in Figure 13-3A
and then became the Master Plan for the Zuiderzee Project.

THE MASTER PLAN IN OPERATION

The modified Lely Plan (Fig. 13-3B) not only extended the area of the reclaimed
polders, but also earmarked a larger water area between Northeast and Flevoland
Polders and a continuous channel on the eastern margin of the Flevoland Polders. Lely's basic design, however, remained intact and formed the principal framework for the

Table 13-1   The Evolution of the Zuiderzee Planning Process

Initial Formulation of Plan	Incremental Master Plan Goals (Fixed)	Incremental Master Plan Goals (Flexible)	
		Urban/Recreation Impact Phase	*Environmentalists* Influence Phase
Hendrik Stevin (1667)	Parliament Enactment of 1918	East Flevoland (1950–7) and South Flevoland (1959–68) Polder's increased non-agricultural uses.	Increasing emphasis in Flevoland Polders for natural landscapes.
Van Diggelen (1849)	Reclamation of Wieringermeer (1927–30) and Northeast (1937–42) Polders		
Wenmaekers (1863–83)			Preservation of Markerwaard as fresh water lake, scheduled to be reclaimed (1963–80) in accordance with the Master Plan
Kloppenburg and Faddegon (1848)	Construction of Barrier Dam (1927–32)	Master Plan base for reclamation unchanged, but agricultural emphasis progressively decreased	
Leemans (1875–7)			
Lely (1891)			
"Wetsontwerp" The bill of 1925			

Master Plan.

In 1919 the Zuyderzee (Zuiderzee) Polder Authority (hereafter called the Authority) was created to carry out the reclamation.[10] In accordance with the Plan, a dike 2.5 km. long was built at the beginning of the 1920s connecting North Holland with the island of Wieringen. The construction of the 30 km. long Afsluitdijk (Barrier or Enclosure Dam) began in 1927 and was completed in 1932. It created Lake IJseel out of the former bay. The lake was eventually turned into freshwater by draining its stored salt water into the Wadden Sea while freshwater from the river IJssel gradually replaced the salt water (Fig. 13-4).

This was in keeping with the development of the plans for the large polders drained in the seventeenth century which show where villages might develop, but they contained no specific village plans, even though the land itself was carefully parceled and surveyed. This is understandable as there was no need for a large village, and development generally took place along the roads. The Haarlemmermeer Polder was planned along the same lines. Reservations of 16 ha each at two points on the map were deemed sufficient, even though it was three times larger than the largest previously drained polder. Farmers, navvies, and other settlers were left to their own devices creating many hardships, poor health conditions, a high infant-mortality rate, and unplanned and unanticipated settling along the edges of the polder. Many settlers had to leave, often ruined. The saying (loosely translated): 'The first farmer takes a dive, the second farmer stays alive, only the third farmer does thrive,' was certainly true in this polder.

Before embarking on a large-scale land reclamation by polder method, the Dutch planners thought it essential to experiment with a smaller area and to avoid repeating the initial experiences of the Haarlemmer Polder. In 1927 such an experiment was conducted near a small village in North Holland, Andijk, where a forty hectare parcel,

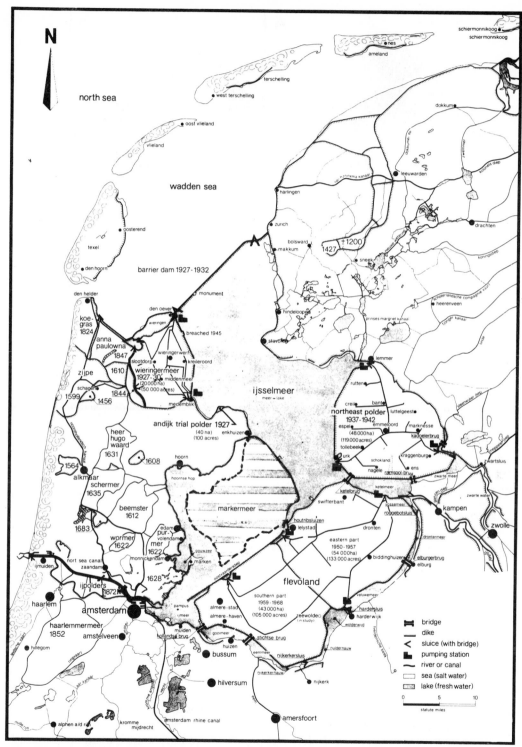

Fig. 13–4 Zuiderzee Polders and Neighboring Reclamations. Dates indicate the Time of Reclamation

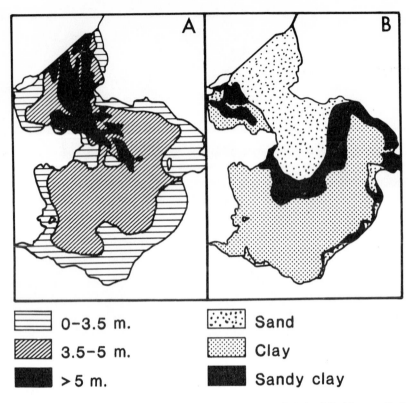

▤	0–3.5 m.	
▨	3.5–5 m.	
■	>5 m.	

Sand	
Clay	
Sandy clay	

Fig. 13-5   The Depth (A) and Soils (B) of the Original Zuiderzee (Lake IJssel)

formerly in the Zuiderzee, was impoldered. The process of draining the sea floor, drying off the drained land, and shrinkage of the soils was studied. Desalinization of the soil, the process of cultivation and choice of crops were perfected. Such useful knowledge was then used by the Authority in the five polders that were to develop thereafter.

Though the processes connected with preparation of land for cultivation and selection of the type of agriculture were carefully researched in Andijk, no serious thought was given to the spacing of settlements, location of central places, or hierarchy of the transport network.

Wieringermeer Polder

Initially, there were indication that the unplanned or spontaneous settlement pattern of the Haarlemmermeer Polder would be used in the Wieringermeer Polder, which fell dry in 1930. At first the village locations were not specified—it was simply stated that 'villages could develop at opportune places at the intersection of roads and canals.' (Canals, besides being water carriers, played an important role as the principal means of transporting farm goods). However, Professor Granpré Molière,[11] the Authority's design advisor, was asked, even before the polders were dry, to look at the problem of the towns, specifically their number and location. Five villages were planned initially,

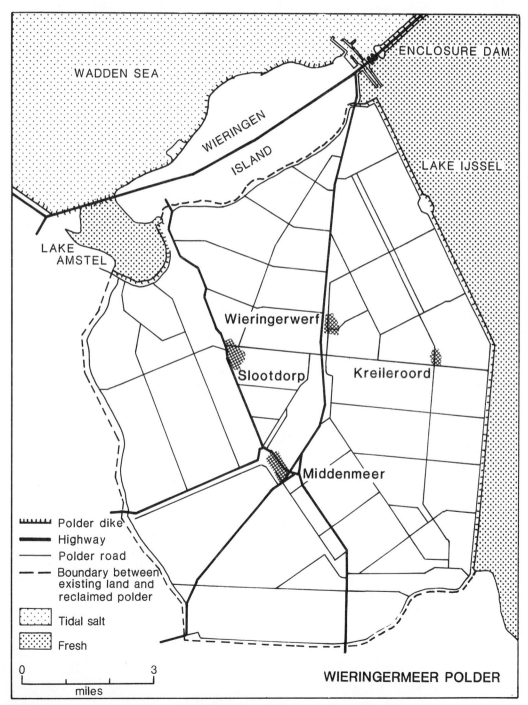

Fig. 13–6   General Plan of Wieringermeer Polder

to be located centrally in the polder, and eight hamlets around its edge where canals and roads came together. But when the Authority made its own calculations on the basis of the number of farms that would be created, it decided that no more than three villages were needed. The locations, though logically situated at intersections of roads and waterways, were unfortunate considering their great distances to the edge of the polder. Nonetheless, the villages were built at their planned locations. Had optimal village siting been the basis of the plan, it would have looked completely different. In the beginning of later polders, the Authority benefited from this experience. In 1931 construction was started on Slootdorp, followed a little later by Middenmeer and Wieringerwerf (Fig. 13-6). As a result of the experiences in Haarlemmermeer, it was decided that the settlement of the new polders should be the responsibility of the national government. The Authority took its task seriously as it was drawn into a regulating and initiating position. It was also the only authority in the new land. It initiated a housing corporation to build inexpensive housing, aided churches through subsidies, helped establish a foundation for the construction of schools, organized health services, supported club life, and in short did its best to get 'normal' rural society 'off the ground' in the shortest time possible. The Authority even decided which people came to the polder to live. Paternalism? Yes, but what else was there in the beginning?

Even before reclamation, the area had been divided among the neighboring municipalities (The Netherlands has no 'unincorporated' areas). However, the polder became a separate entity in 1938, and a legal municipality in 1941. That ended the major involvement of the Authority in the planning process until after the Germans inundated the polder early in 1945, when it again became active in its reconstruction. The destroyed villages were rebuilt in the original locations. A fourth village, Kreileroord, was added in the late 1950s.

As this polder was intended to support a dense population, the parcels had a standard size of 20 ha. or 50 acres. One side of the parcel with a farmhouse bordered a road and the other a canal. Thus a network of parallel roads and canals was developed. This kind of farm settlement was repeated in other Zuiderzee polders. The arable land provides potato, sugar beet, cereal, pulse, and flax-growing with a holding consisting of 2 or 3 parcels (40 to 60 ha.). The dairy holdings consist of 1 or 2 parcels (20 to 40 ha.).

Still predominantly agricultural, with about 87 percent of its total area devoted to farmland in the early eighties, the Wieringermeer Polder is also experiencing some inmigration. Thus an evolution in settlement form is occurring in Wieringermeer since the polder is a recipient of some over-spilled population from the urbanized northern wing of the Randstad.

Northeast Polder

Objectives of the original Master Plan were followed to the letter in the Northeast Polder, as they were in Wieringermeer. Though the work of reclamation started in 1937, the Northeast polder dried up in 1942; its reclamation was delayed by the German occupation, which also hindered the process of land preparation for agriculture. It took almost until 1957 to settle nearly 90 percent of the polder through the leasing of land to farmers. Experience gained from the Andijk Experimental Polder and the Wieringermeer was employed in the preparation of the land.

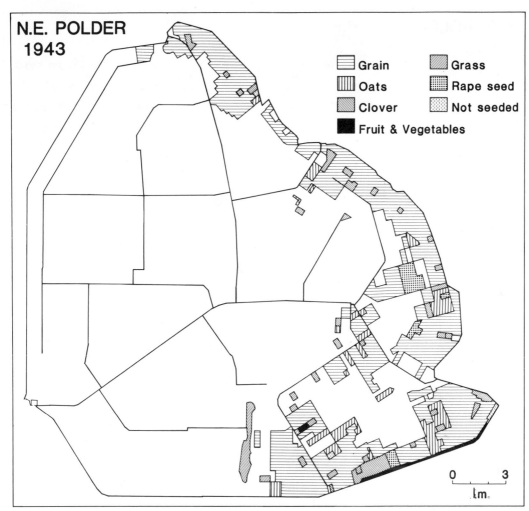

Fig. 13-7   Beginning of Land Preparation in the Northeast Polder. The Reclamation started adjacent to Existing Land where the Depths were Minimal
and Soils were either Clay or Sandy Clay

    The first permanent settlement took place in the northeast corner of the polder and
gradually extended towards the southwest. The series of maps prepared from the
records of the Authority demonstrate successive stages in the land preparation, which
is similar to that followed in other polders and which has been scientifically derived
from experimentation (Fig. 13-7–12). Since government resources and manpower are
limited, the land preparation process is not taken up at once for the entire polder. Each
year several hundred acres are added to the land preparation process. The prepared
land is then turned over to carefully selected farmers.

    Glopper and Smits have summarized the process as follows:[12] When the water is
pumped out of the polder land, the first step is to sow reeds (*Phragmites australis* cav.)
during the first spring. These help to draw water from the subsoil, establish its bearing capacity and discourage weeds from growing. As soon as the land becomes firm

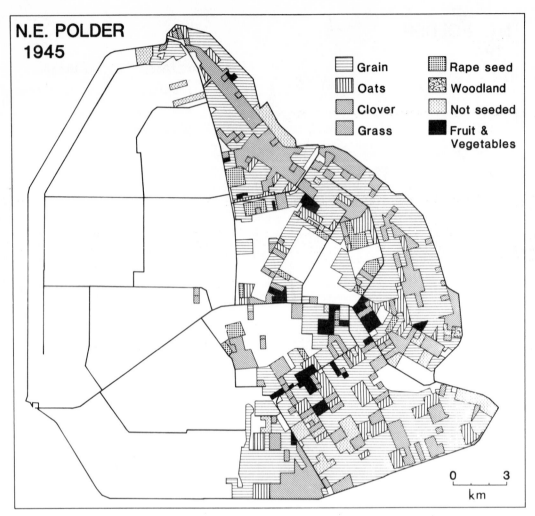

N.E. POLDER 1945

Grain   Rape seed
Oats   Woodland
Clover   Not seeded
Grass   Fruit & Vegetables

0   3
km

Fig. 13–8   By 1945 almost Half of the Northeast Polder Was Reclaimed East of
Major North-South Drainage Canal and a Former Island situated at the
South Center

enough to be capable of bearing machinery, main ditches are dug to drain the parcels
into parallel canals dredged before the emergence of the land. The main ditches eventually turn into underground drainage pipes. Thus their area as a proportion of total
land under processing for agriculture gradually declines and eventually becomes in-
significant (Fig. 13-13). Rapeseed is planted as a first crop after drying, and in rotation
is usually followed by winter wheat, spring barley, sometimes rape again, and oats.
The land is carefully prepared before being leased to farmers for regular cultivation.
Thus, a farmer does not have to face the initial uncertainties of the land as in the
Haarlemmermeer in the nineteenth century.

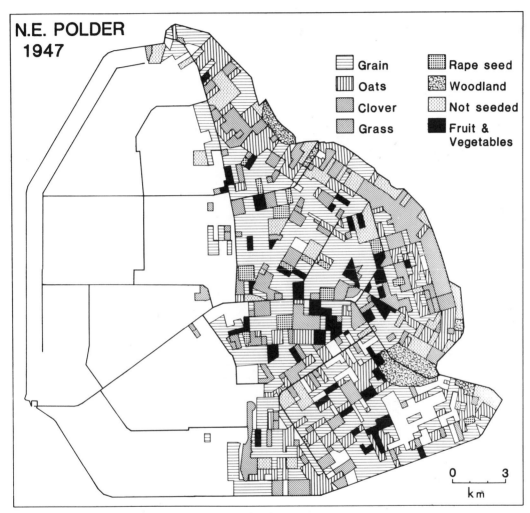

Fig. 13-9   Even Two Years Later the North-South Axis of the Canal remained the
Extent of the Northeast Polder Land Preparation

The Northeast Polder fell dry in 1942. Planting and land preparation or permanent
lease began in the eastern part of the polder adjacent to the mainland, and in the
shallower parts of the Zuiderzee. During the war years (1942–4), reclamation activities
were sluggish. As a result, only a small area of the eastern half of the polder was
undergoing planting. The planting process, however, accelerated after 1947, but until
then the main north-south drainage canal at the center of the polder acted as the boundary line for planting and land preparation.

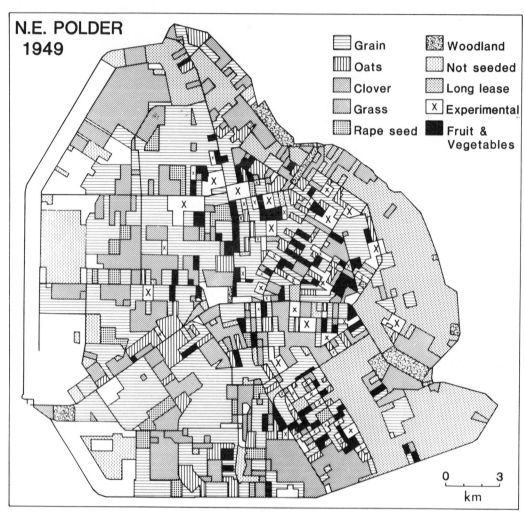

Fig. 13-10   Once the North-South Canal Axis was crossed the Process of Land Preparation was greatly accelerated and within Two Years' Time almost the entire Northeast Polder was brought under Land Preparation. For the First Time, the Farmers were brought in for Cultivation of the New Polder Land under Long-Term Lease Agreements

The accelerated pace after 1947 resulted in almost all the polder land being ready for planting by 1950–2. Thus, because of wartime delays, it took the Authority about 6–8 years to prepare a parcel of land for leasing to farmers, whereas in the past 4–5 years sufficed.

The prepared lands were leased to a number of farmers, beginning in 1948–9, and the process continued until 1957 when there were still some problem lands at the southwestern segment of the polder that were not leased though land preparations had

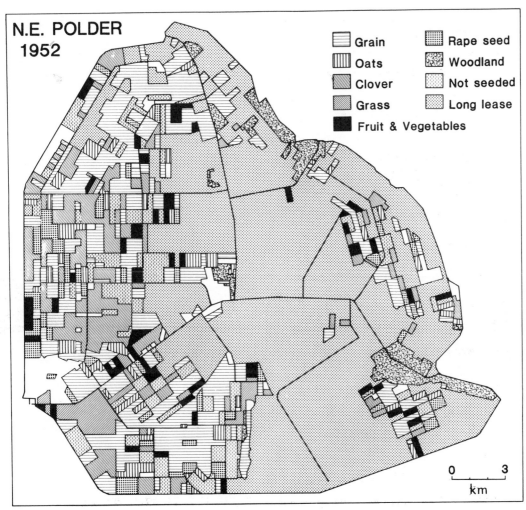

N.E. POLDER
1952

Grain   Rape seed
Oats   Woodland
Clover   Not seeded
Grass   Long lease
Fruit & Vegetables

0   3
km

Fig. 13–11   Three Years Later over Half of the New Polder Land in the Northeast
Polder was given to the Farmers on Long-Term Leases

begun there in the early fifties. There are, thus, some areas which have problem soils
and abnormal relief which take longer to prepare for final lease to farmers than others
that are relatively problem-free.

Figure 6 indicated that when land preparation began (1942–3), almost two-thirds of
the area brought under the initial preparation stage was developed to grain cultivation
by the Authority; this proportion declined progressively, and in 1952, only 17 percent
of the preparation area was allotted to grain, while in 1957, when the Authority had

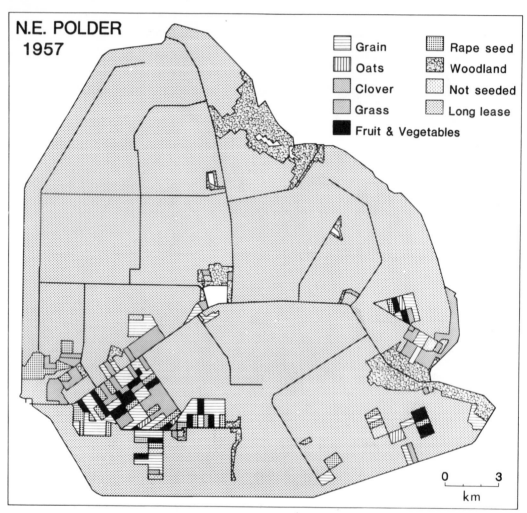

Fig. 13-12 By 1957, Almost All the Cultivable Land was given to the Farmers on a Long-Term Lease Basis

leased 86 percent of the prepared area to the farmers, its own grain area was reduced to 3.3 percent (Fig. 13-13). Virtually no farmland was leased to the farmers before 1947. (Only a negligible 3.9 percent of the total land preparation area was leased that year). However, this jumped to 17 percent in 1949, 47 percent in 1952, and finally to 86 percent in 1957. The purpose of this polder development process was to prepare the land with prior experimentation of grain cultivation and to lease as much of it as possible for farming.

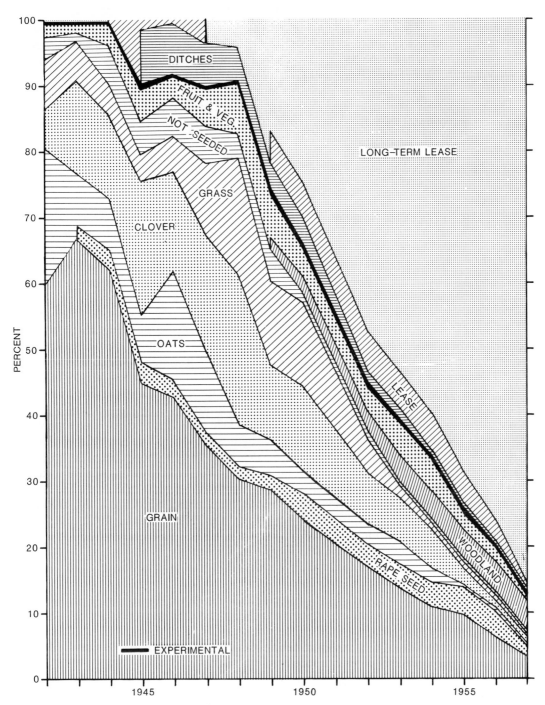

Fig. 13-13   Evolution of Land Use in the Northeast Polder during the Land Prepara-
tion Stage, 1942-57. The 'Percent' on the Vertical Axis indicates the
Relative Shares of Land under Preparation in a Given Year. During the
Early Stages, the Authority planted Grains alternating with Oats, Rape
seed, and Clover for preparing the Land prior to any Attempt to settle
Farmers. At Later Stages, as also indicated by Figs. 13-11, 12, the
Share of Long-Term Lease naturally increased

The farm lands were designated in areas where agriculture was not feasible or otherwise not desirable and their proportions rose progressively to a modest 5.05 percent. The proportionate area not seeded or fallow declined from about 5 percent in 1949 to 1.5 percent in 1957. Thus, in the end all land of the polder was not only designated for specific use but was being used for some purpose.

The mistakes of Wieringermeer in failing to adequately plan for the location of settlements and centers were fully recognized. This realization led to the establishment of a theoretically and empirically stronger basis for the siting of villages in the Northeast Polder. A model of hierarchical centers was adopted in the establishment of a first-order center, Emmeloord, almost at the center of the circular polder, and five new villages as well as the existing village of Kuinre on the mainland, equidistant from each other and from Emmeloord (Fig. 13-14a, b). The six villages would become second-order centers. It was calculated there would be about 45,000–50,000 polder dwellers, of which 15,000 would live outside the centers, 10,000 would live in a centrally located town of regional importance, Emmeloord, and the remainder would be living in the five villages. Distances of 7 to 8 kilometers between nuclei were considered adequate. The other nearest regional centers were identified as the existing towns such as Lemmer, Kuinre and Urk.

This scheme led to objections from those who favored shorter commuting distances. It was argued that experience in the Wieringermeer had taught that the proposed distances were too great (for the bicycle) and a maximum of 4 kilometers was said to be reasonable. Thus a plan was developed for 45 to 55 hamlets, each of which was no more than 4 kilometers from a village and 3 kilometers from the furthest farm. Finally a compromise was reached, and in 1948 a plan was approved which contained one central nucleus, Emmeloord, and ten villages in a ring around it (Fig. 13-14c). The villages were generally located near an intersection of roads (canals had become less important as a mode of transportation). About half of them were located on irregularly shaped parcels, which presumably would benefit the design of the physical plan. Construction on Emmeloord began in 1946. (There had been an abortive beginning during the Second World War). In 1948 village construction began with Ens, Marknesse , and Kraggenburg (planned by F.H. Dingemans). The second group of villages, Luttelgeest, Bant, Rutten (planned by W. Bruin), and Creil, was built between 1950 and 1953. Finally came Nagele (planned by a group called 'the 8'), Espel (planned by Duintjer), and Tollebeek (planned by Nix) in the years 1954–7.

Constandse criticized the above plan because it did not allow for the growing affluence of the people.[13] As automobile ownership increased, the greater mobility of the people led to the weakening of the functions of the centers of the ten villages because most inhabitants found it more convenient to drive to a larger center at Emmeloord and complete their basic shopping needs once a week from there. Moreover, mechanization of farming led to fewer people working on the farms and the number of people in the villages was overestimated.

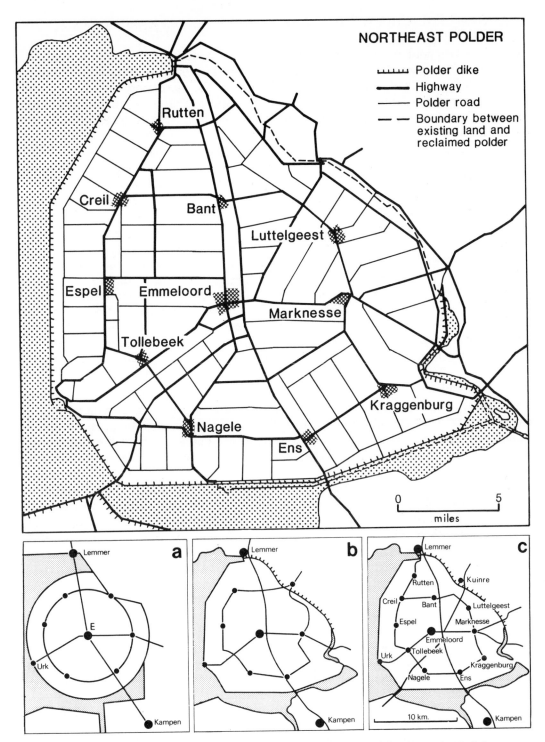

Fig. 13-14   The proposed Location of Towns (a, b) was Based on Christaller's Model of Central Place Theory, but was changed for Northeast Polder (c) to accommodate Larger Numbers of Towns. The Map at the Top represents the implemented General Plan

CHANGING POLICIES WITHIN THE MASTER PLAN FRAMEWORK

In the first two polders the original intent was to provide for agricultural settlement. But several important elements, not apparent in the development of these two polders, began to influence land-use policies. These were: (1) the increasing mechanization of agriculture, making labor-intensive agricultural land use obsolete; (2) the symbiotic relationship between the East Flevoland Polder and Randstad Holland in which urbanization pressures emanating from the Randstad became keenly felt in the East Flevoland Polder; (3) the high level of industrialization in the country generated enough revenue for the purchase of food grains froms the international market, thus lessening the need for agricultural land; (4) policies inherent in the *Second Report on Physical Planning in the Netherlands*, published in 1966, looked to East Flevoland as a region of urban overspill and recreational use for the Randstad residents. The same intentions were strengthened in the *Third Report-Urbanization Report*, in 1976; and (5) the need for a larger area of recreation land use felt.

Therefore, when East and South Flevoland fell dry, one of the basic objectives of the original master plan—creation of new farmland—was no longer emphasized. Later, when Markerwaard was being prepared for drying, a powerful environmental lobby which developed during the 1960s managed to forestall initiation of work on this polder. Thus, from the sixties onward, basic elements of the Lely Plan were called into question and the need to incorporate the new requirements and values of a more affluent and urbanized post-World War II society had to be considered by the planners.

East Flevoland

While the Northeast Polder was being settled, work on the East Flevoland Polder began; and by 1957 the water was out and colonization began. The polder contains 54,000 hectares, comparable in size to the Northeast Polder. In East Flevoland commuting distance figured heavily in the first plans for the siting of towns. A 1954 plan was heavily influenced by experience from the Northeast Polder. A central town of Dronten, comparable to Emmeloord, was set up as a regional center. Ten villages were strewn at equal distances throughout the polder. The average distance between the villages was 7.5 km. In addition, Lelystad was situated along the west edge of the polder, placed there as the super regional town for all the Zuiderzee polders and, possibly, a future provincial capital. As the plans for this polder were made in a period of rapid economic growth in the Netherlands, the validity of small villages with limited shopping and other facilities was questioned. This, and the fact that use of the private car was becoming more and more prevalent, led to a disregard for distance as a norm, and in 1958 there were only six villages left in the plan besides Lelystad and Dronten. These six were further reduced to two villages, Swifterbant and Biddinghuizen, when the plan was finally executed. The first settlers came to live in Dronten in 1962. It is intended to hold 20,000 people eventually. The smaller villages were opened for settlement in 1963. Their eventual size is to be about 5,000 inhabitants each (Fig. 13-15).

In 1961 a report was published entitled *A Structure Plan for the Southern IJsselmeerpolders*. Its publication was evidence that the polders were becoming important on a national planning scale. The report describes the relationship of the polders and their towns to the surrounding country. The polders were losing their

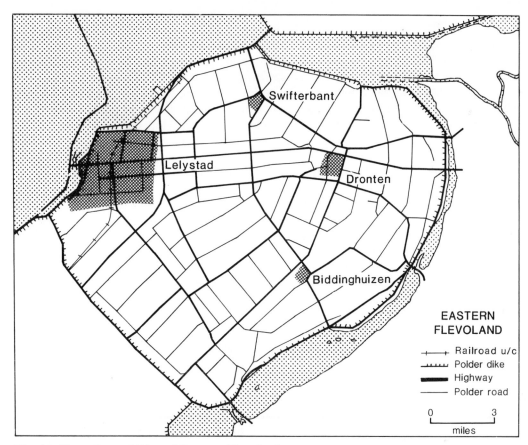

Fig. 13-15   General Plan of Eastern Flevoland

isolation as work progressed on the reclamation of Southern Flevoland. This was the link to the 'Randstad' and the nation realized that the polders could be used to release the pressure of urban population, which had been building up in the Randstad since the end of the World War II. The report called for Lelystad to become a city of 100,000. Another large urban settlement in the southwest corner of Southern Flevoland area was advocated. In 1959 Cornelis van Eesteren was asked to develop a master plan for Lelystad. It was completed in 1964. Construction began in 1966, and in 1983 more than 50,000 people were living there.

East Flevoland provides the most suitable soil base for agriculture because only 4 percent of its total land area is sandy soil in comparison to 16 percent for the Northeast Polder and 31 percent for Wieringermeer. Nonetheless, the pressures for urbanization and reservation of land for recreation prompted the Authority to put only 75 percent of its land area to agricultural use. This compares with 87 percent in both the Northeast and Wieringermeer Polders. Moreover, due to mechanization and the increased income level of the farmers, the average size of the agriculture holding in East Flevoland was raised to 41 hectares.

South Flevoland

The patterns of land use set in East Flevoland were continued in South Flevoland after it fell dry in 1968. Only 50 percent of its total land area has been earmarked for agriculture with 50 hectares as an average farm. As much as 25 percent of its land area has been allocated to woodland and nature conservation, which amounts to about 20 percent more acreage in this category than that of the three earlier polders combined.

The Second Report, published in 1966, clearly showed that polder towns were no longer of local or regional concern, but were of national importance. While the first polders had their villages planned simply as support centers for an agricultural population, in East Flevoland the city of Lelystad was established, to a great extent, independently of its agricultural surroundings.

In South Flevoland the planned urban settlement was no longer to serve exclusively local needs. The intent was to provide space for the spill-over from the north wing of the Randstad—a truly urban plan with heavy ties to the old country. The major settlement is Almere, intended to house to up 250,000 people by the year 2000. In early 1984, its population was 35,000.

In South Flevoland no centers other than Almere and Zeewolde have been planned because previous experience demonstrated that additional centers to serve the farming population were unnecessary in the era of automobiles (Fig. 13-16).

Of all the Zuiderzee polders, South Flevoland has earmarked the largest proportion of its land for urban use because it was reclaimed at a time when the Randstad required overspill land.

Markerwaard

If the Flevoland Polder reclamation altered many of the basic objectives set forth in the original master plan, the Markerwaard may prove to be the plan's undoing because, in the face of objections raised by environmental groups, the Dutch Parliament has not approved any money for the final drying up of this polder. In 1972 the main dike separating the Markerwaard from Lake IJssel was completed, but no further steps have been taken to complete the dikes along the western and southern edges or to pump out the water from Markerwaard.

The environmentalists object to the reclamation of this polder on the following grounds: (a) the fresh waters of the Markerwaard area, in existence since the early thirties, have generated an aquatic ecology which, once destroyed, cannot be replaced; (b) the area has turned into a European bird sanctuary, to which birds from as far away as Siberia migrate during the winter; and (c) this area is the only large body of freshwater available so near to the urban complex of Amsterdam and can be used for both drinking and recreational purposes.

The supporters of the project, including the Authority, argue that so much public money already spent should not be wasted by retaining the Markerwaard area as another freshwater lake. Moreover, this area after reclamation will not only provide for the urban expansion of the northern wing of the Randstad but will be capable of accommodating a number of recreation land uses in its basic plan so that the nearby city dwellers can make use of them.

The Authority has also examined six alternative possibilities and has made a cost-benefit analysis of per-acre reclamation cost for each. Its finding suggest that the sixth alternative with maximum reclamation area is the most economic.

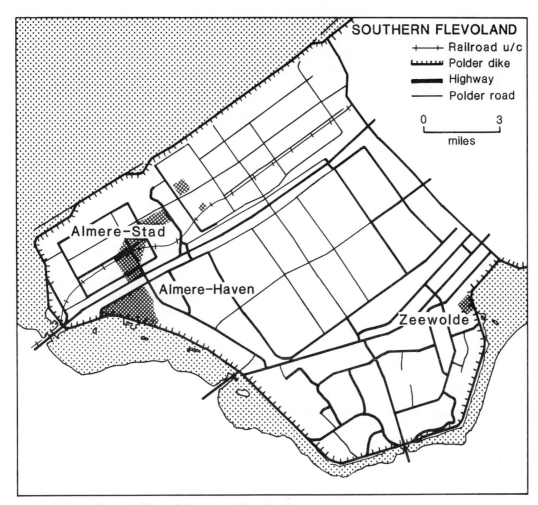

Fig. 13–16   General Plan of Southern Flevoland

Some possible land-use scenarios have also been advanced for the Markerwaard after reclamation. Whatever option is adopted after reclamation of the polder, it is evident that recreation and urban land use will be quite important. Some part of the polder may also be kept as an extensive lake and bird sanctuary.

Other reasons why Markerwaard reclamation has not taken place as yet include the fact that new farm land is no longer a national priority. Natural population growth in the Netherlands has been cut drastically and the prospect of natural disasters such as the 1916 floods no longer exists. Since the mid-1970s the pinch of austerity in public spending is being felt increasingly and as the years pass the possibility of reclamation, because of these factors, will continue to diminish.

INTERVIEW WITH FARMERS

Farmers from the Wieringermeer, Northeast, East Flevoland, and South Flevoland
Polders were interviewed to ascertain (a) their feelings about the move to the new
farmland; and (b) the characteristics of farming that have evolved in the new
polderland. In the last three polders the farmers interviewed were the first generation
farmers who had cultivated the land since it was first leased. In Wieringermeer Polder,
because land was leased there over 50 years ago, no first generation farmer was found
and the person interviewed was a second generation farmer. All the interviews were
carried out in the summer of 1980 by two of the authors (Dutt and Van der Wal).

Interview in Wieringermeer Polder

The farmer interviewed was 50 years old; he had taken over the farm from his father in
1956, who had received it from the Authority in 1938. The father had been a 'polder
worker' in the Wieringermeer for some years before getting the farm. Before that he
had a farm in South Holland, but lost it in the Great Depression of the 1930s. He was
still alive at the time of the interview and lived in a nearby village. The farmer interviewed had a son who was interested in farming but believed that the farm was not
large enough for two families. He discussed the possibility of having his son work with
him on a part-time basis, instead of hiring occasional help, but concluded that this
would not be practical because his son would require additional means to support
himself. This farmer would have liked more acreage, but the initial investment would
be too high. The farmer also has a daughter. Both son and daughter have agricultural
college degrees. His son now works as a farm manager in Saudi Arabia.

The farm is 44 hectares in size and is leased on a basis of a twelve-year term. The
lease is adjusted every three years. He grows sugar beet (25 percent), potatoes (25 percent), and wheat (50 percent). He leases a few hectares to a bulb grower. He manages
the farm alone, though at harvest time he hires additional help and cooperates with his
neighbor on certain harvesting activities. At harvest time he sells the cereals and
stores the potatoes, which he later sells to dealers. Sugar beet is harvested and hauled
directly to a processing plant. He owns three tractors, two wagons, and one machine
each for plowing, sowing, soil tilling, potato planting, potato digging, spraying, straw
bailing, and a combine, which is also used by his neighbor.

The size of farms in Wieringermeer Polder ranges from 8 to 70 hectares. There are
forty farms of between 65 to 70 hectares which is a larger average size than in the
Northeast polder. There have been some changes in the land use. There are few mixed
(dairy and crops) farms left. Shifting from one type of agricultural land use to another
is fairly common in Wieringermeer polder because the government land agent's permission is easier to get here than in other Zuiderzee polders. Crops have changed over
the years; now the rapeseed, and carroway are no longer cultivated. Bulb flower
culture has developed over a number of years and covers an area of 1,250 hectares to
date.

Interview in the Northeast Polder

The farmer interviewed had 55 hectares of land, though the minimum farm size in this
polder is 24 hectares. Some farmers now own two 24-hectare holdings because larger
farms are more profitable. Those who own or lease 24-hectare farms need to undertake

intensive farming, such as growing small onions for canning, carrots, spinach, and seed potatoes. Most devote their land to a single crop, but often combine spinach and potatoes. Small parcel farmers share machines with two or three farmers or rent them at a low cost.

The farmer interviewed (aged 62) came to this polder to lease his farm in 1955, when some parts of the Northwest Polder were still not ready for leasing. He came from Groningen, where he owned 40 hectares and cultivated wheat, oats, green peas, and beans. For him it was not much of a change to produce potatoes and sugar beet on two-thirds of his new land. On the remaining one-third he cultivates wheat, oats, green peas, and beans. Though his family in Groningen had farmed there for six generations, the move to the new farmlands of the polder brought him considerable financial gain and, therefore, he did not regret making the move.

Those who lease the farmlands in the polder cling to them until their retirement, when they move to a nearby village. The farms are generally passed on to their children, who have virtually a legal right to lease them, if they wish. There is, then, little turnover among the farmers.

Consolidation of two 24-hectare holdings is desired by most farmers and some are able to add another holding by making a lease agreement in the name of their sons or in-laws. Not too many farmers end up having a 48-hectare farm because it involves the down payment of cash. If one obtains a bank loan for the land lease purchase, this means a regular mortgage payment at a rate which is frequently too high to be economic. This is the main reason why the small farms fail to consolidate into larger ones.

As the farmhands became to costly and mechanization took over, the 24-hectare farmers farmed the land themselves. Thus, the small government owned houses, which were built for the farmhands, were no longer required for the purpose for which they were built. They are often sold to city dwellers or to the farmers at a low price. The city dwellers use them as a second home or turn them into their permanent residence. Farmers who bought these houses often sell them to city dwellers for a sizeable profit.

Interview in the East Flevoland Polder

The farmer interviewed (aged 55) came from Friesland to lease his land in 1971 and now cultivates 55 hectares. The lease is open-ended and, in effect, permits the farmer and his heirs to lease the land in perpetuity. When he first arrived, such terms of lease were still available, but now the longest-term lease is for forty years or one generation. In the East Flevoland Polder there are two kinds of lease-holders: those with long-term leases (40 years), and those (the majority) with short-term leases (12 years). Only the farmers who invested in farm building from their own funds were offered the more preferred long-term lease.

The farmers have to pay an annual rent, based on the lease agreements, which is subject to revision every six years. Such arrangements are applicable all over the Zuiderzee polders. The farmer interviewed stated that he can pass on to his sons the terms of his lease. He considers the lease arrangement to be as good as private property rights. His rental for one hectare of land in 1971 was Df. 290, but in 1980 this was increased to Df. 700. The rental basis is determined initially by the type of soil, the highest being clay-sand. The revision of rent is made on the basis of a coefficient, the calculation of which is dependent on production and value of production. The highest coefficient (PWC) is considered to be 100. Such a basis of initial rent determination and its subsequent revision is universal for the Zuiderzee polders. The interviewed farmer's land has been given a PWC of 95, while his neighbor's is 100.

Though the farmer voluntarily made his move from Friesland, where he operated a 40-hectare dairy farm, he had no problems in adjusting to the environment of the new polder because the landscape and life-style are similar and East Flevoland is not far from his home in Friesland. Moreover, his new polder farm is not only larger, but also more productive because of the excellent soil. He had only 50 cows in Friesland with a few machines, but during his ten years in East Flevoland he has amassed 210 milking cows, 150 calves, 3 tractors, 2 mowers, 2 self-loading trucks, 2 silos for storing grass, and an electric milking device to milk his cows. He grows all his grass on the farm. He has a modern farm and has put a lot of capital into it.

The East Flevoland farmer may be a crop or dairy farmer and, sometimes a farmer combines the two. The farmer interviewed was bound by the base agreement to maintain his land as a dairy farm because it is classified as a cultural reserve. One end of his land borders a scenic highway and the pastoral view offered by a functioning dairy farm is considered aesthetically desirable. The farmer, however, is not upset by this arrangement. He is happy as a dairy farmer because he knows this kind of farming best.

He plans to retire at the age of 60 or 65, and then the farm may be passed on to one of his sons (aged 26 and 28), who help to run the farm in collaboration with a farmhand who lives in the village.

Interview in the South Flevoland Polder

This farmer (aged 45) moved to South Flevoland in 1979 when the first land was open for lease. There were 400 applicants for 39 farms and he was selected because he was in the process of losing his farm in Gelderland due to land consolidation and because he was a dairy farmer. The soils of the new farmlands were most suitable for dairying and were allocated to those who had experience in dairying. The farmer had farmed in Gelderland for twenty-five years and his father also was a farmer.

The size of his farm (44 hectares) is comparable to that of his Gelderland farm, which, however was scattered over five different areas. As the farmer was interviewed in 1980, he had no idea of his actual profits. He did expect to earn more than he had in Gelderland.

The farmer's lease is for twelve years and he is confident that lease renewal is automatic. In his case the rental payments for the lease are to be revised every three years.

The Authority built his home and barn, though he paid for the interior furnishings and the farming machinery. He was able to make sizeable investments because he had made a profit by selling his Gelderland farm. In his new farm he has 135 cows, 90 calves, 7 horses (a hobby), 2 tractors, 1 feed-spreader wagon, 2 mowers, and an electric milking machine for milking cows. He believes he has an excellent modern farm compared to his older and fragmented one in Gelderland.

His farm is devoted to grass and corn, some of which is stored behind the barn for the winter months and covered by thick plastic and used tires. He grows vegetables for his own use.

CONCLUSION

The Zuiderzee planning process has incorporated ideas and values from many different periods. At the foundation of the process are the initial concepts proposed prior to Lely, whose plan then constituted the second phase. This was followed by a phase of compromise between conflicting goals for development. A shifting or evolving rationale for polder development can be understood when each polder is placed within the context of the policy and values of its period. Thus, the underlying rationale for the Flevoland Polders differs markedly from that for the Wieringermeer and Northeast Polders.

The experience of polder-building in the Zuiderzee also provides a means of understanding evolving land-use policies and the economic condition of the Netherlands. Several distinct stages in the polder building period can be identified:

1. The early period emphasizing agricultural settlement and productivity for an economy still largely based upon agriculture.
2. A later period of shifting priorities in which the need for agricultural settlement was less, but the importance of agricultural productivity was still high (this is reflected in the larger average size of the individual farmstead).
3. The more recent period of allocating increasing amounts of new polder land for 'urban overspill'. The two most recent polders—East Flevoland and South Flevoland—are the sites for two large urban settlements. One of them, Almere, is intended to absorb new population from the older Randstad towns.
4. Allocation of an increasing proportion of new polder lands for recreational use.

Thus, planning objectives have been continually changing since the inception of the polder building period. From an early emphasis upon agricultural settlement to the more recent emphasis upon living space for the crowded populations of the Randstad, the development strategies for the polders have been in large part a reflection of the cultural and economic state of the nation.

NOTES

1. *The Zuyder Zee Works*, seventh edition, The Hague, The Netherlands government information service, 1959; *From Fisherman's Paradise to Farmer's Pride*, The Hague, The Netherlands Government Information Service, 1959; *Zuyder Zee Worker-Land out of the Sea*, The Hague, Board of the Zuiderzee Works, 1964.
2. Ashok K. Dutt and Robert B. Monier, 'Zuyder Zee Project,' *The Journal of Geography*, vol. LXVII, no. 6, pp. 374-7; H. M. H. Van Hulten, 'Plan and reality in the IJsselmeer-polders', *Tijdschr. voor Economische en Sociale Geografie*, vol. 60, no. 2, 1969, pp. 67-76; H. Smits, 'Land Reclamation in the Former Zuyderzee in the Netherlands', *Geoforum*, vol. 4, no. 4, 1970, pp. 37-44; A. K. Constandse, 'The IJsselmeerpolders, an old Project with New Functions', *Tijdschr. voor Economische en Sociale Geographie*, vol. 63, no. 3, 1972, pp. 200-10.
3. A. Rogers, 'Changing Landuse Patterns in the Dutch Polders', *Journal of the Town Planning Institute*, vol. 57, no. 6, 1971, pp. 274-7; A. K. Constandse, 'New Towns in the Netherlands', *Town and Country Planning*, vol. 44, no. 2, 1976, pp. 126-9.

4. H. A. Bruning, H. Hoeve, and F. C. Zuidema, *Development of Flevoland Factors Ruling the Balancing of Rural and Urban Uses*, Lelystad, Rijksdienst IJsselmeerpolders, 1974; A. K. Constandse, *Planning the Creation of an Environment* (a reappraisal), Lelystad, Rijksdienst voor de IJsselmeerpolders, 1976; *Flevoland Facts and Figures, Lelystad, Rijksdient voor de IJsselmeerpolders, 1976.*

5. R. J. de Glopper and H. Smits, 'Reclamation of Land from the Sea and Lakes in the Netherlands', *Outlook on Agriculture*, vol. 8, no. 3, 1974, pp. 148-55; H. Smits, 'Land Reclamation in the former Zuyder Zee', *Agri-Holland*, May 1981, 1-19; B. Fokkens and M. Puylaert, 'A Linear Programming Model for Daily Harvesting Operations at the Large-scale Grain Farm of the IJsselmeerpolders Development Authority', *Journal of Operational Research Society*, vol. 32, no. 7, 1981, pp. 535-47; R. J. de Glopper and W. A. Segeren, 'The Lake IJssel Reclamation Project', *Endeavor*, vol. 30, no. 110, 1971, pp. 62-9.

6. The following articles were published in a special issue of the *Planning and Development in the Netherlands*, vol. 4, no. 1, 1970; O. S. Ebbens, 'The Administrative Organization of the IJsselmeer Polders', pp. 28-41; M. Klasema, 'Water Management', pp. 2-27; J. C. de Koning, 'Social Development', pp. 79-93; P. Loos, 'Recreation in the open air', pp. 107-22; H. Smits, 'Agricultural Aspects', pp. 62-78; A. J. Venstra, 'Villages and Towns in the IJsselmeer Polders', pp. 96-106; L. Wijers, 'The Zuiderzee Works within the frame of Physical Planning', pp. 42-61.

7. *Zuyder Zee Lake IJssel*, The Hague/Utrecht, The Information and Documentation Centre, 1975.

8. Dutt and Monier, *op. cit.*

9. Constandse, *op. cit.* (1976), pp.4

10. The authors refer to the civil service authorities who are at work in the polder simply as: 'The Authority'. A brief history of the different 'authorities' is as follows:

The construction of the first Zuideerzee polder was a task assigned to a new department of the Ministry of Transport and Public Works called the Zuider Zee Project Department (1919). In 1930 another department was placed next to it, the Department for the Cultivation of the Reclaimed Lands of the Wieringermeer, or 'Wieringermeer Direction' for short. It is under the same Ministry. Both departments have moved several times and are now located in Lelystad. The Wieringermeer Direction changed its name in 1962 to IJsselmeerpolders Development Authority.

Civil government duties were left to a 'Public Authority', inititated in the Wieringermeer in 1938 under the Ministry of the Interior. It is an interim government till the establishment of a regular municipal government. In the Northeast Polder in 1942 a 'landrost' (administrator comparable in function to a mayor) was established to head the as yet unincorporated polder area. Almere was under this system of administration till 1, January 1984 when it became a legal municipality.

11. Granpré Molière, M. J. (1883-1972), was a Dutch architect and professor of architecture at the Delft Institute of Technology (1924-53). He searched for: '...eternal truths in architecture. He rejected all other perishable trends. Beauty is truth. Beauty is obtained when one maintains a harmonious relationship between technique and form without letting one dominate the other.' See Giovanni Fanelli, *Moderne Architectuur in Nederland, 1900-1940, Staatsuitgeverij, 's Gravenhage*, 1978, p. 173. The architecture of Granpré Molière and his followers, known as 'the Delft School', is characterized by the use of traditional Dutch forms and materials.

12. *DeGlopper and Smits, op. cit.*, 1974, p. 150.

13. Constandse, *op. cit.*, 1976, pp. 7-8.

14
The New Towns of the IJsselmeerpolders

Coenraad van der Wal

INTRODUCTION

A 'new town' may be defined as a town which in terms of size, physical plan, social and functional content has, to a considerable degree, been decided upon before any construction has taken place. The Netherlands had no history of new towns until 1930, when the Zuiderzee land reclamation project was begun and new land was created by draining large portions of that formerly inland sea. This land, in order to become habitable, needed not only arable acreage, roads, canals, and the like, but also settlements of various sizes to serve various functions, such as housing, shopping, industry, office space, etc., for the support of the rural settlers. The settlements with these facilities for the educational, social, cultural, and religious needs of the population, formed true new towns on new land. The development of the Dutch new town has been simultaneous with the reclamation of the Zuiderzee. The development of this project continues today as does the development of new towns. It is a process that is influenced by changing economic, social, cultural, and technological circumstances. The following is a description of the historic process concerning the physical plans, starting with the formation of the first planned villages, continuing with the present day, and culminating in the planning and subsequent construction of the new town of Almere, designed for 250,000 inhabitants.

To say that new towns did not come into existence until they were situated in reclaimed land, or 'polders',[1] of the former Zuiderzee is in a broader sense not entirely correct. The Netherlands does have some planned settlments in the form of fortifications, or garrisons, which were planned as a whole, containing the necessary military facilities as well as housing for artisans, shopkeepers, their businesses, and of course, churches; so that both the physical and the spiritual well-being of the inhabitants could be catered for. An example of this type of settlement is Willemstad, created under William I in 1583 at a strategic point along the delta waters of the Southern Netherlands to aid in the fight against the Spanish. It is built on the site of the village of Ruigenhil, the plan of which can still be recognized in the present town plan. Another example of this type of settlement is Bourtange[2] in the Northern Netherlands. Other settlements could qualify as new towns in a broad sense, including Heveadorp, built in 1914 to house factory workers and, to choose a large one, Zoetermeer (started in the 1960s) could qualify as it is a planned community whose size is out of proportion with the original village of that name. But the real new towns in modern history are those located in the former Zuiderzee, or, its proper name—the IJsselmeerpolders.

Location of the towns

The previous chapter has explained how, why, and where towns and villages in the IJsselmeerpolders have been located. (See also Fig. 13-1 of the previous chapter for identifying town and village locations in this chapter). The schedule below lists the settlements in order of their development (Table 14-1). When starting on the Wieringermeerpolder the Authority[3] initially emphasized the agricultural aspect of making the land habitable, but soon it attracted the expertise to deal with all aspects necessary to the attainment of a balanced spatial and social development of the new

Table 14–1　Zuiderzee polder settlements

Name of town	planned by	constr. started	date municipal status given	originally planned for	population nucleus	as of rural	1-1-'82 total
Slootdorp	M.J. Granpré-Molière	1931		1,500	1,379	703	2,082
Middenmeer	M.J. Granpré-Molière	1933	1941	2,000	2,795	694	3,489
Wieringerwerf	M.J. Granpré-Molière	1936		1,500	4,685	394	5,079
Kreileroord	W. Bruin	1957		800	769	673	1,442
Wieringermeer polder				total	9,628	2,464	12,092
Emmeloord	M.J. Granpré-Molière Authority	1946		10,000	18,485	857	19,342
Ens	Authority	1948			1,586	1,093	2,679
Marknesse	Authority	1948			2,161	1,146	3,307
Kraggenburg	F.H. Dingemans	1948			699	807	1,506
Luttelgeest	Authority	1950			687	893	1,580
Bant	Authority	1951	1962	2,000	676	600	1,276
Rutten	W. Bruin	1952		max. per	637	885	1,522
Creil	Authority	1953		nucleus	746	756	1,502
Nagele	'De 8'	1954			1,056	886	1,942
Espel	M. Duintjer	1956			763	740	1,503
Tollebeek	Th. Nix	1956			571	815	1,386
Northeast Polder				total	28,067	9,478	37,545
Dronten	J. Van Tol	1960		20,000	10,474	1,470	11,944
Biddinghuizen	R. Hajema	1961	1972	5,000	3,558	1,038	4,596
Swifterbant	W.J.G. Van Hourik	1961		5,000	3,780	558	4,338
Lelystad	C. Van Eesteren Authority	1966	1980	100,000	47,446	731	48,177
East Flevoland				total	65,258	3,797	69,055
Almere	Authority	1974	1984	250,000	20,062	50	20,112
Zeewolde	Authority	1983	1985	8,000	0	493	493
South Flevoland				total	20,062	543	20,605
IJsselmeerpolders (Zuiderzee Polders)				TOTAL	123,015	16,282	139,297

Authority refers to Zuiderzee or IJsselmeerpolder Authority

Source: Compiled by the author.

polders. As can be seen in the schedule, the plans for the villages in the Wieringermeer were made by 'outside' consultants, the Northeast Polder towns were planned partially by consultants, partially by Authority planners. In East Flevoland the Authority planners at first concentrated their efforts on the implementation of the Van Eesteren Lelystad plan, followed by the development of their own plans for Lelystad. For the planning of Almere in South Flevoland a special task force was formed within the Authority to plan the largest town of the polders.

THE WIERINGERMEERPOLDER

The choice of Granpré-Molière[4] as the aesthetics advisor for the Wieringermeerpolder villages was a logical one. He was a well-known architect, professor at the Delft Institute of Technology, had experience with large-scale projects, and his philosophy must have been sympathetic to the Authority, which had been fighting to create an environment fit for human occupancy. He pleaded for an architecture that was 'humble and self-effacing'. He looked for the harmonious proportion between structure and form; his architecture was romantic and conservative. The products of this philosophy are generally described as being of the 'Delft School'. The Delft School had great influence in the Netherlands until well after World War II. Outside the Netherlands this style never received much publicity as it was not innovative and drew its inspiration from traditional, indigenous architecture. Followers of the modern movements in architecture, generally emanating from the 'Stijl' movement[5] were unhappy with the results in the new polder. One of them, a planner named Cornelis van Eesteren,[6] criticized the new villages, in both their plans and their architecture, as being a missed opportunity. His chance came in the fifties when, as part of a group of CIAM[7] designers, he planned the village of Nagele in the Northeast Polder and again when he made the masterplan for Lelystad. He is still a consultant in planning matters for the Authority.

After this introduction it will come as no surprise to the reader that the Wieringermeer village plans had no revolutionary concept behind then, but neither did they have the well-established form of the small-scale centers that manifest themselves generally in Holland as narrow streets, a square, or a combination of both. The concept of the three pre-war towns is basically the same: the main entrance road leads to a wide elongated green area, 60 to 70 m. wide, consisting of long lawns lined with trees. Local traffic is led along the edge of the green. Actually, they are rather un-Dutch, reminiscent of the village greens of England. Shops, important buildings, and churches (usually three, one Roman Catholic and two Protestant churches of different denominations) are located along the edge of the green. That the 'green' is meant as a spatial element only and not as an activity area is borne out by the closeness to the central green of a soccer-size sports field. Industry is traditionally situated along the canal (transportation route). In Middenmeer (Fig. 14-1) the cemetery is rather close to the center, a phenomenon one finds also in some Northeast Polder villages. Sports fields, the ice-skating areas, and other (more recent) facilities complete the amenities, which together with the residential areas were located initially on about 40 ha. per village. In 1936 the trade magazines felt it still worthwhile to mention that all utilities were underground. With regard to the main through-roads, Granpré insisted that they led through the

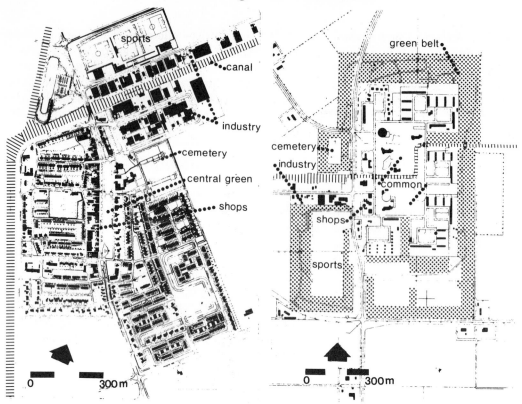

Fig. 14-1   Middenmeer—Plan   **Fig. 14-2   Nagele—Plan**

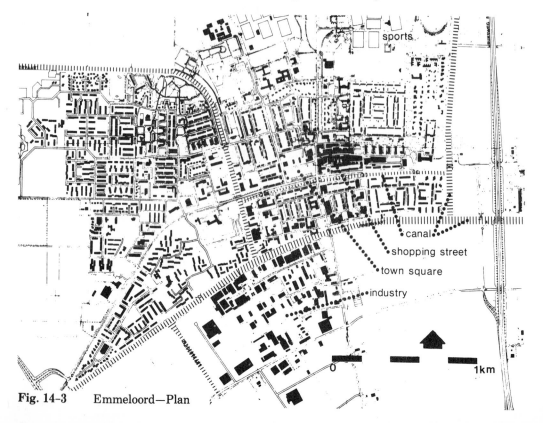

Fig. 14-3   Emmeloord—Plan

town to enliven the local scene[8] In Wieringerwerf, however, the main road bypasses the town.

S.J. Van Embden, an architect from the Delft School, praised the villages in 1933 as the best and purest work that the young science of town planning had delivered: 'every settlement has gotten its own character in harmony with place and function in the polder, because one has related to the differently located parameters in a logical and unbelabored manner'.[9] Of the towns in the Wieringermeer Mumford has stated: 'Although Holland is preeminent in urban culture, the Dutch have not yet given the Zuyderzee development the stamp of the best modern communities around Amsterdam or the Hague.'[10]

Kreileroord was added in 1957 and remains a small village of one main road and a few rectangular housing blocks at the side.

THE NORTHEAST POLDER

Granpré also formulated a plan for Emmeloord, in the center of the Northeast Polder, as did several Authority planners. Professor Wieger Bruin, the planner of Kreileroord, commented: 'Several planners . . . have worked at the concept and subsequently it has become not altogether simple, but lively it is.'[11] Bruin reacted favorably to the plan (Fig. 14-3), claiming it to be thorough, and it does have a pleasant 'ambiance' to it. It has the Dutch small-town flavor, with a canal running along its center, its open space with a tower, and its curved street for shopping. The main roads point straight to the center of town. With its more than 18,000 inhabitants it looks the part of a thriving regional center.

Of the villages in the Northeast Polder it can be said that they follow a pattern which has been set in the Wieringermeer: a wide entrance space with grass, trees, and the road. Shops and principal buildings are situated along the edge of the open space. Industry is placed along the canal. One problem, which has been commented on by several planners, is created by the fact that generally there are three church buildings, none of which may have a dominant position in relation to the others. It is thus impossible to make one church the spatial focal point of the town, as is usually the case in traditional situations. De Boer also mentions that 'one experiences a reduction in (spatial) scale in comparison with the polder'.[12] De Boer deems this a negative quality. Van Leeuwen, on the contrary, argues that 'compactness (togetherness) has not been part of the conceptual planning instructions'.[13] It seems logical and even desirable, considering the wide flat openness of the polder, that one would experience a reduction in scale. In fact, most villages do not seem to have enough of that compactness to satisfy the comfort of the villagers.

Special mention must be made of the town of Nagele (Fig. 14-2). Its form is distinctly different. The basic shape is that of a large rectangle. The center of town is formed by a large rectangular common, consisting of an enormous lawn with trees placed in a grid-like pattern. The common is bordered by a ring road on the outside of which are clusters of dwelling units. The clusters themselves contain their own small green squares. The dwellings are situated on the north, east, and south sides of the common. The fourth side is formed by shopping and service establishments and a cafe-restaurant. To the west of this lies the main thoroughfare. A canal goes through the center common in an east–west direction. Schools and churches are located in the large central common and the whole village is surrounded by swathes of woods to protect it from the wind and to define it as an entity in the open polderland. It was designed by a group called 'the 8'.[14] This group consisted of 'modern' designers from several disciplines and formed part of the Dutch contingent of the CIAM. The group made the plans because they wished to contribute to the 7th Congress of the CIAM, held in Bergamo in 1949, a design solution for a contemporary village. They asked the Authority for a realistic program for one of the as yet unplanned villages. The Authority's reaction was positive. It stated that if the plan were acceptable, it might be used as the design for one of the villages, which in fact did happen.

The first plans show a development which makes use of the irregular corner that is created by an angled road in the southwest corner of the property. The concept of the large green in which public buildings could be located was obvious in an early stage. Using the analytical, rational, and functional approach toward the uses of buildings and space, a simple rectangular plan eventually emerged with differentiated zones for living, shopping, working, and recreational use. It had a simple traffic scheme and the dwellings were optimally oriented towards the sun. The village, by virtue of its plan, has an identity which is distinctly different from the others.

EASTERN FLEVOLAND

As stated in the previous chapter, Eastern Flevoland has four settlements: Dronten as the polder center, Lelystad oriented to the west as an urban center for all southern IJsselmeerpolders, and two villages, Biddinghuizen and Swifterbant. Ir. Van Tol, the planner for Dronten (Fig. 14-4), was commissioned in March 1958 to draw up the 'structure plan'.[15] Dronten's position on the outside bend in the canal was used by the designer as a spatial feature. He stated: 'For this plan I deem essential the grouping of several elements (such as neighborhoods, shopping districts with markets, sports facilities and industrial estates) around the large body of water at the canal. With this concept I have tried to group the different functions of Dronten in such a way that an integrated entity is created.'[16] Major thoroughfares are located outside along the edges of the town, with roads for local traffic coming from different directions going straight to the center. In 1965 plans for a community center were finalized. This center had space under its roof for all kinds of community activities—a meeting-place for the population, or 'a covered square in a pedestrian area', as the architect Van Klingeren called it. As a result of this approach Van Tol was asked to see if the central area could indeed be made car-free. He designed a loop around the center which entailed a drastic change in the structure plan.

The plans for Biddinghuizen and Swifterbant are similar in that they have a simple entrance road with shopping facilities. Both villages have a loop road from which smaller streets go into the neighborhoods. Biddinghuizen has a small square at the end of the entrance road, whereas Swifterbant has a large traffic-free 'green', bordered by a number of housing blocks that have free pedestrian access to the green.

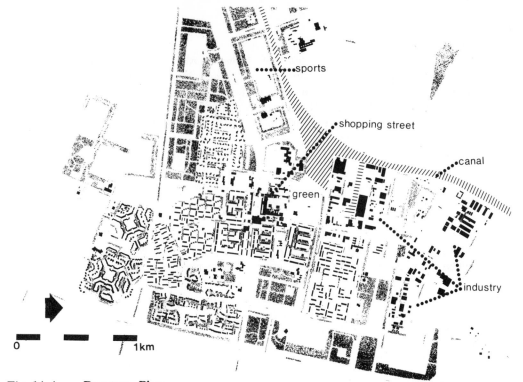

Fig. 14-4   Dronten—Plan

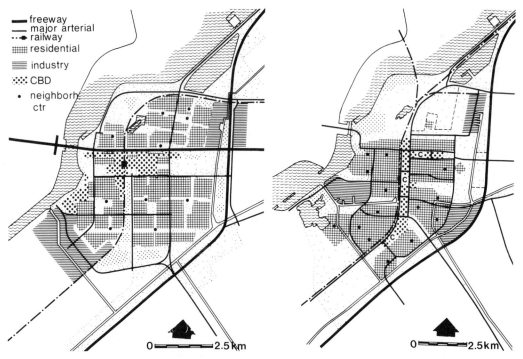

Fig. 14-5   Lelystad Structure Plan 1964   **Fig. 14-6**   Lelystad Structure Plan 1978

Lelystad

Up to this point town and village plans had been made for 'local consumption' only. Even Emmeloord and Dronten were not designed to become more than regional centers, but the position of Lelystad was different from the start. It was to have the 'allure' of a provincial capital, a town that could stand by itself. When Van Eesteren was given the commission to carry out the planning in 1959, he was charged with making a structure plan for 50,000 inhabitants while bearing in mind the possibility of further growth up to 100,000 inhabitants. Following the structure plan he was also to provide the detailed plan for one-third of the town of 50,000. In July 1964 Van Eesteren presented his scheme (Fig. 14-5)[17]. This scheme was considered as a phase in the town's growth to 100,000, after which Van Eesteren envisioned further growth to the west into the next polder. At the time, this polder, the 'Markerwaard', was supposed to have been ready for occupancy by 1980.

The plan presented a rational and, in principle orthogonal, pattern dominated by a grid of highways about 1,500 meters apart. These highways were planned to be on dikes about 3.50 m. above ground level, the idea being that pedestrian and other local roads which had their own network could pass on ground level beneath the main highway grid. This system was not altogether new; it was at the time being employed in the 'Bijlmermeer', a large tenement development extension to Van Eesteren's own Amsterdam. The advantages are obvious, but the disadvantages, particularly in a low-rise, low-density town like Lelystad, would be the high cost of the dikes, viaducts, and bridges; and the effect of so many dikes on the townscape would at the very least be questionable. In accord with CIAM principles, there is a separation of functions: industry in the north and south and the CBD in an east–west zone. The plan met with a great deal of opposition. It was based on a rapid uninterrupted growth to 100,000 (in 35 years), which in 1965 seemed very uncertain. It was, therefore, important to have plans at intermediate stages of 17,000 and 50,000 inhabitants that would have a state of completion, so that, in the event Lelystad would stop growing or grow slower, the town would not have a form or function that would be out of balance with the number of inhabitants. The minister responsible deemed this aspect to be inadequately met in the Van Eesteren plan, particularly with reference to the low housing density and the town's lack of a linkage to the IJsselmeer waterfront. Finally, the minister charged the Authority with the responsibility of making plans for a neighborhood of 2,500 dwelling units within the framework of Van Eesteren's structure scheme. Construction began in 1966 with the first housing complex and main road system, which was, contrary to the original plan, put on ground level. Separation of automobile and slow traffic was accomplished in the new scheme by putting the main roads on ground level, while slow traffic (bikes and pedestrians) routes crossed them via bridges.

The Authority's advisors together with the sociologist E.W. Hofstee, presented a new study of Lelystad in 1969 in which adjustments had been made to the Van Eesteren plan. The rigid grid had disappeared and the CBD had been moved to another location, in a north–south direction parallel to the railroad. The advisors stressed the 'urbanity' of the plan, which meant that they advocated higher densities and an urban life-style with concomitant amenities in the social, cultural, and commercial areas. It was still an automobile-oriented town; little attention was paid to public transit, even though pedestrian and bicycle traffic would be catered for with their own paths, and bridges, across the highways. It was anticipated that car ownership would continue to rise to 400–500 cars per 1,000 inhabitants. As Lelystad gradually built up, a number of adjustments became necessary. The most important was that the densities indicated on the 1969 plan could not be met by using the existing row house form, with backyards, frontyards, public play areas, and other space-consuming areas. The plan had to be expanded to include more residential areas, thus necessitating the elongation of the central north–south zone. This zone would in particular change the character of Lelystad because instead of one shopping area there would be two in the central zone (in addition to the already planned east–west shopping area). The northern one would be the center of all of Lelystad and would include a theater, indoor sports facilities, a swimming pool, and an office-center and a shopping center. The other shopping area would then be the shopping facility for the southern residential districts. The rest of the central zone was to contain all non-residential, non-industrial facilities such as shops, offices, banks, high-density apartments, a hospital, high schools, a hotel, and cultural and social services. In the residential districts small centers would be located near facilities for daily shopping needs with some small-scale business and commercial uses. Another important change was the (re)introduction of a grid of slow-traffic paths. These paths have since become important functional and spatial elements in the design of neighborhoods. The 1978 structure plan (Fig. 14-6) incorporates all the foregoing changes and is the basis for the future development of Lelystad.

Looking at today's map of Lelystad (Fig. 14-7) one notices that the concept of a highway network is still present. The north–south central zone has developed as the central business and commercial zone. The original center is now a district shopping center. The shape of the neighborhoods has gradually changed under the influence of design trends and an increased concern for the rights of the pedestrian, brought about by the deteriorating road manners of Dutch motorists. The first neighborhoods exhibit the rectangular planning of the 1960s, generally having a ring road and some short dead-end streets. Here and there in the early 1970s a daring planner threw in a diagonal or a curve, eventually resulting in the curved free-form road pattern of the middle and late 1970s, wherein cul de sacs, sudden bends, obstacles, bumps, bottlenecks, turns, etc. were to discourage the motorist from speeding. In this way, through-traffic was deliberately hampered or made impossible. On a national level this concern for safety in residential areas has led to legislation which restricts the movement of automobiles in certain residential streets to a walking speed and gives the pedestrian the right-of-way. These areas are called *woonerf*, loosely translated as 'street with an extended yard function', and are identified by special traffic signs. Some areas in Lelystad have been designated as woonerf.

SOUTH FLEVOLAND

Planning for a town of Almere's magnitude required a special approach, and the Authority had to consider carefully how to get the job done. It had taken over the planning of Lelystad in 1965 and had gained experience with the planning of other new towns in the polders. Early in 1971 it was decided not to hire an outside advisor, but to form a task force: a 'project bureau' within the IJsselmeerpolder Development

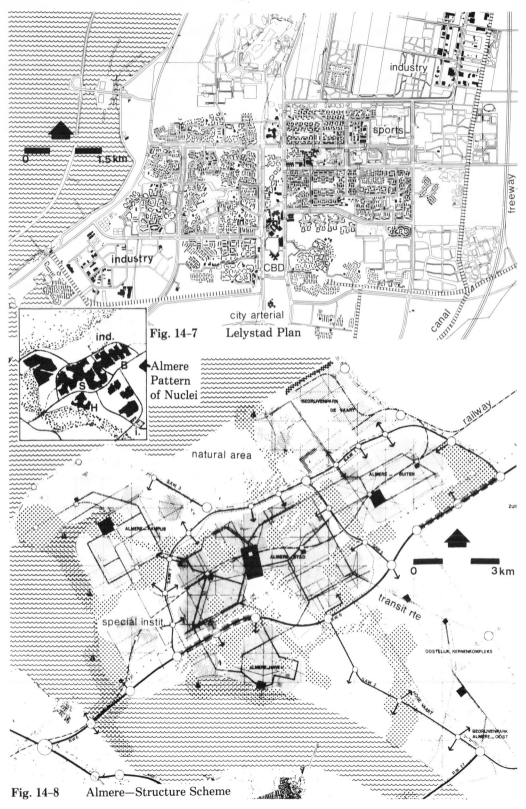

Fig. 14-7   Lelystad Plan

Fig. 14-8   Almere—Structure Scheme

Authority. This bureau, which eventually expanded to include about eighty people—mostly planners of diverse disciplines—with the help of many experts from other departments of the Authority as well as private consulting firms, planned a town with a polynuclear concept. The Project Bureau started by gathering pertinent information with regard to new towns and the growth of cities. They studied new towns in Europe, particularly the British ones. (Milton Keynes was at that time a little ahead in its planning and had similar goals.)

The 1970s were a time of great social change. The 1960s had brought wealth to the Netherlands, more so than to other European countries because of its immense natural gas deposits. Salaries increased and the welfare state arrived. Ownership of an automobile was now within the reach of every worker. We have seen how this affected the Lelystad plan. The high-rise apartment phase of the 1960s had passed and row housing was now to be the answer to mass housing needs, located close to green areas, but also close to schools, shops, and public transport stops. However, this was also the time of the report of the Club of Rome, 'Limits to Growth'[18] and the time of the energy crisis. Bicycle paths and public transport routes were now to be the major communication lines throughout the town.

Almere was to be the town where ordinary people could live in a single-family row house, with a garden, located close to recreation areas and to services, with both a rural and an urban flavor, where the car need not be used to get around, where children could play safely in the streets, and where work was plentiful. At an early stage the planners came up with the concept of the polynuclear city, i.e. a city consisting of several nuclei or townships. This concept would allow for accessibility to continuing green zones throughout the city and would keep major infrastructure out of residential areas. Its other advantage was that it offered great flexibility because final design decisions could be made at various stages regarding the physical structure of the town and its social development. The rate of growth in each nucleus could be kept within the limits of what is technically and socially desirable, i.e. construction could be carried out in a number of areas yielding a high yearly output. Differentiation between nuclei would be a logical possibility—with different trends, times, and planners. The size of the nuclei varies between 100,000 for the central nucleus, large enough to contain a center (CBD) of nuclear and city-wide importance; and 25,000, smaller but able to support a complete shopping and service package. The idea underlying this concept is that hierarchy coupled with complementarity will provide a complete package for the satisfaction of the physical and spiritual needs of the people of Almere.

The structure scheme that emerged (Fig. 14-8) shows how the polynuclear concept has been spatially interpreted. In the north and south are industrial estates (700 and 200 hectares respectively) for those enterprises that cannot be situated close to the residential areas because of their size, extensive land use, or pollution effects. Some areas outside the nuclei are reserved for future specialized use, such as institutions. The major green areas can be divided into intensive recreational use (sports, allotment gardens, etc.), extensive recreational use (parks, woods, etc.), and agricultural use (farms of all sorts). This may be as good a place as any to dwell briefly on the fact that the land as well as the town is new. This means that every tree, shrub, and footpath has to be planned, and that the environment has to be physically shaped: highs and lows, plains and ponds, open space and forests, biotopes for spoonbills, and dirt fields. Cooperation between the urban planner and the landscape architect is essential. The planner must realize that the landscape architect can only provide a framework for development. An urban planner has a tendency to want to 'finish' his environment, at least in the physical sense, which is fine as long as he realizes that he too is providing a framework for the development of the community that eventually makes up the real substance of the town.

The major infrastructure is the railway that runs southwest–northeast through Almere with six stops and connects the Randstad with Lelystad. It is scheduled to come into operation in 1988. The possibility of a connection from Amsterdam via a northern route across a future dike in the IJsselmeer is being considered. Local mass transit will be taken care of by separate routes in the form of a network connecting all neighborhoods with important points like stations, centers, and other mass facilities. Another separate and more or less independent system is that of the slow traffic routes, i.e. bicycle and pedestrian routes. They cross auto-routes on different levels, as they do in Lelystad, except that in Almere the path usually goes through a tunnel, because this requires less height than would a bridge across the highway. Last but not least, the auto-routes have been designed to keep vehicular through-traffic out of the neighborhoods as much as possible. Major highways are situated along the edges of the residential districts in order to keep through-traffic out. In Almere-Haven this principle has led to a tree-like road structure: from the outside, on one trunk, the road branches off into the neighborhoods with dead-end streets. This keeps through traffic out but it is very inconvenient for service traffic and frustrating for the unwary motorist, who knows where he wants to go but does not know how to get there. This system has therefore been adjusted in other nuclei so that, while it is possible to go through, it is definitely not worth one's while. It should be clear from the above that a major feature of the Almere plan is the separation of large parts of its traffic system from other functional spaces. This approach was adopted for reasons of safety and convenience, but is somewhat contrary to the principle of the integration of functions which, it was intended, should be adhered to in the planning of Almere. Unlike Lelystad, which is something of a patchwork quilt, Almere has been planned with an express and explicit regard for continuity, both spatially and functionally, i.e. spaces and functions are considered in their relationship to adjacent spaces and functions.

The first nucleus to be developed was Almere-Haven (Fig. 14-10). The concept for the basic plan is quite simple: a public transit loop is formed by a string along which a number of beads, the stops, have been evenly spaced. The stops form the central points of neighborhoods (90 percent of all dwellings must be within a 400 m. radius from a transit stop), with their highest density around the stop and their lowest around the periphery. Near the centers are the neighborhood schools and shopping. The center of Almere-Haven was deliberately located near the water, as are traditional Zuiderzee towns. Siting the town near the water was an important factor in deciding where to locate the first nucleus. It was thought that 'the psychological effect of visual contact with the old land' would enhance the attraction of the new town to newcomers.[19] The idea of a romantic town appealed to the planners, who were reacting against the plans of the 1960s with their dull rectangular patterns of 'row-house' neighborhoods and with their 12 to 15 story high-rise apartment slabs placed parallel to one another in a Corbusian manner. Lelystad never considered high-rise housing and neither did Almere. Almere-Haven was to have row-housing designed in such a way as to form 'cozy' spaces, hospitable neighborhoods, not with 90° angle corners

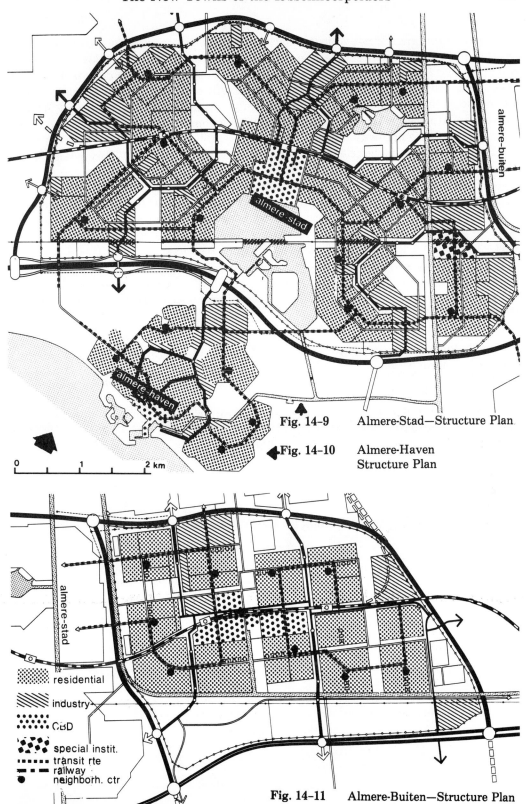

Fig. 14-9   Almere-Stad—Structure Plan

Fig. 14-10   Almere-Haven
Structure Plan

0   1   2 km

residential

industry

CBD

special instit.

transit rte
railway
neighborh. ctr

Fig. 14-11   Almere-Buiten—Structure Plan

but with obtuse angles, not wide but narrow, car-free streets, and a canal through the center of town. The architecture also reverted to the small scale, with low roofs, small windows, and facades segmented into pieces with a discontinuity in design. This trend was aided in Almere by the philosophy of the traffic engineers. It has been mentioned in the description of Lelystad, but it actually originated in the design of Almere-Haven. In Almere the traffic system adheres to a consistent hierarchy of auto-roads, from the four-lane highway down to the small neighborhood streets. The more direct the contact with the pedestrian, the narrower and shorter the road. This meant that at the neighborhood level roads had to make pronounced turns at intervals of no more than 45 meters. This explains why the Almere-Haven plan has a non-directional quality about it. Almere-Haven's design philosophy is not unlike that of the villages conceived in the first Zuiderzee polder: traditional, recognizable forms must be used and the new and experimental, at least in spatial form, must be shunned. This philosophy was criticized in a 1934 trade magazine by Van Eesteren, et. al.:

The heart of the matter is this, that in a landscape with its own very special character, as that in the Wieringermeerpolder, a landscape of business-like directness and contemporariness, as in the rest of Europe can hardly be found; the deliberate romanticism, as found in the concept of the villages, is uneqivocally misplaced.

And of the architecture the article states:

The possibilities that existed here for grand and important but naturally risky experiments have been completely cut off. One has remained Dutch sober and realistic and one is extremely satisfied with that. It is an attitude whose consistency and honesty one has to respect. Should one, on the other hand, be proud of it . . . ?[20]

Almere-Haven's center has integrated shopping, business, and living (often vertically). There has been an attempt to make the townscape continuous with 'seamless' transitions to create an urban environment.

Table 14–2   The target populations for the Almere nuclei

Name of Nucleus	Targeted Population	
	Minimum	Maximum
Almere-Stad	80,000	100,000
Almere-Haven	20,000	25,000
Almere-Buiten	30,000	40,000
Almere-Pampus	40,000	60,000
Rest	5,000	25,000
Total	175,000	250,000

Recent economic development have brought pressure to bear on the population density, increasing each of the Almere-Stad and Almere-Buiten figures by approximately 10,000.

This sense of continuity has played an important part in the planning of Almere-Stad as well (Fig. 14-9 and 14-12). The central nucleus is expected to have a population of 100,000. It has been designed on the same premises as Almere-Haven, but by different planners at a later date. The public transit route has a prominent place in this plan as a spine for the residential districts which radiate out from the CBD. The curvilinear quality of Almere-Haven has been abandoned and the straight line reintroduced as an aid to orientation toward the center. This center (Fig. 14-13) of 50–60 hectares lies between a man-made lake in the south and the main railroad station in the north. Its character is completely different from the romantic old-town flavor of Haven. It has a center of grander proportions, rectilinear, with a high density of buildings, shopping streets, avenues, etc. The architecture reflects this different approach , with the designs tending towards neo-rational ('post modern') form language. The residential districts also follow rectilinear patterns, with long streets reserved for slow traffic. They generally parallel the transit routes. Rowhouses are arranged in blocks enclosing relatively quiet areas, consisting of individual gardens and small common playgrounds. When closed blocks are used the corner-building solutions are usually expensive and often awkward. The economic recession that started in the late 1970s has caused architects and planners to shy away from this type of solution. Other less expensive plans have therefore been made, and one sees that the more recent neighborhoods, towards the extremities of residential districts, have architecturally simpler plans. Since Stad is much larger that Haven, a number of main highways loop through it from which automobiles can branch off into the different districts via the hierarchical pattern of streets. As in Haven, measures have been taken to slow traffic in the neighborhoods so that there is no threat to pedestrians.

The third nucleus, Almere-Buiten (Fig. 14-11), was designed within the same parameters as Haven and Stad, but (as can be readily seen from the plan) with its own interpretation regarding the use of space, volumes, and lines. The plan has been simplified to the point where there are only two major directions. These directions have been taken from the polder's ditch pattern. The layout of in-town green areas has been planned so that green swathes intersect the urban area so as to go 'through' the town, to bring the out-of-town landscape not only in but right through. An almost geometrical pattern of twelve neighborhoods, each with 1,200 dwelling units, based on the neighborhood school concept, make up the residential districts. Each neighborhood, consisting of about 50 hectares, contains one transit stop, two elementary schools, a gymnasium, some small stores, and a small commercial area. Three neighborhoods form a district with some community facilities such as a medical center and a neighborhood house. There are two railroad stations; the main business and shopping center is situated near the westerly one. The neighborhood plans show the same straightforward approach that is apparent in the overall plan.

The physical plan of Buiten is in fact a reaction to the plans of Haven and Stad, a reaction to the rather arbitrary directions of both nuclei, and to the denial of both the design-philosophical as well as the physical parameters that the polders lends to the urban settlement built therein. Although one must say in all fairness to Almere-Haven that the polder had barely come into existence when Haven was being planned, the planners can hardly be blamed for not expressing Almere's relationship with its surroundings in a more sympathetic fashion. Almere-Haven's plan is in fact an answer to the inhospitable, open, bleak landscape of the new polder. That answer was composed

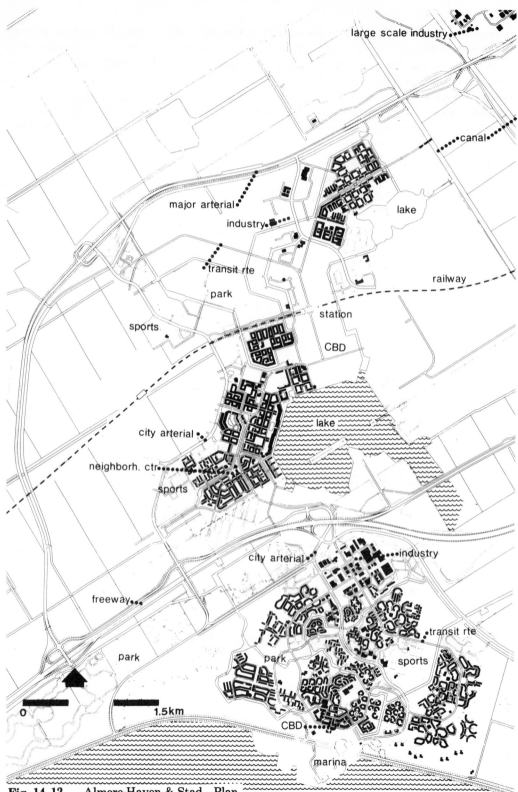

Fig. 14-12   Almere-Haven & Stad—Plan

in the form language of the day which was to bring the human scale back into forming both interior and exterior spaces. Later trends were contrary to this because it was felt that preoccupation with the details to achieve comfort, and too great an emphasis on 'cuteness' and old-hat answers, were untrue to the art of giving form to space. The more rationalistic forms, in some ways akin to the new movements in design of the twenties, later referred to as the 'international style', are in vogue again in modern architecture and planning in the expression of geometrical forms, rather than the comfortable condescension to the old-town style. Grid-like designs are coming back in Dutch planning, often mixed with a little 'city beautiful' philosophy, in which axes and vistas figure prominently. The latest plans for a new residential district of 3,400 dwelling units in Almere-Stad exhibit this tendency very well. Almere-Buiten has similarly been planned within the reaches of this philosophy. One has to wait and see how people will enjoy living in a neighborhood of this straight-forwardness, as compared to the neighborhoods of Haven, which generally have been well received.

Zeewolde's structure plan has recently been approved. Plans for the first neighborhoods are on the drawing boards. A linear, grid-like design employed in Almere-Buiten, also forms the basis for the physical plan of Zeewolde. No definite plans have been finalized at this date. (Fig. 14-14)

THE FUTURE

Apart from Zeewolde in the eastern portion of Southern Flevoland, Almere will be the last major town planned in the Zuiderzee polders for some time to come. The draining of the last polder, the Markerwaard, is in doubt, though some of the dikes, locks, and bridges of that project have been constructed. Political pressure to preserve the status quo is building up. The Authority, however, is going ahead with the research and planning for this last great polder.

Present plans show no large-scale urban settlements in the new polder (Fig. 14-15), only villages to support the local rural population. A few years ago towns the size of Almere were envisioned in the Markerwaard, but the latest calculations, which take into account the sobering trends in respect of the housing needs and housing desires of the population, attempt to show that the inflated expectations of the sixties and seventies are not likely to be fulfilled or even desirable in the Markerwaard. A recent report[21] on that polder also discounts the possibility of large urban settlements and envisions the Markerwaard as being similar to the Northeast Polder in that respect. Eighty thousand is mentioned as realistic eventual population. In the event of major urban pressure from the Randstad in the future, it is conceivable that an urban settlement might be located in the IJsselmeer north of Almere, for which the Markerwaard would have to be enlarged.

This may end the cycle of new town planning on the bottom of the former Zuiderzee, a process which has shown itself to be a search for perfection, to make the very best environment for future inhabitants. The Authority has been aware of and has lived up to its responsibilities. The most cogent criticism directed toward the Authority has been that it has tended to overplan and has guided the development of the polders to the point where nothing was left to chance. In that sense it is understandable that the planning of towns has been largely conservative (i.e. there has been a shying away

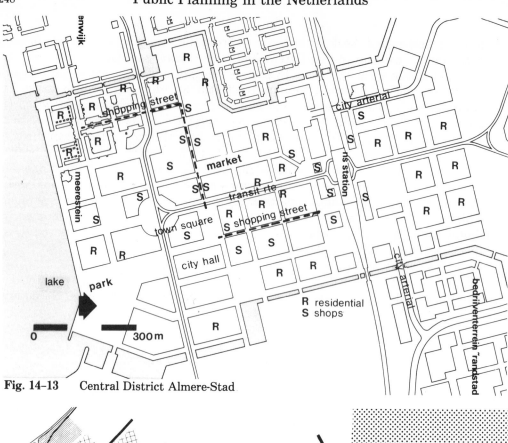

Fig. 14–13   Central District Almere-Stad

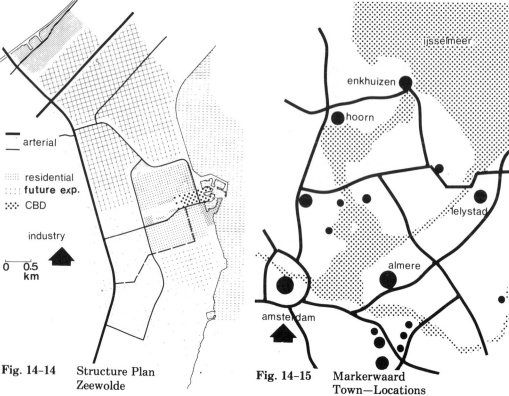

Fig. 14–14   Structure Plan Zeewolde

Fig. 14–15   Markerwaard Town—Locations

from large-scale experiments) starting with the Wieringermeerpolder towns, planned by the conservative Granpré-Molière, up to the planning of Almere where a search for readily identifiable forms has so far given shape to the townships of Almere-Haven and Almere-Stad.

NOTES

1. A 'polder' is any level area that would be inundated, permanently or periodically, if by mechanical means the water were not kept at a certain specified level.
2. Bourtange is a fortification started in 1580 under Prince William I. It is situated between the towns of Groningen (Neth.) and Oldenburg (Ger.). It was intended to help control the northern province against the Spanish in the eighty-year war (1568–1648).
3. For an explanation of 'Authority' see note 10 of the previous chapter.
4. See note 11 of the previous chapter.
5. 'De Stijl' movement was started in 1917 by Van Doesburg and Mondrian, who 'wished to express through their work a universal truth'. The form language, which Mondrian referred to as 'neo-plasticism', had developed out of a search to bring all forms back to their essentials: the straight line and the rectangular plane. Colors similarly were reduced to red, yellow, and blue, and white, gray, and black. The group adhered to the principle of complete abstraction and banished the subjective and individual. Oud, Rietveld, and Van Eesteren were all members at one time. The movement can be said to have ended with the death of Van Doesburg in 1931.
6. Van Eesteren, Cornelis, 1897– . Dutch architect and urban planner. Planned several residences with Van Doesburg in France. Became interested in city planning while on a study tour in Germany, 1921. Worked in the City Planning Department of Amsterdam from 1929 to 1959. Was president of CIAM (see footnote 7) from 1930 to 1947, where he was instrumental in the writing of the 'Charter of Athens'.
7. CIAM: Congres Internationaux d'Architecture Moderne. 'The purpose of CIAM was to establish contemporary architecture's right to existence against the antagonistic forces of offical architectural circles, who controlled the major building enterprises. The aim was to deal with problems that could not be solved by the single individual...' (Le Corbusier according to Giedion). First congress was in Las Sarraz, Switzerland in 1928, the last in Dubrovnik in 1956. The fourth congress produced the 'Charter of Athens', which laid down the principles of contemporary city planning.
8. On this point Granpré went against the prevailing opinion of his principals. He argued that motor traffic would diminish eventually and stated: 'movement is characteristic for becoming, rest is characteristic for being'.
9. S. J. Van Embden, 'Bouwen in het Nieuwe Land', *Bouwkundig Weekblad Architectura*, V. 154, no. 49, 1933, pp. 428–41.
10. Lewis Mumford, *The Culture of Cities*, New York, Harcourt Brace Jovanovich, 1970, p. 401.
11. Wieger Bruin, 'Over de dorpen van de Noordoostpolder', *Forum*, vol. 10, no. 1, 2, 1955, pp. 23–6.
12. N. A. De Boer, 'Vormgeving van Nieuwe Dorpen', *Stedebouw en Volkshuisvesting*, vol. 44, no. 4, 1963, pp. 84–7.
13. H. Van Leeuwen, 'Impressies en Kanttekeningen over het Wonen in Oostelijk Flevoland', *Stedebouw en Volkshuisvesting*, vol. 44, no. 4, 1963, pp. 88–92.
14. 'De 8', a group of designers who together with another affiliated group, 'De Opbouw', formed the Dutch segment of the CIAM. The designers of Nagele were: W. Van

Bodegraven, A. Bodon, J. T. P. Bijhouwer, C. Van Eesteren, P. Elling, A. Van Eyck, W. Van Gelderen, M. Kamerling, J. P. Kloos, B. Merkelbach, J. Niegeman, G. Rietveld, M. Ruys, and H. Salomonson.

15. A 'structure plan' is a master plan showing, to scale,the different functional zones of towns or districts in their approximate size and their relationship to each other. Major facilities (such as shopping centers, neighborhood centers), and major communications lines (such as highways, railroads, transit lines, canals) are shown in their approximate location. The plan is a programmatic guide rather than a physical plan.

16. Rijksdienst voor de IJsselmeerpolders, *Dronten, Nieuwe Gemeente in Nieuw Land*, 's Gravenhage, Staatsuitgeverij, 1972, p. 76.

17. C. Van Eesteren, *Stedebouwkundig Plan voor Lelystad*, 's Gravenhage, Staatsuitgeverij, 1964.

18. Dennis L. Meadows, *The Limits to Growth, A Report for the Club of Rome Project on the Predicament of Mankind*, New York, Universe Books, 1972.

19. H. A. Bruning, P. Davelaar, W. A. Segeren, H. Van Willigen, *Verkenningen omtrent de Ontwikkeling van de Nieuwe Stad 'Almere' in Flevoland*, Flevobericht No. 78, Lelystad, Rijksdienst voor de IJsselmeerpolders, 1970, p. 137.

20. C. Van Eesteren, B. Merkelbach, L. C. Van der Vlugt, W. Van Tijen, 'Bebouwing Wieringermeerpolder', *Tijdschrift voor Volkshuisvesting en Stedebouw*, vol. 15, no. 1, 1934, pp. 4–7.

21. Ministerie van Verkeer en Waterstaat, *Denkbeeld voor een Struktuur van het IJsselmeergebied*, Lelystad, Rijkswaterstaat, directie Zuiderzeewerken and Rijksdienst voor de IJsselmeerpolders, 1981, p. 37.

15
Dutch Planning in the Twenty-First Century

Ashok K. Dutt and Frank J. Costa

In recent decades Dutch society has gone through many economic and social changes. Changes in the processes of production, distribution, and the relationship between management and labor have been augmented by changes in social values favoring the development of the nuclear family and even non-family relationships. The creation of a powerful state welfare system and greater public participation in government have also contributed to a greatly altered society. To all these can be added the recent introduction of significant numbers of non-Dutch ethnic minorities into the general population. Thus since the end of the Second World War, Dutch society has undergone a change surpassing that experienced in any other equivalent period. The question therefore arises as to the extent of change that is to be expected over the last years of this century. The answer will have far-reaching effects on the theory and practice of planning in the next century.

The content of Dutch planning in the twenty-first century will depend upon the nature of the political compromise reached among the major contrasting sets of ideological perspectives concerning development and on the constraints imposed by the enveloping national environment.

Figure 15–1 depicts the anticipated process of planning policy creation. Dutch planning institutions and their policies will be affected by two sets of external impacts. These include prevailing ideological or value perspectives on what ought to be planned and constraints imposed upon planning by environmental circumstances such as physical resources, social conditions, and the level of economic development. Future planning in the Netherlands must avoid adoption of a single ideological perspective. Rather it should adopt a conprehensive synthesis based upon the resolutions of environmental constraints and ideological contrasts.

These impacts, however, will not evolve in isolation from one another. The pure bases of political compromise are derived from differing and often opposing ideological perspectives. But these frequently opposing arguments are either lessened or confirmed by their advocates via hard facts from the environment. Structural unemployment has pushed many welfare economists toward a market-oriented approach to economic policy. The introduction of diverse population groups has at times had the effect of reversing long-standing attitudes towards social equality. These facts from the envionment are the decisive circumstances at work in the evolution of ideological perspectives. In totalitarian societies they can often be repressed by force, but in democratic societies like the Netherlands they impose themselves upon the political process.

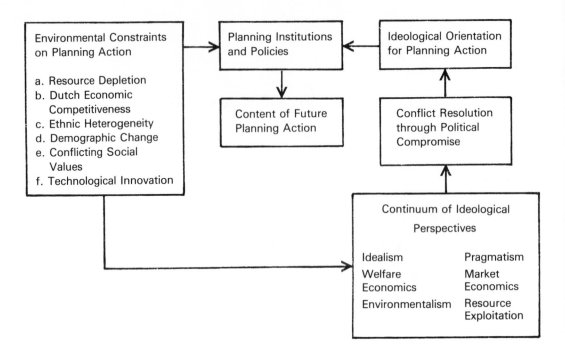

Fig. 15-1   Forces affecting the Development of Future Planning Policies for The Netherlands

Economic and social developments will greatly affect the future of the Netherlands. The nature of the impacts of these developments upon the Dutch will be determined by the effectiveness of planning. The Netherlands is an open economy. The nature of the free world economy in the twenty-first century is unknown, but the high growth rates of the post World-War II decades of the 1950s, 1960s, and early 1970s are unlikely to return, and the Netherlands, along with other countries, will have to contend with smaller economic growth rates into the twenty-first century. Public planning, consequently, may have to adjust to conditions of greater austerity and to the reduced resources of a more limited welfare system.

A limited welfare system, however, does not imply elimination of the social and economic legislation that the Dutch have adopted in recent decades in the fields of unemployment, health care, education, and housing. To eliminate these welfare measures would be politically impossible. The welfare system guarantees the unemployed about 80 percent of his previous income for a period of 30 months and a minimum wage thereafter until reemployment. In 1983 the unemployment rate reached Great Depression levels. Severe economic difficulties do not afflict the Dutch worker as they did in the 1930s. Nonetheless, politicians and planners in the future will have to redesign Dutch welfare programs to take into account the stability or possible decline in the service levels of these programs.

The maintaining of high service levels is dependent upon the wealth created by an economy. A nation such as the Netherlands can retain its place among the developed nations only if it continually enhances its technological innovativeness, competitiveness, and productivity. The Netherlands became a highly developed nation after World War II and its place within this select group in the twenty-first century depends on an effectively planned economy with an advanced technology.

Recent experience indicates that fewer people are needed to produce increasing amounts of goods and, similarly, a smaller number of people can manage a greater number of administrative and transport operations. An even larger proportion of the labor force has been absorbed into the services or tertiary sector of the economy (Figure 15-2). All these changes are the result of automation, robotization, and computerization. The greater the use of such technological innovations the more competitive a nation will become in improving its place in the ranks of the highly developed nations. The Netherlands like other developed nations, is undergoing great change in its technology and in its economic condition, and this change has created a new problem: structural unemployment, which during the recession of the early 1980s reached a high of about 16 percent.

The crux of the structural unemployment issue is that the occupational requirements of the emerging economy are reduced quantitatively and enhanced qualitatively. Thus, a significant sector of the work force will remain idle or unemployed.

How are Dutch planners seeking to solve the problem of structural unemployment? If the welfare system has to take care of all the unemployed for decades to come, the system is likely to collapse, particularly after the depletion of Dutch natural gas resources. A response aimed at reemploying the structurally unemployed is needed by the Dutch for the economic survival of the Netherlands in the front ranks of the highly developed nations.

The future of the Dutch economy is bound up with trends in productivity and labor costs, not only in Europe but throughout the world. Structural unemployment in the advanced economies of the West is found most frequently in the coal-mining, older metals, metals fabricating, and related industries such as machine tools, plastics, and chemicals. These industries have been unable to remain competitive vis-'a-vis their newer and lower labor-cost counterparts in other parts of the world.

Economic growth or its lack can be explained by the concept of frontiers. A frontier is a geographic opportunity space in which a combination of resources, available markets, and human skills work together to create profits for investors. Frontier settings, in an earlier era, were associated with different periods in the same nation. The American rural frontier was eventually supplemented by an urban frontier, which in turn, through the impetus of suburbanization, became a metropolitan frontier.[1] Within nations, including the Netherlands, the concept of regional frontiers is quite readily understood. Randstad Holland has been the economic frontier for generations and the other regions of the Netherlands have suffered losses to this more attractive region. In the 1960s and 1970s international frontiers began to emerge. East Asia is one of the best examples. Entire nations began to witness declining economic conditions occasioned in part by the extremely high competition of the newer industrial states. The older industrial economies were entering a 'post-industrial' era. Structural unemployment began to emerge as a significant problem.

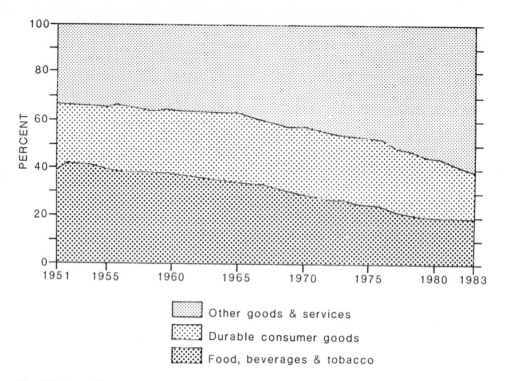

Fig. 15-2   Consumption Structure of The Netherlands (1951–83) (Source: *Jaarverslag Rijksplanologische Dienst 1982*, S-Gravenhage, Staatswitgeverij, 1983, p. 17)

Dutch planners and public officials must begin the task of creating a new frontier of opportunity for the Dutch economy. The new frontier will come about as the result of many specific policies, all aimed at creating a profitable setting for Dutch economic life. These policies would probably foster the creation of new products for international consumption. Such a course of action requires the development of a major commitment to technological innovation by Dutch industry and the support of the Dutch government. Policies aimed at reducing labor costs must also be pursued. Ultimately, in order to absorb the structurally unemployed into the labor force again, the present wage and benefit level of all Dutch workers may have to be kept at internationally competitive levels.

The tri-partite nature of Dutch planning makes it an extremely important element in the transition from the current condition of economic stagnation and decline to an expanding economy based, in part, upon new products and services. The reforming zeal of economic planners must be tempered by the human awareness of the social planner. Both benefit from the physical planner, who can identify the physical impacts of the new technologies and new social conditions imposed upon workers in a period of economic transition.

Along with the economic structure of the nation, the number and characteristics of the population will also help to determine the future of planning in the Netherlands. Considering the two decades of rapid population growth (about 1.4 percent annually) following World War II, demographers in the mid-1960s projected that the Dutch population would reach 21 million by the year 2000. However, the lower birth-rates achieved since the mid-1960s and widespread acceptance of family planning techniques by both Protestants and Catholics, resulted in a dramatically low population increase in the 1970s (0.87 percent annually). This happened despite the arrival of about half a million guest workers from the Mediterranean nations and immigrants from Caribbean countries during the sixties and seventies. Most demographers now believe the Dutch population may never reach 21 million. Current projections place it at about the 15.5 million mark by the year 2000. Thereafter a zero level of population increase is probable, followed by population decline. The positive side of this picture is that the planners will then have to deal with declining numbers in terms of housing units, employment, school space, recreation areas, hospital beds, and other community facilities. The 'problem' side of the picture is the issue of absorption of overbuilt facilities and declining use of already built-up space.

Another demographic issue in the Netherlands is the recent increase in the ageing population and consequent decline in the younger population. In 1900 only 6 percent of the Dutch population was sixty-five years and above, increasing to 11 percent in 1977, while in 1982 it reached 11.7 percent. With a further increase in life expectancy resulting from improved medical treatment, the percentage of the population in the older age group will continue to increase. Along with an ageing population is the parallel development of smaller household size resulting from increasing numbers of older-single person households and younger one- and two-person households (see Figure 15-3).

The evolution of the Netherlands into a multi-ethnic community from a Teutonic, Dutch-speaking, Christian nation since the 1960s has brought about new planning problems not only in the large cities, but throughout the country. Over 200,000 people from the Mediterranean basin, primarily Islamic Turks and Moroccans, over 130,000 Surinamese (mainly Hindustanis) and Dutch Antilleans, and 32,000 Moluccans have created a wide diversity in terms of color, race, language, and religion. Their relative importance in the population should increase because some of them, particularly the Turks and Moroccans, have a very high birth-rate. Culturally these minority groups maintain their own distinct identity. Will these minorities ever be assimilated into Dutch society in the twenty-first century, or will they form distinct individualized crystals in the melting pot? Planners will have to understand the sociological implications of heterogeneity in order to plan for all the people.

The reversibility of long-term trends upon which planning objectives are based is the 'bête noire' of most traditional planners. The apparent end of economic growth is but one example, but there are many others. Since the 1950s, planners in the Netherlands at all levels have designed space and planned facilities to suit the needs of motorists. As long as the world's gasoline demands do not outstrip supply, motorists will stay on the road, but the supply of petroleum products may decline and by the 1990s demand could outstrip supplies. Thus, a global gasoline shortage may occur by the turn of the century. Another seemingly irreversible trend may be changing. Dutch planners are aware of the problem, especially since 1973 Arab oil embargo. In the

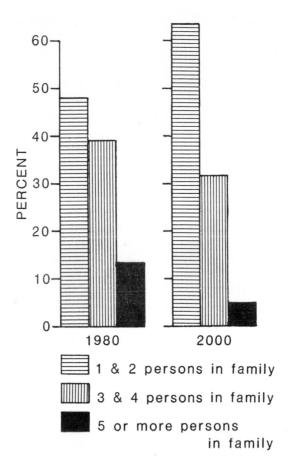

Fig. 15-3   Households by Type in The Netherlands
for 1980 and 2000 (projected) (Source:
Jaarverslag Rijksplanologische Dienst 1982, p. 42)

Netherlands there is an alternative public transport system consisting of railroad, bus, tram, and ferry, which is purposely kept in operation, despite sizeable operating losses, by governmental subsidy. New social and economic realities set the stage for new planning issues and a new planning environment. Dutch planners must try to understand how these realities will affect their work. The maintenance of public transportation is an example of the capacity of Dutch planners and political leaders to anticipate long-term needs.

Thus, before the beginning of the next century, Dutch planners must address three fundamental problems: structural unemployment, increasing ethnic and racial divisions, and an ageing population. Each is vast in itself, but the three in concert create an even more emotionally charged environment for decision-making. But if past achievements can be replicated in the future, then the current dilemmas should be resolved. Dutch political and social institutions solved the problems of protection from sea floods. Reconciliation of serious denominational strife in the nineteenth century through the establishment of the 'pillars' is further evidence of the flexibility of Dutch social and political institutions.

Resolution of the fundamental problems discussed here can be achieved through the development of new social policies capable of supporting new technologies in product development and distribution. Countries that are able to develop these social policies will possess an economic future.

Innovation in and expansion of the scope of publicly supported education in the Netherlands is the most important single social policy. The fostering of new technologies through an expansion of educational opportunities for the structurally unemployed and the ethnic minorities can address simultaneously all three of the fundamental problems we have identified. Once again the Dutch past provides us with reassuring evidence of the country's capacity to turn a potential social dilemma into economic opportunity. The great migrations of religious dissenters to the Netherlands in the sixteenth and seventeenth centuries did not result in societal fragmentation but rather societal and economic enrichment. Similar opportunities exist in the social and economic crises of the 1980s.

Whatever the state of the economy and whatever the social complexities of the twenty-first century, it is certain that the effectiveness of Dutch planning during the twentieth century will continue into the twenty-first century. The degree of success, however, will depend on both the economic health of the country and the theoretical ingenuity of the planning profession.

NOTES

1. Daniel J. Elazar, *Cities of the Prairie*, Basic Books, New York, 1970.

Index